Helmut Germer

The German Novel of Education
1792–1805
A complete Bibliography and Analysis

German Studies in America

Edited by Heinrich Meyer

No. 3

Helmut Germer

The German Novel of Education
1792–1805
A complete Bibliography and Analysis

Herbert Lang

1968

The German Novel
of Education
1792-1805
A complete
Bibliography and Analysis

by

Helmut Germer

Herbert Lang

1968

TABLE OF CONTENTS

STATISTICAL STUDIES OF LOST AND FORGOTTEN BOOKS

Introductory Remarks by Heinrich Meyer

Professor Germer's study of the Novel of Education *(Erziehungsroman)* on the basis of his own readings, on the basis of the review journals of Nicolai, and of the bibliographers aiming at completeness is not in danger of becoming the kind of statistics which Professor Bell, the late historian of mathematics, liked to call numerology, it is rather the kind of statistics that Tönnies advocated and that Schlözer founded at the very time that is here under consideration, the tabulation of facts as concrete data.

We need not go into statistics as a mathematically developed discipline except in order to say this: when a number of comparable data reveal a deviation that is greater than chance would suggest, let us say, when among the births happening in the clinics more end in death than among the births happening at home, as Semmelweiss observed, then there must be a "reason" that can be found. Semmelweiss thus had the statistics before he had the hypothesis accounting for the fact. Dr. Germer did not go into this problem at all, though his material is rich enough to allow even for such deductions. But deductions were not needed and opportune, for they could not have been verified, since most of the books under discussion are known to us only through their reviews.

There is another problem involved, the term "novel of education", which is here meant as *Erziehungsroman* and not as *Bildungsroman*. Was there such a genre and how numerous was it and what were its characteristic content and formal structure? Obviously it was up to Professor Germer to establish first the existence of the genre itself; he did so with great skill.

In English, "novel of education" serves equally to cover the *Bildungsroman* in the sequence of Rousseau and Goethe. Yet a distinction had to be made. *Bildung* is self-formation and involves the development, growth and maturing of innate, native gifts and needs. *Bildung*, as Goethe meant it, had a biological component of the naturally given that takes on its varied shapes. *Formation* is therefore a better translation than *education*. The latter term implies too much our later connotations, connected with schooling and purpose and social standing, all of which were not meant when the word "Bildung" originated and became fashionable at first.

Bildung therefore has a component of natural endowment, of something given and not acquired or subject to choice and will. *Education,* on the other hand, is used to designate our formation insofar as it is wilful, a matter of purpose and intent, of social aims and ends. When Professor Germer speaks of the *Novel of Education* he is concerned only with this second kind of education, the purposeful, moral, wilful formation for good ends, not with the irrational factors that may enter into a man's growth and development.

What distinguishes a novel of education, an *Erziehungsroman,* from the *Bildungsroman*? This is itself a very interesting project which Dr. Germer is investigating at present. It has to do with topics that go to the heart of literary structure. A novel of education is rational, like More's *Utopia* or the tales of Voltaire and Dr. Johnson, of Zschokke or the modern Detective Story, rational and carefully knit like a fable or a comedy worth its name. Each character has his given place in the plot, and the plot results from the interplay of the characters so conceived. Nowhere does the author intrude personally and express his own whims or feelings, as does the author of the lyrical novel of confession and autobiography, which is the *Bildungsroman.* One most obvious difference is this: the *Bildungsroman* reflects the present state of an author's self-knowledge and therefore has no clear ending that must result from the antecedents. The constructed novel of rational "ends" *has* such an end. Also, the rational novel sets up an environment of its own choice, a Robinson's Island, a world of Gulliver's vision, a village peopled with drunkards, or a world of noblemen or robbers or knights as kind as the Gospels, others as fiendish and brutal as only plot constructors can invent them, and we accept these conditions as we accept the world of the opera or the detective novel, though no such world exists in reality; it is the world of pure fiction. The novel of self-revelation, of lyrical self-expression, of *Bildung,* on the other hand, is encumbered with a certain amount of reality that may strike us as highly poetic, but which nevertheless is not entirely created by us and thus is generally beyond the range of free manipulation through art. Other studies in this area are now being undertaken by Professor Finto and Mr. Angevine, the former dealing with Zschokke, the latter with the motif of Travel in plot construction.

Dr. Germer chose the *Erziehungsroman* for his theme. This was a bold move that required considerable technical ingenuity and thus led to results that will remain unassailable for all times, a complete bibliography of the genre for a given period, a complete tabulation of its substance and structure and some of its formal characteristics in terms of the statistical basis chosen. Nothing mades man so immortal as a complete bibliography which need never again be made. Nothing is such sound scholarship as that which presupposes constant application until a topic is fully exhausted. The years spent in this manner save everyone else at least that many years. — During the high time of positivism, factual compilations were popular, as the Berlin theses of the eighteen-eighties, nineties and thereabouts show. But unfortunately none of these studies ever envisaged completeness for a large enough period or a significant enough subject;

thus the "results" of these dissertations cannot as a rule be tallied and used by anyone else. The ensuing period of *Synthese,* which soon merged with the fashion of deductive verbalism from mere names, called *Geistesgeschichte,* and the next phase, literary interpretation and emphasis on the *art* side of literary production alone, these all suffer equally from subjectivism and arbitrariness. Why should we care to read any "interpretation" of a play at all? Why not read the play itself and know what we ourselves feel? Why discuss interpretations which, in the nature of the aim, must be and must remain subjective and therefore beyond final arbitration? No reason for *not* doing so; for this is perhaps "literary criticism" and worthwhile in itself, but it is not scholarship in the sense here considered. Unless a study saves another person years of work because years of hard work have gone into it, I cannot consider it scholarly, whatever its other qualifications may be. Dr. Germer was happily equipped for just this kind of scholarship.

He had and still has a flighty imagination and a very pronounced gift for combinatorics, and he could easily have combined some facts and some of his gifts to come forth with a verbal artifact of considerable charm and sufficient general appeal to pass for sound work. Many do no more, many do even less. But Dr. Germer is also a man of strong will and, a phenomenon unique in my experience, of uncanny memory. He can read through hundreds of volumes when he makes up his mind to do so, decide which of the books discussed are treatises and tracts, which textbooks, and which novels of "Education", and thereby first establish the fact that there actually *are* "novels of education" hitherto unrecognized. But having done so, he can also recall the concrete detail that, in the nature of the theme, must be rather uniform and difficult to keep apart from similar material in many of the hundreds of other titles found. And he can then organize this material successfully till it is all transformed into objective classifiable data which can even be statistically tabulated.

This requires a great deal of self-sacrifice and devotion, but also of good humor and good nature. Dr. Germer had ample opportunity to develop these traits, for he grew up in difficult times. Born in 1938 in Berlin, he came to America in 1951, where his father had already gone before him. His father had obtained several important patents on various high vacuum lamps etc. and ought by rights to be one of the richest men in the world, but the Custodian of Alien Property only took care that these important patents were used and that the proceeds should not accrue to an "enemy alien", and the German Governments which were supposed to repay those damaged in this manner made it impossible to do so by making themselves immune from being sued. Thus only others profited from the Germer inventions. Yet Helmut Germer was not daunted. He graduated from an American highschool, went to Muhlenberg College and then to Vanderbilt University, and is at present teaching in a state university in Ohio. His extraordinary vitality and balance of mind are combined with his eagerness to prove himself with a work of utter perfection; and we are the beneficiaries of these circumstances.

Dr. Germer describes the facts of his investigations in very few words, but having seen him at work was an experience I shall not forget. For it is by no means easy to read through hundreds of volumes and to keep track of one and only one aim, then to tabulate these thousands of pages in such a way that a worthwhile result is obtained. In the process, initial vagueness changed to ultimate factuality, and we got a bibliography that is as original as his father's research and can serve as a pilot study for many similar studies.

Germer also discovered the incompleteness of Nicolai's review journals, even when they were meant to be all-inclusive, because he had the advantage of our collections of eighteenth century novels which I got for Muhlenberg College and myself (these latter are now available at Vanderbilt University). Though these collections of ours yielded only about fifty novels of education, there were quite a few of them which had escaped the attention of the reviewers at the time of publication. Nor is every book published ever listed in later bibliographies, even where they are meant to be inclusive. The limits of Kayser's *Bücherlexikon* and Goedeke become as apparent as those of similar books once we begin to know the original material. (I could cite similar instances in other areas, including the one best worked-over, American bibliography proper.)

Thus Professor Germer had to correlate several bibliographies with the original review journals under consideration and both with the individual novels he had in hand. This yielded another source of information. He could now judge from his own reading as to the accuracy of the reviewers where they reviewed the books he knew. Here his prodigious memory came most happily into play. All of this appears here only in the lists and as tables. The tabulation of themes and contents and formal characteristics is peculiarly entertaining since here we get a picture of writers and readers during the period under consideration, a picture which we can obtain only because the material is brought together under *one* heading.

Many of the books then reviewed are now lost for ever. Even authors who once were important or who survive with one or two works, like Moritz or Kortum, or who were controversial, like Starck and Plessing, are not fully extant anywhere; some of their works seem to be completely lost by now. The novels of education may not be significant as literature, but they are indicative of a trend and of an interest, even if they were published in small numbers, as most of them no doubt were — they tell us that the "period", which the *Stil- und Geistesgeschichtler* subsume under such designations as *Klassik und Romantik*, was actually still the period of Rationalism and Enlightenment, if indeed such "periods" make any sense at all. Just as Church history shows us independently, the years covered by Dr. Germer and the *Neue Allgemeine deutsche Bibliothek,* were far more clearly marked by the reforming spirit than by the flight into romantic poeticalness and political "Restauration".

The remark just made as to "*periods* making sense at all" is perhaps in need of a short explanation. Since it is *we* who call and select the *period,* the only correction for circularity and arbitrariness must obviously be a basis wide enough to cover *all* the material supposedly designated by our "period". This has also been pointed out by Professor Richards in his study of the twentieth century bestseller (Vol. 2 in this series). It is, for instance, only *ex post facto* evaluation, not history, when a style historian focusses on Expressionism as characteristic of the nineteen-twenties; for, as Richards shows, the vast mass of the material published and read at the time was by no means "expressionistic". Unless we therefore measure the writers now subsumed under "Expressionism" against all others writing at the same time or at least against those most widely read at that time, we merely substitute our later opinion of stylistic changes, tastes, programs and so forth for the opinion held by the majority of the readers in those days. A pertinent other example is given in Rust Hills' review of the critic Podhoretz in *Esquire* (vol. LXIX, 4. April 1968). Too often do we regard as the past only that which we happen to know of it; yet that which we never heard of also existed and must be considered equally. Where are we to find out about the unknown past? Only the review journals can give us enough material to work with. This is the chief lesson of Professor Germer's study.

More complex is another lesson. We have become so accustomed to the notion of evolution, development, inherent purpose that we still tend to interpret history as being meaningful in the sense of Herder, Ranke or Hegel and Marx. Yet is there a *Geist* which has a history? Is this not a construction on insufficient data? Is perhaps *Geist* not rather that which has *no* history? Omar Chajjam (cf. Nordmeyer's Translation in vol. 1 of this series) seems to have thought of *Geist* as that which *remains* behind the changing forms! There is an amusing example in the area of *Bildungsroman,* presupposing an evolution, and *Erziehungsroman,* presupposing only a purpose. Another example is the historical novel insofar as it is *Erziehungsroman.* When Xenophon wrote "The Education of Cyrus", when others wrote their *Fürstenspiegel,* when the Archbishop of Cambray wrote his *Telemaque* and Lord Hardwicke his *Athenian Letters,* they combined an historical theme with a moral purpose. With Fenelon's *Telemaque* this is obvious, but Hardwicke's story of Athens during the Peloponnesian war, as seen through the letters of a resident foreigner, is no less educational. Only it is informative, as were the later books by the eminent specialists Dahn or Ebers. We are not discussing their taste or their literary merits, just their educational aspect. For here they and many others have a common quality. This is a fact, but has it any "historical" significance? It certainly is every time another fact, a new fact, independent of similar facts before and after!

The young Cambridge students around Lord Hardwicke wanted to bring back to life what the sources about the Peloponnesian war had recorded as mere events and opinions. Their book appeared in 1740, yet I knew nothing of it when I taught a boys' class at the Schule am Meer in 1928; and yet I hit on exactly the same device, though none of our professors had ever thought of giving us such "projects" as every American pupil now undertakes from his ninth year on, or even earlier. When the Provençal Abbé Barthelemy thought of a suitable theme for reviving the past, he chose the travel theme, *Voyage du jeune Anacharsis* (1788). He said that he had not been aware of Hardwicke's book, else he would have profited from it. A similar novel of education with an historical slant is Böttiger's *Sabina. Morgenszenen im Putzzimmer einer Römerin,* which is a marvellous predecessor of Friedländer's book, of interest to scatologists, pornographers, historians of culture and classicists more proper. Again this book owes nothing to its predecessors, though Böttiger probably knew them when he published his in 1808. And yet a hundred years later, another book appeared, somewhat in the vein of one of Thornton Wilder's historical novels, which again was not aware of the predecessors. O.F. Grazebrook, an English industrialist, had also devoted his leisure hours to the writing of a novel about Greece during the Peloponnesian war. The delightful volume is called *Nicanor of Athens, The Autobiography of an Unknown Citizen* (University Press, Cambridge, England. 1946). These examples prove that there is often no conscious tradition and that history can freely repeat itself when writers with a need for liveliness decide to write about the remote past. Such writers want to made the past intelligible by seeing it through the eyes of a contemporary.

This side of the historical novel, its educational content, should certainly be investigated with care. It is rather too cheap to belittle Dahn and Ebers for having brought the past up to nineteenth century understanding, as Bulwer had done before them. They did it with consummate skill and should therefore be studied in earnest. Nothing at all can be gained by ridiculing them. Adolf Stern, Riehl, C.F. Meyer, Raabe and many others did it differently; so did George Moore in *Heloise and Abelard* or Stevenson in *A Lodging for the Night,* that marvellous story about Francois Villon. Yet nobody has seriously studied the various techniques and their results.

When Professor Germer first thought about his theme, I suggested a simple working hypothesis: that the reform spirit of the age of the Revolution might have kindled some of the plots. For I had noticed just such revolutionary themes in some of the historical novels of the time, especially in those of Lafontaine. It seemed plausible that others might have imitated him, who was after all the most successful novelist of the age and one of the few who could live by his pen. (Jean Paul could not. Goethe might have been able to, had he but decided to write for the public, as he intended for a while when he came back from Italy and thought of turning out plays for his theatre. But then he was not aware of his popularity even later, because Cotta cheated him, as Goeschen had cheated his authors before, when they reprinted whole editions without paying royalties. This has been established by Kurrelmeyer and Faber du Faur, himself a descendant of Cotta.) At any rate, Lafontaine was successful and liked to use revolutionary and other contemporary themes in the disguise of past history. But Dr. Germer found little of this in his novels of education.

This allows us to make perhaps a cautions deduction that the writers of Germer were after all and on the whole not literary men, but educators, and perhaps only students hoping for a post as tutor in a nobleman's house or, if their imagination took a higher flight, a charge as a minister or rector who would help a noble Prince or kindly Baron to change a village full of dirty children and habitual drunkards into a paradise, perhaps even a paying paradise. We shall probably never know for certain, except in rare instances like that of Zschokke, whom Dr. Germer rightly used as a foil and counterweight to the many unknowns he dealt with. But Germer's studies show that even an indirect approach can bring back to us a great deal of solid information that we would otherwise lack. Such studies are bound to succeed if the writer has the stamina and the imagination and the character that will not rest until a certain area is exhaustively and completely studied. His reward is the satisfaction of having done a piece of research that will stand for all time.

Vanderbilt University   Heinrich Meyer

INTRODUCTION

Among the genres and subgenres of the novel, taken
from various frames of reference, there are a number of
types defined by their contents: Picaresque novel, pasto-
ral novel, Utopian novel, Robinsonade, Bildungsroman, Erziehungsroman, and in some respects even Trivialroman. We
shall concern ourselves with the Erziehungsroman, the Novel of Education, which can be defined as a novel that attempts to improve and educate its reader. It may show the
disastrous consequences of vice and thereby hope to divert
the reader from the wrong path; it more frequently shows
the beneficial effects of sound conduct and thereby means
to help the reader on his road to virtue. While the German
genre of Bildungsroman is, in more than one respect, also
concerned with education, its "education" is, as the name
Bildung and its Goethean connotation show, directed at the
individual's "formation"; moreover, it always follows the
picaresque technique of biography, though not necessarily
autobiography, which puts its hero into a peculiar situa-
tion: he must pass more or less passively through various
experiences, he learns from life as a whole. The author as
well as the reader are interested in the hero's ever new
unique experiences and adventures in life. Persons whom

the hero meets early are not likely to appear again later.
The Novel of Education, on the other hand, considers more
general themes. It devotes itself to showing how a whole
village is transformed or a widely regretted vice is eradi-
cated. It is not interested in mere personal formation for
the sake of the individual hero, it only takes this hero
as a model and prototype. The author's main concerns are
the common experiences of life with which the reader is
familiar and from which he can learn. Hardly a single fig-
ure in the Educational Novel is a rounded character. For
it suffices for the purpose of the novelist of education,
as for the teller of fables, to have his character represent the particular virtues and vices he wishes to depict.

This allegorical quality, which reminds us both of
the medieval drama and the contemporary comic strips,
could also be connected with the dialogue and the fable.
Traces of these relations which are inherent in the educational aim, need neither have occurred to the writers con-
sciously nor need they be thought of as proving an earlier
model. Quite a few authors proceed by dialogue to make
their point; we might even see in these works an attenu-
ated form of the drama rather than the impact of Socrates
or other famous partners in dialogue. Others are constructed as simply as a fable. But all of them are meant
to tell a story for the sake of entertainment or confes-

2

sion.

This design then, to teach by entertaining, to teach a particular form of life or virtue, is the chief feature of the novel of education. It does not depict complex human beings in their various irrational and psychological relationships, but emphasizes design, rationality, and purpose.

The plot and the content of the Novel of Education center around man. The fantastic, grotesque, ironic and idyllic are as much avoided as are complicated characters, parallel plots, indirect characterizations, difficult motivations, and dialogues and letters which do not develop or directly explain the principal incidents. The Novel of Education makes frequent use of questions and answers in dialogues; incidents are narrated without relying on accounts by other characters; a linear structure prevails, and the Rahmenerzählung is not found at all. The characters are mostly stereotypes and their attributes seldom overlap. Thus good and bad qualities are clearly distinguished. Occasionally an individual changes his life of vice to one of virtue. Incidents of the Novel of Education have a causal relationship: the good is rewarded and the bad punished. The happy end is an essential part of the definition of the genre. Frequent use of conversational ordinary language, a limited vocabulary, and a relatively simple sentence structure are its predominant style.

Our generic term "Novel of Education" need, however, include not only novels as such, but also other forms of prose fiction: the Erzählung, the calendar story[1] and other narratives found in Lesebücher, Taschenbücher, Almanache and periodicals; for these were more likely than long novels to reach the uneducated, farmers and burghers alike. At any rate, the German novel of the late eighteenth century, in spite of the excellent models of Wieland, Heinse and Goethe and the treatises on the genre by Blankenburg, Sulzer, Adelung and J. J. Engel, was not a clearly defined genre. The popular Journal der Romane, for example, intended to print long novels as well as stories "da die Romantheorie wahrscheinlich keinen wesentlichen Unterschied zwischen dem Roman und der kleineren Erzählung machen wird."[2] All fiction was to be printed "worinn ein romanhaftes Interesse herrscht, aber dennoch nicht von der Wirklichkeit abweicht."[3] Educational and moral advice for many problems appeared in long and short narratives and the more it

---

[1] "Der Kalender ist doch außer dem Gebetbuch oder der Bibel die einzige zuverläßige Lektüre des Handwerkers und hauptsächlich des Landmannes." Quoted in the review of Pestalozzi's Lienhard und Gertrud in Allgemeine Deutsche Bibliothek (Berlin: Friedrich Nicolai, 1765-1792), Vol. LII, Part 1, p. 149.

[2] Journal der Romane (Berlin: Unger, 1800), p. 5.

[3] Ibid.

made use of the narrative façade, the closer it came to be a "novel." Basedow's Elementarwerk (1770-1774), Bertuch's Bilderbuch für Kinder (1790ff), both based on Comenius' encyclopaedia Orbis sensualium pictus (1658), J. L. Ewald's Die Kunst, ein gutes Mädchen, eine gute Gattinn, Mutter und Hausfrau zu werden. Ein Handbuch für erwachsene Töchter, Gattinnen und Mütter (Bremen: Wilmans, 1798)[4] and many others do not have a fictional façade at all. Adelung's Leipziger Wochenblatt für Kinder (1772-1774) and its sequel Kinderfreund, edited by C. F. Weisse, Briefwechsel der Familie des Kinderfreundes (1784-1792) and Rochow's Bauernfreund (1773-1776) were patterned after the Moralische Wochenschriften. Campe's Kleine Kinderbibliothek (1783ff) also contained many fables, poems and moral stories. In all of these one finds traces of the Abenteuerroman, the plot of which is here interrupted with instructive dialogue and comments by the author.

Concrete Examples of the Novel of Education

The names of Rousseau and Pestalozzi, possibly of Fénelon and Madame de Genlis or Wieland, Campe, Hermes, Zschokke and even Gotthelf can give an indication of the range of the educational novel. It varies in artistic per-

---

[4]Neue Allgemeine Deutsche Bibliothek (Berlin: Friedrich Nicolai, 1801), Vol. LXVII, Part 1, p. 270.

fection according to whether its author was a great artist
like Gotthelf or merely a competent story-teller like
Zschokke or only a well-intentioned educator like Salzmann,
Campe or Rochow. The fictional characteristic is always
present and obvious. While an essay or treatise will proceed by themes, the Novel of Education rests on types or
"characters." A fictionalized account serves the purpose
to educate better than a treatise. "Fiction [ist] die beste Lehrerinn für die lebhafte jugendliche Phantasie."[5]
"Selbst die denkende Klasse von Menschen nimmt in gewissen
Beziehungen . . . die durch sinnliche Darstellungen mitgetheilte Belehrung williger an, als den Unterricht, welchen
sie in gerader Beziehung auf sich erhält."[6] It may well be
that the first form of the Educational Novel was the Moralische Wochenschrift,[7] the impact of which on the development of English fiction is known. But it would be rash to
draw conclusions as to the history of a genre when its bibliography and content are still unexplored. Such investigations must await the completion of a tabulation of the

---

[5]Ibid., Vol. XL, pt. 1, p. 188.

[6]Ibid., Vol. XXIX, pt. 2, pp. 484-485.

[7]Christian Friedrich Timme writes in the forword to
the fourth part of his Faramonds Familiengeschichte in Briefen (4 vols. 2d ed. Erfurt: Keyser, 1782): "Zu einer anderen Zeit würde ich meine Sammlung brauchbarer Wahrheiten in
die Form der moralischen Wochenschrift gebracht haben, aber
heutzutage liest das Publikum nur noch Romane und Schauspiele."

concrete material and require moreover many detailed studies in biography and history. Gottsched, for example, introduces fictional characters, as had his English counterparts and predecessors, to illustrate his educational aims. But whether he thereby influenced Pestalozzi or Jung-Stilling or Rudolph Zacharias Becker would be impossible for us to determine, unless these authors said so themselves. In our undertaking we shall avoid all deductions, however plausible, and not draw conclusions that would depend on surmise. When the whole material is tabulated and the content and the form of many such books is known, whether from a first hand reading or from the extensive and generally factual reviews that were once in use, it will perhaps be possible to see how different forms derive from different models, but it is obvious that the first prerequisite for further research is a factual and bibliographical investigation.

Method of Investigation

The first chapter of this dissertation is an extension of a Master's thesis.[8] It is a tabulation of all the novels of education that appear in the appropriate groupings of Friedrich Nicolai's <u>Neue Allgemeine Deutsche Bi</u>-

---

[8]Helmut Germer, "The German Novel of Education from 1792 to 1805: A Bibliography." Unpublished Master's thesis, The Graduate School, Vanderbilt University, Nashville, Tennessee, 1965.

bliothek (1793-1805). The headings under which these books
are listed are "Romane" (abbreviated in this study as R),
"Erziehungsschriften" (abbreviated as E), "Vermischte
Schriften" (abbreviated as VS), and occasionally "Staats-
wissenschaft," "Handlungswissenschaft," and "Arzneygelahrt-
heit." Each of these titles is checked against Kayser's Bücher-Lexicon,[9] which in intent at least was all-inclusive.
But actually it was not. Quite a few titles reviewed in the
Neue Allgemeine Deutsche Bibliothek do not appear in Kayser.
Nicolai's review journal attempted to review all publications
from all fields of knowledge. Nicolai wanted to have reviews
of all books published in Germany and proclaimed in several
of his prefaces this critical intent also as his patriotic
aim:

> "Ich hatte bey meiner A[llgemeinen] B[iblio-
> thek] eine andere und höhere Idee, die bloß auf
> Deutschland gerichtet war. In diesem unserm all-
> gemeinen Vaterlande, wo die Literatur nicht auf
> eine einzige Hauptstadt beschränkt ist, und wo
> daher der so wohlthätige mündliche Gedankenwech-
> sel seinen Einfluß nicht in so großem Umfange
> äußert, kann die literarische Verbindung nur
> schriftlich, und durch offenen Druck unterhal-
> ten werden. Selbst das ernste Streben nach Ver-
> besserung der prosaischen Schreibart und in den
> Werken der Einbildungskraft, ward durch Journale
> befördert, durch die Belustigung des Verstandes
> und des Witzes, durch die Bremischen Beyträge
> u.a., daher sind Journale in Deutschland für die

---

[9]Christian Gottlob Kayser, Index Locuplentissimus Librorum . . . Vollständiges Bücher-Lexicon enthaltend alle
von 1750 bis zum Ende des Jahres 1832 in Deutschland gedruckte Bücher (3 vols.; Leipzig: Ludwig Schumann, 1834-1836).

Literatur viel wichtiger, als z.B. in England
oder Frankreich."[10]

   "Wer wird nicht mit Überzeugung und Vergnügen
   erkennen, daß unter unsern Universitätsgelehrten
   in Deutschland berühmte und vortreffliche Männer
   in großer Anzahl von jeher gewesen sind, und noch
   sind, auch daß die deutschen Universitäten auf
   den Fortgang der Wissenschaften immer einen viel
   ausgebreiteteren und wohlthätigern Einfluß gehabt haben, als die Universitäten in andern Län-
   dern."[11]

If our tabulation is necessarily still incomplete, it

is nevertheless the best that can be had, short of trying

to find publications that may have been omitted or missed

by the most comprehensive review journal ever issued in Ger-

many. Thirteen books published between 1792 and 1805 have

been found in the "Meyer Collections" of the Joint Univer-

sity Libraries which had not been listed in the Neue All-

gemeine Deutsche Bibliothek. These (as well as a few nov-

els by Zschokke, Salzmann and J. H. Meynier which were not

published between 1792 and 1805) have therefore been added

separately to the bibliography as they show the continuous

success of the genre. It was first thought useful to check

the list against Goedeke's Grundriß, but this soon proved

unnecessary. Goedeke's listings lack too many of the titles

here offered, while they add none that could clearly be

assigned to the genre here under discussion.

---

[10]Neue Allgemeine Deutsche Bibliothek, Vol. CV, p. VI.

[11]Ibid., pp. XV-XVI.

The first chapter of this study offers then a cata-
logue of all the appropriate titles of novels of education
listed in the Neue Allgemeine Deutsche Bibliothek (abbreviated as N) with precise reference to the particular volume, part of the volume, page and heading under which it
is reviewed; they are indicated, for example, by N: Vol.
VI, pt. 2, pp. 367-370. (R). Anonymous works were checked
in Holzmann and Bohatta's Anonymen-Lexikon.[12] If they were
listed in this work their authors are indicated in the bibliography by brackets. Many reviews give the indexes of
those books containing more than one educational novel.
These indices have also been included in the bibliography.
The novels were then checked in Kayser's Bücher-Lexicon
(abbreviated as K) and the volume, part and page number
were noted. This gives us a first, and, for the periodical
under consideration, complete table of educational novels
between 1792 and 1805.

After completion of our unpublished Master's thesis,
1965, new material from the Joint University Library hold-
ings and other sources came to light. Besides, the tables
of contents of collections, reviewed in the Neue Allgemeine Deutsche Bibliothek, have since been searched and, when

---

[12]Michael Holzmann und Hanns Bohatta, Deutsches Anonymen-Lexikon 1501-1850 (7 vols.; Hildesheim: Georg Olms
Verlagsbuchhandlung, 1961 [reprographic reprint of the Weimar edition, 1902-1911]).

appropriate, included. Other additions were necessary to make the tabulations that are here first offered, more useful, especially as regards the form and survival of the genre.

All the publications are numbered according to their alphabetical sequence. These numbers are then used as the briefest reference in the chronological table at the end of the first chapter which gives the years of publications of the educational novels. This new table may give an indication of the statistics of the genre.

The second chapter lists all the themes of the novels of education that are given in the Neue Allgemeine Deutsche Bibliothek. To these were then added the predominant themes of the forty-three novels which I myself have read in full. Often it was difficult to find the ideal borderline between significant and less significant themes. Not all the reviews are equally explicit. Next, short summaries of the stories which illustrate these themes have been given. The numbers following these summaries correspond to the numbered titles of the bibliography in the first chapter. No doubt other categories might be set up. But as long as the listing gives a picture of the content of the novels, not biased to yield preconceived results, the arrangement is of no importance. It would, for instance, be possible to select "reform" themes and to correlate them with revolutionary movements, but when all themes are considered, such a selection would be biased.

The theme of "revolution" will therefore appear under many headings: education, reform by princes, squires, teachers, pastors, etc.

Christian Gotthilf Salzmann already called for a collection of educational fiction when he said:

> "Ich wünsche, daß man doch einmal aus den vielen Erzählungen, mit denen der gute Gott unser Jahrhundert gesegnet hat, besonders aus den Campischen, Weisischen, Rochowschen, und--(wenn nicht etwas Eigenliebe mich verleitet, sie hinzuzusetzen), aus den Unterhaltungen für Kinder und Kinderfreunde, einen guten Auszug machte, in dem die Erzählungen in eine bestimmte Ordnung gestellet, und unter gewisse Kapitel gebracht würden, so, daß jeder Lehrer mit leichter Mühe ein Geschichtchen, zur Beförderung der Ältern-, Menschen- und Gottesliebe, der Geduld, zur Steuerung des Eigensinnes, der Trägheit, u. d. gl. so oft er es nöthig hätte, finden könne."13

The third and final chapter contains a list of predominant formal characteristics of the Novel of Education. Again the numbers refer to the bibliography.

This dissertation does not attempt to come to any specific conclusions as to novel and story techniques, the personal traits of writers, changes in focus and interest, or even as to possible trends in the choice of the themes. It would be arbitrary to attempt such discussions on the basis of the material here covered, because it is of too short-range a run, comprising, as it does, only the years from 1792 to 1805. Nor can we give the history of the genre,

---

13Christian Gotthilf Salzmann, Über die wirksamsten Mittel Kindern Religion beyzubringen (Leipzig, 1787), p. 90.

influenced perhaps by the English novels of Defoe, Smollet and Richardson. or the Moralische Wochenschriften without considering first the novels of education of an earlier period. And finally we will not attempt to develop dependencies and relations between the Novel of Education and such books as Jung-Stilling's autobiography, K. P. Moritz' Anton Reiser (1785-1790), J. K. Wezel's Hermann und Ulrike (1780), Wieland's Agathon (1766-1768), Nicolai's Das Leben und die Meinungen des Herrn Magister Sebaldus Nothanker (1773-1776) and Hippel's Lebensläufe nach aufsteigender Linie (1778-1780). The works of Friedrich Eberhard von Rochow, Bernhard Overberg, Johann Ignaz Felbinger, Joseph Schreyvogel (Das Sonntagsblatt, 1807-1809), Matthias Claudius and Johann Peter Hebel can also be related to the Novel of Education, but such investigations may only be undertaken after further study of each author. It is hoped that our dissertation will have prepared the ground. For we do give as complete a tabulation of titles, contents and formal elements as the extant sources permit for the vital period when the transition from the Enlightenment to Romanticism took place. 1792, the first year of the reviews in the Neue Allgemeine Deutsche Bibliothek, was the year of which Goethe said "Von hier und heute geht eine neue Epoche der Weltgeschichte an." Fichte was writing his first book, Grundlage der gesamten Wissenschaftslehre (1794) which was to in-

fluence a generation of Germans in Jena where later some
of the Romanticists gathered. 1805 was the last year of
the reviews in the Neue Allgemeine Deutsche Bibliothek.
The journal ceased to appear in 1806, the same year when
Prussia was defeated at Jena and when the Heilige Römi-
sche Reich Deutscher Nation ended.

"Aufklärung" and the Educational Novel

It has not been attempted to evaluate the Educational Novel in terms of various concepts of "Enlightenment." It is nevertheless obvious that our chapter 2, with
its tabulations of character and plot characteristics, and
our chapter 3, with its listings of formal characteristics,
can serve as compendia not only of the late eighteenth century novel, but also of its social structure, moral aims,
human values, and aesthetic aspirations. The writer hopes
to follow up these questions in later studies.

The Allgemeine Deutsche Bibliothek

The Allgemeine Deutsche Bibliothek was founded in
1765 by Friedrich Nicolai (1733-1811). While other journals
with the exception of Haller's Göttingensche Anzeigen von
gelehrten Sachen had a local appeal,[14] the Allgemeine Deut-

---

[14]Joachim Kirchner, Das Deutsche Zeitschriftenwesen,
seine Geschichte und seine Probleme (Wiebaden, Otto Harrassowitz, 1958), Vol. I, p. 77.

"soll [ihrer] Absicht nach, eine allgemeine Nachricht von der ganzen neuen deutschen Litteratur von 1764 an, in sich enthalten. Man wird also darinn von allen in Deutschland neu herauskommenden Büchern und andern Vorfällen, die die Litteratur angehen, Nachricht zu ertheilen suchen. Schriften, von einiger Wichtigkeit, sonderlich deutsche Originalschriften, wird man ausführlich recensiren, so daß sich der Leser von dem ganzen Werke selbst aus der Recension einen richtigen Begriff machen kann. Die Leser sind in vielen Dörfern und Städten, zum Theil in kleinen Städten wo nicht einmal ein Buchladen befindlich ist, zerstreuet, und ihnen ist also sehr damit gedienet, zuverläßige Nachrichten von den neuen Büchern und von ihrem wahren Werthe zu erhalten."[15]

To effect his plan, Nicolai had 25 contributors for the journal in 1765,[16] almost 40 in 1767,[17] 50 in 1769,[18] almost 100 in 1778,[19] 130 in 1791,[20] and almost 150 in 1806.[21] These reviewers lived in all parts of Germany and, although they were "Männer von so bekannten Talenten, daß ihre Namen allein das Lob des Werkes ausmachen könnten, . . . wenn man sie veröffentlichen wolle,"[22] remained

---

[15] Allgemeine Deutsche Bibliothek, Vol. I, "Vorrede," p. 2.

[16] Ibid., Vol. I, p. 3.   [17] Ibid., Vol. IV, p. 2.

[18] Ibid., Vol. VIII, p. 4.   [19] Ibid., Vol. XXXVI, p. 3.

[20] Ibid., Vol. LXXXVI, "Anhang," pt. 5, p. 2.

[21] Neue Allgemeine Deutsche Bibliothek, Vol. CV, "Vorrede," p. 26.

[22] Allgemeine Deutsche Bibliothek, Vol. I, "Vorrede," p. 3.

anonymous.[23] In 1765 the journal consisted of two **Bände**
or four **Stücke**, but an increasing number of books forced
Nicolai to publish in future years as many as nine volumes
annually (1785, 1797, 1802, 1804), ten in 1793 and 1805,
eleven in 1780 and 1801, twelve in 1802 and thirteen in
1791. He meant to provide an all-encompassing review journal:

> "Die Verfasser . . . sind überhaupt bemühet
> gewesen, die allgemeine deutsche Bibliothek so
> vollkommen zu machen, als es die vielen Schwie-
> rigkeiten, die mit diesem Unternehmen verknüpft
> sind, haben zulassen wollen. . . . Wir werden
> uns ferner bemühen, die allgemeine deutsche Bi-
> bliothek so vollständig zu machen, als es mög-
> lich ist. Man wird, gesetzt, daß sie nicht ganz
> vollständig seyn konnten, doch in diesem Journa-
> le die ganze deutsche Litteratur vollständiger
> übersehen können, als es sonst irgend wo durch
> geschehen könnte. . . . Unser Zweck bleibt also,
> ausser den oben ausgenommenen Arten von Schriff-
> ten [Dissertationen, Predigten, Auszüge und Dis-
> positionen von Predigten, ganz kleine Tractät-
> chen, desgleichen Journale], alle neuen Bücher
> anzuzeigen, so viel uns nämlich bekannt werden."[24]

> "Es ist ausgemacht, daß man alsdann den An-
> wachs der deutschen Litteratur in diesen fünf
> Jahren, vollständiger wird übersehen, und bes-
> ser beurtheilen können, als sonst durch irgend-
> eine gelehrte Zeitung, oder eine andere gelehrte
> periodische Schrift geschehen kann. Der Haupt-

---

[23]The reviewers remained anonymous until Gustav Parthey
revealed their identity in his important work entitled Die
Mitarbeiter an Friedrich Nicolais Allgemeinen Deutschen Bibliothek nach ihren Namen und Zeichen in zwei Registern geordnet. Ein Beytrag zur deutschen Literaturgeschichte (Berlin: Nicolai, 1842). Cf. comments on this work by Oscar
Frambach, "Zur Jenaischen Allgemeinen Literatur-Zeitung
(JALZ)" in DVLG XXXVIII (1964), 4, pp. 576ff.

[24]Allgemeine Deutsche Bibliothek, Vol. VIII, p. 4.

zweck dieses Werkes ist, daß man daraus die Voll-
kommenheiten und die Mängel, die Veränderungen
und die Besserungen; kurz, den jetzigen Zustand
unserer Litteratur, theils soll kennen lernen,
theils mehr im Ganzen soll übersehen können, als
es sonst möglich ist. . . . Ohne Zweifel würde
eine periodische Schrift, die dieses thäte [bloß
wichtige und gute Bücher anzeigen], dem Leser eine viel angenehmere Aussicht öffnen, aber sie
würde ihm nicht den wahren Zustand der Litteratur vor Augen legen. . . . Man muß die Vollkom-
menheiten unserer Litteratur wissen, dieß ist
nöthig, aber ihre Mängel kennen lernen, um diese mit gutem Erfolge zu verbessern. Man lernt
diese Mängel am besten aus den mittelmäßigen
und schlechten Büchern kennen, mit denen Deutschland jährlich in ungeheurer Anzahl überschwemmet
wird. Sie entdecken aufs deutlichste, wie unvoll-
kommen die Kenntniße vieler unserer Mitbürger
sind, ja wie finster es noch in manchen ganzen
Provinzen Deutschlands aussiehet. Diese, obgleich
traurigen Bemerkungen, muß sich der nicht entge-
hen lassen, der von dem wahren Zustande unserer
Litteratur sich einige Begriffe machen will."[25]

In spite of his ambitious plans, Nicolai's <u>Allgemeine</u>

<u>Deutsche Bibliothek</u> had to become somewhat selective as early

as 1771.

"Es weiset die Erfahrung immer deutlicher,
wie unmöglich es sey, alle neu herauskommenden
Bücher, keines ausgenommen, anzuzeigen. . . .
Die Anzahl der Bogen dieses Anhanges selbst,
so enge er gedruckt ist, doch einen solchen Um-
fang hat, als vier Stücke oder zween Bände,
zeigt die Nothwendigkeit, künftig unter den Büchern eine Auswahl zu machen, wenn die a. d. B.
nicht allzu weitläufig werden soll. Das Bücher-
erscheinen wird ohnedies nicht weniger, sondern
mehr. Man wird bey der Fortsetzung dieses Werkes
beständig die ganze Deutsche Litteratur vor Augen haben. Man wird Bücher von allen Arten anzeigen, Von wichtigen wird keines ausgelassen
werden."[26]

---

[25] <u>Ibid</u>., Vol. XII, p. 3.   [26] <u>Ibid</u>., Vol. XII, p. 2.

"Es ist unglaublich, wie sehr das Bücherschrei-
ben zunimmt. Man hat einigemal in öffentlichen
Blättern, aus allgemeinen Meßverzeichnissen, Be-
rechnungen von der Anzahl der jährlich herauskommenden Bücher machen wollen. Sie sind aber unzu-
verläßig: denn es steht bey weitem nicht die Hälfte derselben in Meßverzeichnissen, besonders feh-
len fast alle im Katholischen Deutschland herauskommenden Bücher; sehr viele Schriften, die in
großen Städten, als Wien, Berlin, Hamburg u. a.
geschrieben und auch nur in diesen Städten gelesen werden; viele Bücher, die, auf Kosten der Verfasser gedruckt werden, u. a. m. Es sind gewiß
jährlich 5000 Bücher."[27]

When Nicolai published the last volume of the Neue

Allgemeine Deutsche Bibliothek in 1806, he wrote:

"Im Jahre 1765 kamen jährlich nur vier Stücke
oder zwey Bände heraus, jetzt, gegen Ende sind einigemal jährlich achtzehn [!] Bände gedruckt worden. Demungeachtet, und obgleich jetzt die A. D.
Bibl. viel enger gedruckt ward als am Anfange, war
es doch unmöglich, alle herauskommenden Bücher anzeigen zu lassen. Doch ist es meine beständige Sor-
ge gewesen, daß kein wirklich vorzügliches neues
Buch unangezeigt bliebe, und dass in jeder Wissenschaft oder Kunst von guten und schlechten Büchern
jeder Art so viele angezeigt würden, als mir nöthig
schien, treue Umrisse des Gemäldes der neuen deutschen Literatur zu zeichnen."[28]

Nicolai's efforts made the Allgemeine Deutsche Biblio-

thek one of the most widely distributed journals. 1800

copies of each volume were printed in 1785.[29]

In 1792 Nicolai ceased to be the editor of the review

---

27 Ibid., Vol. XXXVI, "Anhang," p. 3.

28 Neue Allgemeine Deutsche Bibliothek Vol. CV, p. XXVI.

29 Kirchner, loc. cit.

journal because he thought himself to be too old and
his son's death had caused him great grief:

> "Ich glaube, jetzt in einer Lage zu seyn, daß
> ich der a. d. B. nicht mehr so nützlich seyn kann,
> als sonst."[30]

In 1801, in the "Vorrede" to the fifty-sixth volume
of the Neue Allgemeine Deutsche Bibliothek, Nicolai reveals
that secret societies had prevailed on the successor of
Frederik the Great to prohibit the journal in Prussia. In
the last "Vorrede" (Vol. CV) Nicolai summarizes:

> "Daß ich wegen hämischen Verläumdungen und we-
> gen nachherigen Verfolgungen der sogenannten Exa-
> minationskommission im Jahre 1792 die Herausgabe
> der A. D. Bibl. in andere Hände zu geben genöthigt
> war; daß Hermes und Hilmer demungeachtet im Jahre
> 1794 bewirkten, daß dieses Werk in allen preußi-
> schen Ländern streng verbothen ward, unter dem Vor-
> wande: Es sey ein gefährlich Buch wider die Reli-
> gion, ist bekannt."[31]

In 1793 the journal merely changed its name to Neue
Allgemeine Deutsche Bibliothek and was published in Kiel.
Carl Ernst Bohn, its new editor, added a new section to
the journal:

> "Vom Jahre 1793 an wird der Allgemeinen Deutschen
> Bibliothek ein allgemeines deutsches litterarisches
> Intelligenzblatt beygefügt werden, worin jederman,
> gegen billige Gebühren, litterarische Nachrichten
> bekannt machen, und selbst Vertheidigungen gegen
> Recensionen in der a. d. B. oder in anderen Jour-
> nalen einrücken lassen kann, wenn sie in anstän-
> diger Schreibart abgefasset sind."[32]

---

[30] Allgemeine Deutsche Bibliothek, Vol. CVI, p. 5.

[31] Neue Allgemeine Deutsche Bibliothek, Vol. CV, p. 26.

[32] Allgemeine Deutsche Bibliothek, Vol. CVII, p. 2.

No other changes were made in the transition from the
Allgemeine Deutsche Bibliothek to the Neue Allgemeine Deutsche Bibliothek.

Already eight years later in 1800 the journal was
again edited by Nicolai in Berlin. The factual and rationalistic tenor of the Neue Allgemeine Deutsche Bibliothek
meant, however, nothing to the new generation in Weimar,
Jena and Berlin. Its circulation fell to 750 copies.[33] The
last volume was published in 1806 and concluded with reviews
of "all" books published in 1805.

A total of 251 volumes, each containing circa 550
pages, had appeared during the forty-one years of its existence. Each volume is divided into two Stücke and reviews
books under specific headings. Since 1766 (Vol. II, pt. 2)
all novels published in Germany, original works as well as
a few translations, were reviewed. Other journals also commented upon selected novels, notably the Göttingensche gelehrte Anzeigen (1739ff), Deutsches Museum (1776-1791), Der
Teutsche Merkur (1773-1810), Jenaische Allgemeine Litteraturzeitung (1785-1848) and Hallische gelehrte Zeitung (1766-
1792), as well as the minor periodicals edited by the Classic and Romantic poets, but they represent an altogether
different type of review. This can best be illustrated by
the Frankfurter gelehrte Anzeigen, from which one could

---

[33]Kirchner, loc. cit.

gather as little as from Claudius' Wandsbecker Boten as to which books came on the market and what they contained; for the reviewers did not feel the need to be objective and informative, they wanted to give vent to their own notions, feelings and values. The common quality of the Göttingensche gelehrte Anzeigen might perhaps be said to have been its emphasis on historical and philological fact and factual natural science, tinged with a strongly Hanoverian and British philosophy of government (English freedom versus French Revolution). It is defined by relatively few contributors: Albrecht von Haller, the orientalist Johann David Michaelis (1717-1790), the archeologist Christian Gottlob Heyne (1729-1812), the historian Arnold Heeren (1760-1842), Jacob (1785-1863) and Wilhelm Grimm (1786-1859) and the philologist Rudolph Hermann Lotze (1817-1881).[34] All the other periodicals are even more strongly governed by the particular writers and their ties of friendship and interests: one knows how Goethe could launch any kind of review in his own production, the Jenaische allgemeine Literaturzeitung. Nothing like this seems to have existed in the Berlin review journals which Nicolai himself edited.

Many of the books of the eighteenth century were published only once in small editions. Since novels were not deposited regularly in the universities or town libraries

---

[34]Wilhelm Kosch, Deutsches Literatur-Lexikon (2d ed.; Bern, A. Francke A. G. Verlag, 1949), Vol. I, p. 692.

they frequently disappeared altogether after their owners and the lending libraries discarded them. Other copies which might have been preserved through the nineteenth century were probably destroyed during the World Wars. Today there are few libraries which have as rich a selection of the German popular novel of the eighteenth century as the library of Muhlenberg College and the Meyer Collections in the Joint University Libraries in Nashville, Tennessee. The _Allgemeine Deutsche Bibliothek_, however, remains the only factual source left to us of many novels published between 1765 and 1805.

CHAPTER I

THE BIBLIOGRAPHY

Anonymous.   (1)
    Die Abendstunden einer glücklichen Familie, ein
    Lesebuch für Kinder von reiferm Alter.
    VI ⨍ 216 S.
    Nürnberg: Grattenauer, 1793.
    N: Vol. VI, pt. 2, pp. 508-509. (R).
    K: Vol. I, pt. 1, p. 10 b.

Anonymous.   (2)
    Amalie Seckendorf. Geschichte eines kleinen Mäd-
    chens aus der Schweiz. Ein Sittenbüchlein für die
    frühe, vorzüglich weibliche Jugend.
    96 S.
    St. Gallen: Huber und Compagnie, 1795.
    N: Vol. XXVIII, pt. 1, p. 206. (E).
    K: Vol. III, pt. 5, p. 208 b.

Anonymous,   (3)
    Annalen der Bürgerlichen Tugend, oder wahre Facta
    zur Bildung des Geistes und Herzens.
    1. Sammlung, 17 Bogen; 2. Sammlung, 16 Bogen.
    Flensburg und Leipzig: Kortensche Buchhandlung,
    1796.
    N: Vol. III, pt.1, p. 77; Vol. XXXI, pt. 1, p. 272.
    (VS).
    K: Vol. I, pt. 1, p. 76 b.

Anonymous. (4)

Anthologie für Knaben und Mädchen. Ein unterhal-
tendes Lesebuch zur Bildung des Verstandes und
Herzens.
Nürnberg: Raspesche Buchhandlung, 1804.
"Beyspiele der Weisheit und Tugend." (a)
"Erzählung von der Dürftigkeit eines Pfarrers."(b)
N: Vol. CI, pt. 2, pp. 391-392. (E).
K: Vol. I, pt. 1, p. 81 a.

Anonymous. (5)

Armins biographische Geschichte, ein Buch für El-
tern, Erzieher und Jünglinge.
13 Bogen.
No place or publisher cited. 1792.
N: Vol. IV, pt. 2, p. 512. (E).
K: Vol. I, pt. 1, p. 106 a.

Anonymous. (6)

Auguste und Hieronimus: oder Briefe über die moralische Bildung des Menschen, nach den Bedürf-
nissen unserer Zeit.
1. Theil, 6½ Bogen; 2. Theil, 11 Bogen; 3. Theil,
17 Bogen.
Schleßwig: Röhß, 1796-1797.
N: Vol. XXXV, pt. 1, pp. 98-100; Vol. LVI, pt. 2,
pp. 378-380. (R).
K: Vol. I, pt. 1, p. 123 a.

Anonymous. (7)

Auswahl kleiner Liebesgeschichten in sittlichen
Erzählungen aus deutschen Zeitschriften.
1. Bändchen, 240 S.
"Die Stärke des Vorurtheils." (a)
"Glück aus Unglück." (b)

"Eine gefährliche Probe." (c)
Berlin, 1799.
<u>N</u>: Vol. XLIX, pt. 1, pp. 77-79. (R).
<u>K</u>: Vol. III, Romane, p. 11 b.

Anonymous. (8)
Der Bauernfreund, ein allgemein nützliches Lesebuch für Bürger und Landleute, wie auch für Stadt
und Landschulen.
31 Bogen.
Frankfurt und Leipzig, 1794.
<u>N</u>: Vol. XXII, pt. 2, p. 406. (VS).
<u>K</u>: Vol. I, pt. 1, p. 161 a.

Anonymous. (9)
Beyspiele von allerley Unglücksfällen, zur Belehrung und Warnung besonders für die Jugend.
168 S.
Göttingen: Dieterich, 1798.
<u>N</u>: Vol. LI, pt. 1, pp. 276-277. (VS).
<u>K</u>: Vol. I, pt. 1, p. 187 b.

Anonymous. (10)
Braut und Bräutigam, oder das neunundzwanzigste
Kapitel vor dem Ende. Ein züchtiger Roman, voller
Laune und Witz, für Alt und Jung zum Trost und
zur Erbauung geschrieben.
253 S.
Leipzig: 1803.
<u>N</u>: Vol. XCII, pt. 1, p. 91. (R).
<u>K</u>: Vol. III, Romane, p. 21 b.

Anonymous. (11)
Geheime Briefe an die gesunde Vernunft; Etwas

für (nach schlechter Waare) lüsterne Leser.

19½ Bogen.

Constantinopel, 1794. K: Rostock: Stiller, 1794.

N: Vol. XII, pt. 2, pp. 485-486. (VS).

K: Vol. I, pt. 1, p. 355 b.

Anonymous.   (12)

Die geheime Brieftasche.

1. Bändchen, VIII ╪ 196 S.

"Vierzigjährige Briefe zweyer Frauenzimmer."   (a)

"Gespräche im Olymp."   (b)

"Reiseblätter."   (c)

"Amaliens Geschichte."   (d)

2. Bändchen, 182 S.

"Über weibliche Freundlichkeit, an Sophie X.
von Elisa."   (e)

"Julie Wanner, eine wahre Geschichte."   (f)

"Das Impromptu."   (g)

"Reiseblätter."   (h)

Berlin und Leipzig, 1805.

N: Vol. XCVII, pt. 1, pp. 86-87. (R).

K: Vol. III, Romane, p. 22 a.

Anonymous.   (13)

Cäciliens Briefe an Lilla. Ein Handbuch für Bräute, Gattinnen und Mütter, oder solche, die es
werden wollen.

1. Band, 344 S.; 2. Band, 313 S.

Tübingen: Cotta, 1803.

N: Vol. LXXXIX, pt. 2, pp. 498-504. (VS).

K: Vol. I, pt. 1, p. 402 a.

Anonymous.   (14)

Edelsinn und Tugendhöhe der Weiblichkeit, in Beyspie-

len aus der wirklichen Geschichte.
XXX ≠ 745 S.
Münster und Leipzig: Theissing, 1803.

N: Vol. LXXXV, pt. 1, p. 241. (VS).

K: Vol. I pt. 2, p. 97 a.

Anonymous.   (15)

Erdmann Hülfreichs erfahrne Hausmutter auf dem
Lande, in der Beschreibung der Wirthschaft seiner Frau Katharine (,) zur Belehrung für Bauersweiber und Töchter (,) die auch gute Hausmütter
werden solen.
200 S.
Leipzig: Schlegg, 1802.

N: Vol. LXXVII, pt. 2, p. 520. (Haushaltswissenschaft).

K: Vol. II, pt. 3, p. 211 b.

Anonymous.   (16)

Erzählungen lustiger und trauriger Begebenheiten zur Unterhaltung, Belehrung und Warnung für
den Bürger und Landmann.
388 S.
Leipzig: Solbrig, 1793.

N: Vol. VI, pt. 2, pp. 549-550. (VS).

K: Vol. I, pt. 2, p. 156 a.

Anonymous.   (17)

Erzählungen und Gespräche von Ereignissen und
Vorfällen im gemeinsamen Leben. Kindern zum Unterricht, und Erwachsenen zur Erinnerung.
8 Bogen.
Leipzig: Hilscher, 1796.

N: Vol. XXIX, pt. 1, p. 50. (E).

K: Vol. I, pt. 2, p. 156 b.

Anonymous. (18)

Erzählungen zur Unterhaltung für alle Stände und
Vorbereitung tieferer Kenntniß menschlicher Schick-
sale.
29 Bogen.
    "Das edle und große Weib." (a)
    "Der Ball." (b)
    "Das Tagebuch eines Frauenzimmers. (c)
    "S. Nachlaß." (d)
    "Unglück aus Speculation." (e)
    "Die verwandelte Feindin." (f)
    "Der schöne Wechsel der Zeit." (g)
    "Der Einzige in Allem." (h)
    "Die edle Findlingin." (i)
Augsburg: Stage, 1793.
N: Vol. IX, pt. 1, p. 278. (VS).
K: Vol. I, pt. 2, p. 158 a.

Anonymous. (19)

Etwas über den Selbstmord, in einer wahren Ge-
schichte zur Warnung.
146 S.
Frankfurt am Main: Hermann, 1802.
N: Vol. LXXX, pt. 2, pp. 532-534. (VS).
K: Vol. I, pt. 2, p. 167 b.

Anonymous. (20)

Die glückliche Familie und der ungerathene Sohn.
Ein Lesebuch für Bürger und Landleute.
359 S.
Koburg: Ahl, 1803.
N: Vol. XCIV, pt. 1, pp. 87-90. (VS).
K: Vol. I, pt. 2, p. 191 a.

Anonymous.   (21)

    <u>Kleine Familiengeschichten.</u>

    194 S.

       "Ida: Eitle Erziehung und ihre Gefahren."   (a)

    Aarnheim: Neue Gelehrten Buchhandlung, 1801.

    <u>N</u>: Vol. LXXV, pt. 2, pp. 392-394. (R).

    <u>K</u>: Not listed.

Anonymous.   (22)

    <u>Ferdinand Ehrenfels Jugendjahre. Ein Beytrag zur</u>

    <u>Pädagogik.</u>

    VIII / 438 S.

    Leipzig: Supprian, 1798.

    <u>N</u>: Vol. LIX, pt. 2, pp. 525-526. (E).

    <u>K</u>: Vol. I, pt. 2, p. 102 b.

Anonymous.   (23)

    <u>Ferdinand Sternheim. Zur Lectüre für junge Leute</u>

    <u>in den Musestunden (Mußestunden!).</u>

    112 S.

    Erfurt: Vollmersche Buchhandlung, 1796. <u>K</u>: Leip-

    zig: Andrä; Anst: Hildebrand, 1796.

    <u>N</u>: Vol. XXX, pt. 1, p. 96. (R).

    <u>K</u>: Vol. III, Romane, p. 135 b.

Anonymous.   (24)

    <u>Floride, oder die Liebe zur Natur.</u>

    262 S.

    Jena: Cröker, 1804.

    <u>N</u>: Vol. XCIII, pt. 2, p. 415. (R).

    <u>K</u>: Vol. III, Romane, p. 43 b.

Anonymous.   (25)

    <u>Frans Grünbergs Abendunterhaltungen mit seinen</u>

    <u>kleinen Kindern über die Erde, Natur und Menschen.</u>

1. Band, 24 Bogen; 2. Band, 21 Bogen. <u>K</u>: 3 Bände,
Nürnberg: Raspesche Buchhandlung, 1803.
<u>N</u>: Vol. XCI, pt. 2, pp. 442-443; Vol. C, pt. 2,
p. 377. (E).
<u>K</u>: Vol. I, pt. 2, p. 444 b.

Anonymous. (26)
   <u>Franz Weichenberg; eine Lectüre für Wohllüstlin-</u>
   <u>ge.</u>
   326 S.
   Breslau: Hirschberg, 1796; Lissa in Südpreußen:
   Korn d.ä, 1796.
<u>N</u>: Vol. XXX, pt. 2, p. 380. (R).
<u>K</u>: Vol. III, Romane, p. 149 a.

Anonymous. (27)
   <u>Friedrich Bickerkuhl. Ein Roman aus dem Leben und</u>
   <u>für dasselbe.</u>
   408 S.
   Dortmund: Mallinckrodt, 1802.
<u>N</u>: Vol. LXXXIII, pt. 2, pp. 362-363. (R).
<u>K</u>: Not listed.

Anonymous. (28)
   <u>Neueste Gallerie edler und unedler Menschenhand-</u>
   <u>lungen. Lectüre für Leser feinern Gefühls.</u>
   1. Bändchen, 9 Bogen; 2. Bändchen, 9 Bogen.
   Budissin: Arnold, 1792-1793.
<u>N</u>: Vol. III, pt. 2, p. 390; Vol. IX, pt. 2, pp. 340-
341. (VS).
<u>K</u>: Vol. I, pt. 2, p. 295 a.

Anonymous. (29)

Einige geographische, historische und moralische
Gegenstände für gute und fleißige Kinder. Ein
Weihnachtsgeschenk.
15 Bogen.
Leipzig: Gräff, 1804.
N: Vol. XCI, pt. 2, pp. 439-442. (E).
K: Vol. I, pt. 2, p. 322 b.

Anonymous. (30)

Geniestreiche älterer und neuerer Erzieher. Oder
wichtige Beyträge zur Geschichte der Pädagogik
des verflossenen achtzehnten Jahrhunderts.
VIII ≠ 438 S.
Leipzig: Supprian, 1801.
N: Vol. LXXIV, pt. 1, p. 272. (VS).
K: Vol. III, Romane, p. 50 a.

Anonymous. (31)

Geschichte der Familie von Bernheim. Ein angeneh-
mes und lehrreiches Lesebuch.
16 Bogen.
Braunschweig: Verlag der Schulbuchhandlung, 1795.
N: Vol. XXIV, pt. 1, p. 57. (E).
K: Vol. III, Romane, p. 51 b.

Anonymous. (32)

Graf Wildburg, oder Unglück durch Temperament
und Pfaffenränke.
1. Theil, 279 S. K: 4 Theile.
Halle: Ruff, 1800. K: Halle, Fr. Ruff, 1801.
N: Vol. LXII, pt. 2, pp. 352-353. (R).
K: Vol. III, Romane, p. 151 b.

Anonymous.   (33)

    <u>Gustav Mehrwelt, oder die Quelle der Glückselig-</u>
    <u>keit. Ein satyrischer Roman.</u>
    272 S.
    Leipzig: Martini, 1798; <u>K</u>: Leipzig: Knobloch,
    1797.
<u>N</u>: Vol. XLVII, pt. 2, pp. 327-329. (R).
<u>K</u>: Vol. III, Romane, p. 58 a.

Anonymous.   (34)

    <u>Heinrich Goswin, eines noch lebenden Mannes, Le-</u>
    <u>ben und Schicksale.</u>
    219 S.
    Stuttgart: Ehrhard und Löflund, 1792.
<u>N</u>: Vol. V, pt. 2, pp. 595-596. (R).
<u>K</u>: Vol. III, Romane, p. 55 b.

Anonymous.   (35)

    <u>Huldigung dem Genius des weiblichen Geschlechts.</u>
    <u>Über die Würde, die Pflichten, die Rechte und</u>
    <u>die Bildung des weiblichen Geschlechts.</u>
    300 S.
    Breslau: Schall, 1801.
<u>N</u>: Vol. LXXVII, pt. 1, pp. 270-271. (VS).
<u>K</u>: Vol. II, pt. 3, p. 211 a.

Anonymous.   (36)

    <u>Jahrbuch zur belehrenden Unterhaltung für Damen.</u>
    <u>Für das Jahr 1802.</u>
    16 Bogen.
        "Liebesnoth und Liebesglück."   (a)
        "Die kurze Ehe."   (b)
    Leipzig: Seeger, 1802.
<u>N</u>: Vol. LXXIII, pt. 2, pp. 545-549. (VS).
<u>K</u>: Not listed.

Anonymous.   (37)

    <u>Julie Wolmar. Ein Bild des Weibes, wie es sich</u>
    <u>der Weise denkt und der Mann von Geiste und</u>
    <u>Herz träumt. Als Seitenstück zur Sophie, dem</u>
    <u>Bilde edler Jungfräulichkeit.</u>
    406 S.
        "Über Herzensverbindungen in Beziehung auf
          das weibliche Geschlecht."   (a)
        "Julie Wolmar und ihres Mannes Portrait."   (b)
        "Privatleben Wolmars und Juliens."   (c)
        "Weise Einrichtung des Wolmarschen Hauses,
          in Beziehung auf die Dienerschaft."   (d)
        "Julie als Erzieherinn ihrer Kinder."   (e)
    Leipzig: Martini, 1803.
<u>N</u>: Vol. XCIV, pt. 1, pp. 129-132. (R).
<u>K</u>: Vol. III, pt. 6, p. 284 a.

Anonymous.   (38)

    <u>Für gute Kinder und solche die es werden wollen.</u>
    2. Bändchen, 204 S.; 3. Band.
        "Folge der Verschwendung, eine Erzählung."   (a)
        "Der Vorwitz bestraft sich immer selbst."   (b)
        "Edelmuth eines Mohren."   (c)
    Leipzig: Joachim Müller, 1792.
<u>N</u>: Vol. VII, pt. 1, p. 291; Vol. XXV, pt. 2, p. 330.
    (E).
<u>K</u>: Vol. II, pt. 3, p. 338 b.

Anonymous.   (39)

    <u>Neues moralisches Kinderbuch. Ein Neujahrge-</u>
    <u>schenk.</u>
    7½Bogen.
    Leipzig: Rein, 1800.
<u>N</u>: Vol. LIX, pt. 1, p. 223. (E).
<u>K</u>: Vol. II, pt. 3, p. 338 b.

Anonymous. (40)

> Die Kunst zu Vermögen und Ansehen zu gelangen.
> Lebensbeschreibungen von Personen, die als Mu-
> ster zur Nachahmung aufgestellt zu werden ver-
> dienen.
> 1. Bändchen, X / 220 S.
> Berlin: Sander, 1801.

N̈: Vol. LXXIV, pt. 1, pp. 183-186. (VS).
K: Vol. II, pt. 3, p. 446 b.

Anonymous. (41)

> Der Kutscher und sein Herr, oder Lob des schnel-
> len Reitens und Fahrens in volkreichen Städten
> und engen Straßen. Mit philosophisch- politisch-
> und physiognomischen Bemerkungen.
> 72 S.
> No place of publication cited, 1799.

N: Vol. XLIX, pt. 2, pp. 405-406. (VS).
K: Not listed.

Anonymous. (42)

> Laterna Magica, ein satyrisch-moralischer Roman
> ohne Vehmen, Ritter und Pfaffen.
> 1. Theil, 416 S.
> Hamburg: Hoffmann, 1795.

N: Vol. XXI, pt. 1, pp. 190-194. (R).
K: Vol. III, Romane, p. 80 a.

Anonymous. (43)

> Leben und Meinungen des Dorfschulmeisters Wenzel
> Caseus. Ein wichtiger Beytrag zu den Selbstbiogra-
> phien großer Männer.
> 1. Theil,406 S.
> Hamburg: Barth, 1800.

N: Vol. LXVII, pt. 2, pp. 328-330. (R).

<u>K</u>: Not listed.

Anonymous.   (44)

    <u>Leben und Thaten eines Weltbürgers. Mit Seiten-</u>
    <u>hieben auf manche Modethorheit unsers Jahrhun-</u>
    <u>derts</u>.
    1. Theil, 132 S. 2. Theil, 272 S.
    Berlin: Vieweg, 1798-1800.
<u>N</u>: Vol. XLI, pt. 2, pp. 309-314; Vol. LXV, pt. 2,
    pp. 358-359. (R).
<u>K</u>: Vol. III, Romane, p. 83 a.

Anonymous.   (45)

    <u>Lebensgeschichte der Maria Weinerin, oder jen-</u>
    <u>seits muß Vergeltung sein? eine Geschichte zur</u>
    <u>Belehrung, Trost und Unterhaltung für Leidende</u>.
    14 Bogen.
    Leipzig: Link, 1800.
<u>N</u>: Vol. LXV, pt. 2, pp. 352-354. (R).
<u>K</u>: Not listed.

Anonymous.   (46)

    <u>Lebensgeschichte Siegfried Habermanns, eines gu-</u>
    <u>ten Landmanns in Mahrendorf</u>.
    264 S.
    Magdeburg: Keil, 1804.
<u>N</u>: Vol. LXXXIX, pt. 2, pp.504-506. (VS).
<u>K</u>: Vol. II, pt. 3, p. 500 a.

Anonymous.   (47)

    <u>Lesebuch in Beyspielen, für dienende Mädchen und</u>
    <u>solche,die es werden wollen</u>.
    1. Sammlung, 6½ Bogen.
    Berlin: Müller, 1802.

N: Vol. LXXVII, pt. 1, pp. 236-237. (E).
K: Vol. II, pt. 3, p. 529 a.

Anonymous.   (48)

    Die Leuchte (,) oder die weisse (weiße) Frau.
    Ein Geistermärchen aus dem achtzehnten Jahrhun-
    dert.
    236 S.
    Leipzig: Kaven, 1797.
N: Vol. XXXVIII, pt. 2, pp. 443-444. (R).
K: Vol. III, Romane, p. 85 b.

Anonymous.   (49)

    Louise, ein Weib, wie ich es wünsche.
    384 S.
    Breslau: Korn, 1802.
N: Vol. LXXXIII, pt. 2, pp. 355-362. (R).
K: Vol. III, Romane, p. 98 a.

Anonymous.   (50)

    Ludwig Waghals. Ein Gemälde menschlicher Sitten,
    Thorheiten, Laster u.s.w. in allen Himmelstrichen.
    Seitenstück zu Hans Kiekindiewelts Reisen.
    25 Bogen.
    Leipzig: Gera, 1795.
N: Vol. XXIV, pt. 1, p. 93. (R).
K: Vol. III, Romane, p. 146 b.

Anonymous.   (51)

    Ludwig Wildau, oder Reue versöhnt. Ein Familien-
    gemälde des achtzehnten Jahrhunderts.
    116 S.
    Leipzig: Supprian, 1798.
N: Vol. XLIV, pt. 2, p. 384. (R).
K: Vol. III, Romane, p. 89 b.

Anonymous.   (52)

    <u>Natalie Normann, das Mädchen im Thale; oder die</u>
    <u>Gefahren der Einsamkeit</u>.
    25½ Bogen.
    Leipzig: Jacobäer, 1803. Neue Ausgabe; Altona:
    Aue, 1805.
<u>N</u>: Vol. LXXXII, pt. 2, pp. 364-365. (R).
<u>K</u>: Vol. III, Romane, p. 101b.

Anonymous.   (53)

    <u>Die sonderbare Nonne, oder die erfüllten Gelübde</u>.
    255 S.
    Breßlau: Korn, 1801.
<u>N</u>: Vol. LXXXVIII, pt. 2, pp. 384-385. (R).
<u>K</u>: Vol. III, Romane, p. 101 b.

Anonymous.   (54)

    <u>Novellen zur angenehmen Unterhaltung</u>.
    2. Bändchen, 300 S.
      "Minchens Lebenslauf.Eine Warnung für Mäd-
      chen."   (a)
    Weissenfels und Leipzig: Severin, 1798.
<u>N</u>: Vol. XLI, pt. 1, pp. 59-60. (R).
<u>K</u>: Vol. III, Romane, p. 102 a.

Anonymous.   (55)

    <u>Pächter Martin über die moralische Anwendung der</u>
    <u>französischen Revolution. Nebst Anhang über die</u>
    <u>Abschaffung der französischen Sprache im gemeinen</u>
    <u>Leben</u>.
    Göttingen: Dietrich, 1796.
<u>N</u>: Vol. XXXVII, pt. 2, p. 272. (VS).
<u>K</u>: Vol. II, pt. 4, p. 36 a.

Anonymous.   (56)

    <u>Peter Lebrecht. Eine Geschichte ohne Abentheu-
    erlichkeiten</u>.
    1. Theil, 144 S.
    Berlin und Leipzig: Fr. Nicolai, 1795.
    <u>N</u>: Vol. XXIII, pt. 2, pp. 526-527. (R).
    <u>K</u>: Not listed.

Anonymous.   (57)

    <u>Pöcile für studirende Jünglinge und ihre Führer</u>.
    1. Bändchen, 164 S.
    Leipzig: Kummer, 1801.
    <u>N</u>: Vol. LXXIII, pt. 2, pp. 461-463. (E).
    <u>K</u>: Not listed.

Anonymous.   (58)

    <u>Die Reise auf den Brocken. Eine Geschichte am En-
    de des philosophischen Jahrhunderts</u>.
    1. Theil, 14 Bogen; 2. Theil, 14 Bogen; 3. Theil,
    14 Bogen.
    Leipzig: Dyk, 1801.
    <u>N</u>: Vol. LXXXII, pt. 2, pp. 359-360. (R).
    <u>K</u>: Vol. II, pt. 4, p. 476 a.

Anonymous.   (59)

    <u>Reisen und Genesungen eines am Geiste seltsam ge-
    fesselten jungen russischen Edelmanns</u>.
    302 S.
    Leipzig und Kopenhagen: Schubothe, 1804.
    <u>N</u>: Vol. XCIX, pt. 2, p. 324. (R).
    <u>K</u>: Vol. II, pt. 4, p. 476 b.

Anonymous.   (60)

    <u>Robinson der Jüngste. Ein Lesebuch für Kinder</u>.
    1. Theil, 364 S.

Riga: Hartknoch, 1797.

N: Vol. XL, pt. 1, pp. 192-194. (E).

K: Vol. III, Romane, p. 114 b.

Anonymous. (61)

Kleine Romane, Feenmärchen, und unterhaltende Er-
zählungen.

1. Bändchen, 256 S.

Leipzig: Sommersche Buchhandlung, 1799. K: Leipzig: Nauck, 1792.

N: Vol. LIV, pt. 1, p. 41. (R).

K: Vol. III, Romane, p. 115 b.

Anonymous. (62)

Rosamundens Feierstunden. In Erzählungen, klei-
nen Romanen und Gedichten. Für Geist und Herz zur
Unterhaltung.

188 S.

Budißin und Leipzig: Arnold, 1798.

N: Vol. XLVII, pt. 1, p. 125. (VS).

K: Vol. III, Romane, p. 116 b.

Anonymous. (63)

Sammlung moralischer Erzählungen, oder Wahrheit
und Dichtung zur Beförderung wahrer Lebensweis-
heiten und Sittlichkeit.

1. Bändchen, 21 Bogen.

Erfurt: Rudolphi, 1804.

N: Vol. XCV, pt. 1, pp. 256-259. (E).

K: Vol. III, pt. 5, p. 23 b.

Anonymous. (64)

Die Schule der Erfahrung für Alle, welchen Zufrie-
denheit, Leben und Gesundheit etwas werth sind.
Warnende Thatsachen, zur Verhütung alltäglicher

Unglücksfälle.
1. Theil, 245 S. 2. Theil, 336 S. Auch unter dem
Titel: Durch Schaden wird man klug, 1. Theil;
und Werdet glücklich durch mein Unglück, 2. Theil.
3. Theil, 274 S. Auch unter dem Titel: Durch
Schaden wird man klug. Zweyhundert ein und drei-
ßig Geschichten aus der wirklichen Welt.
4. Theil, 174 S. Auch unter dem Titel: Durch
Schaden wird man klug. Einhundert vier und drei-
ßig Geschichten aus der wirklichen Welt.
Berlin: Maurer, 1797-1800.
N: Vol. XLIII, pt. 2, p. 540; Vol. LII, pt. 2,
p. 404; Vol. LV, pt. 2, pp. 434-435; Vol. LXXIV,
pt. 2, pp. 479-480; Vol. LXXXVIII, pt. 1, p. 194.
(VS).
K: Vol. III, pt. 5, p. 170 b.

Anonymous.   (65)
Sophrosyne, oder Reinheit der Seele und des Kör-
pers für Familienglück und Bürgerwohl.
164 S.
Leipzig: Jacobäer, 1799. K: Altona, Aue, 1799.
N: Vol. LXIII, pt. 1, p. 144. (VS).
K: Vol. III, pt. 5, p. 278 a.

Anonymous.   (66)
Angenehmer goldener Spiegel für Jünglinge und
Mädchen zum Vergnügen und (zur) Belehrung, mit
Gedichten, Erzählungen, Anekdoten und kleinem
Roman.
6 Bogen.
  "Der gute Vorsatz."   (a)
  "Der weinerliche Knabe."   (b)
  "Der unvorsichtige Knabe."   (c)

"Grausamkeit gegen Thiere." (d)
"Geschichte eines unartigen Kindes." (e)
"Das eitle Mädchen." (f)
"Der Zänker." (g)
"Die Wirkungen des Beyspiels." (h)
"Goldener Spiegel für kleine stolze Mädchen." (i)
"Die Unordnung." (j)
"Der unglückliche Fall." (k)
"Das Kinderfest." (l)
"Die Wohlthätigkeit." (m)
"Die Misgunst." (n)
"Die Lüge." (o)
"Die zwey unglücklichen Brüder." (p)
No place of publication cited, 1792.

<u>N</u>: Vol. III, pt. 2, pp. 530-531. (E).

<u>K</u>: Not listed.

Anonymous. (67)

Der Staarstecher. Zum Nutzen und Frommen aller
französischgesinnten deutschen Bürger.
Germanien, in Donnersberg am linken Rheinufer,
1799.
32 S.

<u>N</u>: Vol. LIV, pt. 2, pp. 366-367. (VS).

<u>K</u>: Vol. III, pt. 5, p. 299 a.

Anonymous. (68)

Taschenbuch für den Bürger und Landmann.
8 Bogen.
Berlin: Hayn, 1796.

<u>N</u>: Vol. XXIX, pt. 1, p. 268. (VS).

<u>K</u>: Vol. III, pt. 5, p. 396 a.

Anonymous. (69)

    <u>Theodor Hardenberg, oder die Folgen der Erziehung</u>.
1. Theil, 16½ Bogen; 2. Theil, 19 Bogen, 3. Theil,
20 Bogen.
Königsberg: Göbbels, 1802. <u>K</u>: Neue Ausgabe; Kö=
nigsberg: Unzer, 1817.

<u>N</u>: Vol. LXXXI, pt. 1, pp. 110-113. (R).

<u>K</u>: Vol. III, Romane, p. 59 b.

Anonymous. (70)

    <u>Der Triumph der Unschuld oder die Stiefmutter</u>.
<u>Eine Geschichte in Briefen</u>.
368 S.
Stendal: Franzen und Grosse, 1793.

<u>N</u>: Vol. XXVIII, pt. 2, pp. 308-314. (R).

<u>K</u>: Vol. III, Romane, p. 141 a.

Anonymous. (71)

    <u>Neue Unterhaltungen für Kinder und Kinderfreunde</u>.
Halle: Buchhandlung des Waisenhauses, 1792.

<u>N</u>: Vol. III, pt. 2, pp. 438-439. (E).

<u>K</u>: Vol. III, pt. 6, p. 18 a.

Anonymous. (72)

    <u>Das Weib ohne physische Liebe. Eine wahre Ge-
schichte</u>.
348 S.
Zeitz: Webel, 1803.

<u>N</u>: Vol. XCI, pt. 2, pp. 348-351. (R).

<u>K</u>: Vol. III, Romane, p. 149 a.

Anonymous. (73)

    <u>Wilhelmine Reinhard. Ein Pendant zu dem Leben
und Thaten eines Weltbürgers</u>.
194 S.

Berlin: Vieweg, 1802.

N: Vol. LXXXIII, pt. 2, pp. 368-369. (R).

K: Vol. III, Romane, p. 111 a.

A., N. (74)

Der rechtschaffende Professionist, ein Taschenbuch für alle Handwerker.
1. Theil, 165 S. 2. Theil, 130 S. Auch unter dem
Titel: Allgemeines Handbuch beym Handel und in
bürgerlichen Haushaltungen.
Meißen: Uz, 1804.

N: Vol. CIII, pt. 1, p. 222. (VS).

K: Vol. II, pt. 4, p. 403 b.

Adelbert. (75)

Amathusia, oder über die Geheimnisse der Toilette.
Ein Geschenk für Damen.
236 S.
Leipzig: Reinicke. No date given.

N: Vol. X, pt. 2, pp. 387-382. (VS).

K: Vol. I, pt. 1, p. 51 a.

Adlerjung, Johann Ludwig. (76)

Unterhaltungen eines Lehrers mit seinen Schülern,
in belehrenden und warnenden Erzählungen, zum Un-
terrichte der erwachsenen Jugend beyderley Ge-
schlechts.
17 Bogen.
 "Der gute Anton." (a)
 "Anton Schieferstein." (b)
 "Thomas." (c)
 "Hermann." (d)
Prag und Leipzig: Widtmann, 1792.

N: Vol. III, pt. 2, p. 440. (E).

K: Vol. I, pt. 1, p. 31 a.

[Ahlefeld, Charlotte Sophie Louise Wilhelmine von.] (77)
 Die Bekanntschaft auf der Reise, oder Liebe und
 Zweifelsinn.
 1. Theil, 307 S.; 2. Theil, 320 S.
 Leipzig: Widtmann, 1804.
 N: Vol. XCV, pt. 1, pp. 70-72. (R).
 K: Vol. III, Romane, p. 5a.

Albrecht, S. (78)
 Legenden.
 1. Bändchen, 124 S.
  "Das höfliche Gespenst." (a)
 Altona und Leipzig: Bechtold, 1797.
 N: Vol. XLV, pt. 2, pp. 367-368. (R).
 K: Vol. III, Romane, p. 83 b.

Ambornberge, B. W. (79)
 Vorträge an seine Schüler; Lesebuch für Jünglin-
 ge und Wißbegierige.
 Auch unter dem Titel: Spiegel für die Bildung jun-
 ger Herzen. Ein Sittenbuch für Jedermann.
 216 S.
 Prag: Neureutter, 1793; Prag und Leipzig: Al-
 brecht und Compagnie, 1795.
 N: Vol. XXII, pt. 1, pp. 143-144. (E).
 K: Vol. I, pt. 1, p. 51 a.

Armbruster, Johann Michael. (80)
 Gemälde aus der Kinderwelt. Zur Belehrung und Un-
 terhaltung.
 9 Bogen.
 St. Gallen: Huber und Compagnie, 1794.
 N: Vol. XVI, pt. 2, p. 476. (E).
 K: Vol. I, pt. 2, p. 333 b.

44

———————————.

Johann Caspar Lavaters Regeln für Kinder, durch
Beyspiele erläutert. Zum Gebrauch in Schulen und
im Privatunterrichte.
19 Bogen.
St. Gallen: Huber und Compagnie, 1794.
N̲: Vol. XIX, pt. 1, p. 179. (E).
K̲: Not listed.

Augusti, Karoline, See Fischer, Caroline Augusti.

B., R.   (82)
Paul Werner, oder Geschichte meines Freundes.
Für Universitätsjünglinge.
156 S.
Breslau und Leipzig: Gehr und Compagnie, 1799.
N̲: Vol LXII, pt. 1, pp. 83-84. (R).
K̲: Vol. III, Romane, p. 105 a.

Bachmann, W. A. A.   (83)
Sophron, oder der erfahrene Lehrer für Eltern,
Jünglinge und Mädchen, etc., vorzüglich für Er-
zieher und Lehrer auf dem Lande.
260 S.
Altona: in Commission der Verlagsgesellschaft,
1796.
N̲: Vol. XXXIX, pt. 1, pp. 100, 111-112. (E).
K̲: Vol. I, pt. 1, p. 136 b.

[Baczko, Ludwig Adolph Franz Josef von.]   (84)
Erzählungen zur Beförderung guter Gefühle und
stiller Tugenden.
260 S.
    "Edelmuth und Liebe."   (a)

"Man ist doch etwas seinem Stande schuldig." (b)
Königsberg: Göbbels und Unzer, 1804.

N: Vol. CII, pt. 2, p. 303. (VS).

K: Vol. III, Romane, p. 37 b.

Becker, Rudolph Zacharias.   (85)
Noth- und Hülfsbüchlein für Bürger- und Bauersleute.
2. Band, 360 S. darin für den Bürger- und Bauern-
stand viel Nützliches, Angenehmes und Belehrendes
verzeichnet steht.
Grätz: Zaunrith, 1793.

N: Vol. VI, pt. 1, pp. 236-237. (VS).

K: Vol. I, pt. 1, p. 179 a.

_____.   (86)
Noth- und Hülfsbüchlein. Oder lehrreiche Freuden-
und Trauergeschichte der Einwohner zu Mildheim.
Andrer Theil.
Gotha: Beckerische Verlagsbuchhandlung, 1798.

N: Vol. LII, pt. 2, pp. 394-395. (VS).

K: Vol. I, pt. 1, p. 179 a.

Becker, Huber, Lafontaine, Lindenau, u.a.m.   (87)
Spiegel menschlicher Leidenschaften.
340 S.
    "Der leukadische Felsen, oder die Folgen der
    Unvorsichtigkeit."   (a)
    " Henriette Dufort."   (b)
Leipzig: Michaelis, 1801.

N: Vol. LXXIX, pt. 1, p. 90. (R).

K: Vol. III, Romane, p. 133 a.

Becker, Wilhelm Gottlieb B.   (88)
Darstellungen.

1. Bändchen, 320 S. 2. Bändchen, 328 S.
Leipzig: Voß und Compagnie, 1798.

N: Vol. XLIX, pt. 1, pp. 115-116; Vol. LIV, pt. 2,
p. 373. (VS).

K: Vol. I, pt. 1, p. 179 a.

Belchart, Ernst Heinrich.   (89)
Die Rosenfelsische Familie. Ein Unterhaltungs-
buch, besonders für die Chursächsische Jugend,
zur Kenntniß der vaterländischen Gesetze, zur
Beförderung der Vaterlandsliebe und der Tugend
überhaupt.
1. Bändchen, 8½ Bogen; 2. Bändchen, 9½ Bogen.
Leipzig: Müllersche Buchhandlung, 1793.

N: Vol. XII, pt. 2, p. 313; Vol. XV, pt. 2,
pp. 358-359. (E).

K: Vol. I, pt. 1, p. 196 b.

[Benkowitz, Carl Friedrich.]   (90)
Natalie, oder die Schreckensscene auf dem St.
Gotthard. Eine Geschichte zur Beherzigung aller,
denen Gewalt auf Erden verliehen ist.
346 S.
Leipzig: Gräff, 1801.

N: Vol. LXIX, pt. 1, pp. 117-118. (R).

K: Vol. III, Romane, p. 15 b.

[Berghofer, Amand.]   (91)
Der Mann von warmen Herze. Es ist gut, daß der
Mensch Verfolgung leidet, sonst geht er dem Wohl-
leben nach und bleibt sich selber unbekannt.
10 Bogen.
Prag und Leipzig: Krappe, 1796.

N: Vol. XXXI, pt. 1, pp. 275-276. (VS).

K: Vol. III, Romane, p. 91 a.

Blum, Ed.   (92)
    Die deutsche Xantippe, oder der zerstörte Haus-
    friede. Ein Warnungsspiegel für junge Ehemänner.
    14 Bogen.
    Weißenfels und Leipzig: in Commission der Bösischen
    Buchhandlung, 1805.
    N: Vol. CI, pt. 1, pp. 169-170. (R).
    K: Vol. III, Romane, p. 154 a.

Böckh, Christian Gottfried Friedrich   (93)
    Der Rathgeber junger Leute beyderley Geschlechts.
    2. Band, 1. Stück. 2. Band, 2. Stück, 12 Bogen.
    Leipzig: Gräff, 1793-1794.
    N: Vol. XI, pt. 2, p. 362; Vol. XIX, pt. 1, pp. 274-
    275. (E).
    K: Vol. I, pt. 1, p. 299 b.

Bolten, Johann Heinrich.   (94)
    Sittenbuch, oder die ersten Grundsätze einer heil-
    samen Lebensordnung und eines guten Verhaltens
    für Knaben und Mädchens (Mädchen). In Erzählun-
    gen, Gesprächen, Regeln und Bildern.
    188 S.
    Neu-Ruppin: Kühn, 1792.
    N: Vol. II, pt. 1, pp. 154-155. (VS).
    K: Vol. I, pt. 1, p. 310 b.

[Brakebusch, Johann, Georg Lorenz.]   (95)
    Elisa, kein Weib, wie es seyn sollte. Ein höchst-
    nöthiges Wort zur richtigen Schätzung der Schrift:
    Elisa, oder das Weib, wie es seyn sollte.
    2. Theil. Auch unter dem Titel Musterkarte von Wei-
    bern, Männern, Jünglingen und Kindern, wie sie
    sind, seyn können und seyn sollen.

Hildesheim: Gerstenberg, 1801.

N: Vol. LXXIV, pt. 2, pp. 326-334. (VS).

K: Vol. III, Romane, p. 35 b.

───────────────.   (96)

Karl Trautmann, Geschichte seines Lebens und seiner Geistesentwicklung bis ins männliche Alter.
Kein Moderoman.
432 S.
Hannover: Ritscher, 1792. K: Hannover: Hahn,
1791.

N: Vol. III, pt. 1, pp. 265-272. (R).

K: Vol. III, Romane, p. 141 a.

Braubach, Daniel.   (97)

Der gelehrte Handwerker. Eine komische Erzählung.
12 Bogen.
Altona: Kraven, no date. K: Altona: Hammerich,
1797.

N: Vol. XL, pt. 2, pp. 329-330. (R).

K: Vol. III, Romane, p. 59 a.

[Braunschweig, Johannes Daniel von.]   (98)

Nützliche und unterhaltende Aufsätze für junge
Frauenzimmer, zur Bildung ihres Geistes und Herzens.
12 Bogen.
    "Beyspiele von guten und schlechten Hausmüt-
    tern."   (a)
    "Der Ehemann, ein Beichtvater."   (b)
    "Der würdige Ehemann."   (c)
    "Miß Kery und Sophie Gallen; eine moralische
    Erzählung."   (d)
Breslau: Gutsch, 1794.

N: Vol. XV, pt. 1, pp. 177-179. (E).

K: Vol. I, pt. 1, p. 121 a.   49

[Büchner, Johann Friedrich.]   (99)
   Kurze Geschichte eines Onanisten, der sich selbst
   kuriert hat. Für Eltern, Erzieher, besonders aber
   für seine leidenden Mitbrüder.
   70 S.
   Gera: Rothe, 1793.
   N̲: Vol. XXI, pt. 2, p. 462. (E).
   K̲: Vol. I, pt. 2, p. 363 a.

Christiani, O. C.   (100)
   Ceciliens Flucht nach Berlin. Eine Schule für die
   Mädchenwelt.
   14 Bogen.
   Braunschweig: Reichard, 1800.
   N̲: Vol. LXVI, pt. 1, pp. 98-101. (R).
   K̲: Vol. I, pt. 1, p. 442 b.

_____.   (101)
   Elisa's Schwestern. Eine Schule für die Jüng-
   lingswelt.
   2 Theile, 23 Bogen.
   Braunschweig: Reichard, 1800.
   N̲: Vol. LXVI, pt. 1, pp. 98-100. (R).
   K̲: Vol. I, pt. 1, p. 442 b.

Claudius, Georg Karl.   (102)
   Sechzig kleine Geschichten und unterhaltende Ge-
   spräche für Kinder, die lesen können und nun
   auch denken lernen wollen.
   Hamburg: Hoffmann, 1803.
   18 Bogen.
   N̲: Vol. LXXXIV, pt. 2, p. 545. (E).
   K̲: Vol. I, pt. 1, p. 459 a.

_____ .

Neue Kinderbibliothek.

13 Bogen.

"Die Flucht aus dem väterlichen Hause, oder
die Gefahren des jugendlichen Leichtsinnes,
eine wahre Geschichte zur Belehrung und
Warnung." = Joseph Freeland, 1788.   (a)

"Familie Wilmann."   (b)

Heilbronn und Leipzig: Claß, 1803.

N: Vol. LXXXIV, pt. 2, pp. 545-547. (E).

K: Vol. I, pt. 1 p. 459 b.

_____ .

Kleine Kinderwelt, oder neues Lesebuch zur ersten Bildung des gesunden Menschenverstandes
für das Alter von fünf bis acht Jahren.

2 Bändchen.

Leipzig: Höfer, 1797.

N: Vol. XXXVII, pt. 1, p. 184. (E).

K: Vol. II, pt. 3, p. 430 b.

_____ .

Über die Kunst sich beliebt und angenehm zu machen.

Leipzig: Böhme, 1797.

N: Vol. XXXV, pt. 1, pp. 275-276. (VS).

K: Vol. I, pt. 1, p. 459 a.

[_____ .]

Marianens Schäferstunden. Ein Gemälde aus der
wirklichen Welt.

VI ≠ 246 S.

Rostock und Leipzig: Stiller, 1800.

N: Vol. LXV, pt. 1, pp. 75-76. (R).

K: Vol. III, Romane, p. 92 a.

Collenbusch, Daniel.   (107)

    <u>Der aufrichtige Volksarzt</u>.

    156 S.

    Eisenberg: in der Expedition des aufrichtigen
    Volksarztes, 1796; Leipzig: Grieshammer, 1797.

<u>N</u>: Vol. XXXII, pt. 1, pp. 35-38. (Artzneygelahrt-
    heit).

<u>K</u>: Vol. I, pt. 1, p. 469 b.

Cramer, Karl Gottlob.   (108)

    <u>Hans Stürzebecher und sein Sohn. Ein Beytrag</u>
    <u>zur Geschichte meiner Zeit</u>.

    1. Theil, 280 S. 2. Theil, 261 S.

    Leipzig: Fleischer, 1798.

<u>N</u>: Vol. XLVI, pt. 1, pp. 99-100. (R).

<u>K</u>: Vol. III, Romane, p. 29 b.

    _____.   (109)

    <u>Leben und Meinungen, auch seltsame Abentheuer</u>
    <u>Paul Ysops, eines reduzirten Hofnarren</u>.

    1. Theil, 25 Bogen. 2. Theil, 22 Bogen.

    Leipzig: Fischer, 1792-1793.

<u>N</u>: Vol. III, pt. 1, pp. 170-180; Vol. VII, pt. 1,
    p. 110. (R).

<u>K</u>: Vol. III, Romane, p. 29 a.

    _____.   (110)

    <u>Ysopiana. Als Anhang und Nachtrag zu dem Leben</u>
    <u>des Paul Ysops, eines reduzirten Hofnarren</u>.

    238 S.

    Leipzig: Friedrich Fleischer, 1799.

<u>N</u>: Vol. LIII, pt. 2, p. 431. (R).

<u>K</u>: Vol. III, Romane, p. 29 b.

Dassel, Christoph Conrad.   (111)
    Merkwürdige Reisen der Gutmannischen Familie.
    1. Theil, 237 S. 2. Theil, 258 S. 3. Theil,
    268 S. 4. Theil, 268 S.
    Hannover: Gebrüder Hahn, 1795-1798.
    N: Vol. XXII, pt. 1, p. 141; Vol. XXIX, pt. 2, pp. 313-
    314; Vol. XLV, pt. 1, pp. 194-197. (E).
    K: Vol. I, pt. 2, p. 16 b.

Demme, Christoph Gottfried.   (112)
    Erzählungen in Karl Stille's Manier und Absicht.
    1. Sammlung, 204 S.
    Jena: Akademisches Leseinstitut, 1795.
    N: Vol. XIX, pt. 2, pp. 401-403. (R).
    K: Vol. III, pt. 5, p. 335 b.

————————————.   (113)
    Sechs Jahre aus Carl Burgfeld's Leben. Freund-
    schaft, Liebe und Orden.
    Leipzig: Göschen, 1793.
    N: Vol. II, pt. 1, pp. 65-66. (R).
    K: Vol. III, Romane, p. 68 a.

————————————.   (114)
    Der Pächter Martin und sein Vater.
    1. Band; 2. Band; 3. Band, 308 S.
    Leipzig: Göschen, 1792-1802.
    N: Vol. VI, pt. 1, p. 176; Vol. XIV, pt. 2, pp. 497-
    500; Vol. LXXXII, pt.2, pp. 542-543. (R), (VS).
    K: Vol. II, pt. 4, p. 36 a.

Diehls, J. M. dem Jüngern.   (115)
    Verirrungen des menschlichen Herzens, darge-
    stellt in drey moralischen Erzählungen aus der
    wirklichen Welt .

13 Bogen.

Frankfurt a. M.: Jäger, 1800.

N: Vol. LX, pt. 1, pp. 108-109. (R).

K: Vol. III, Romane, p. 31 b.

Durach, Johann Baptiste. (116)

Eleonora del Monti. Eine Geschichte aus dem achtzehnten Jahrhundert.

328 S.

Berlin: Königlich. Preuß. akad. Kunst- und Buchhandlung, 1796.

N: Vol. XXX, pt. 2, pp. 518-528. (R).

K: Vol. III, Romane, p. 35 b.

Dyck, Johann Gottfried. (117)

Lesebuch. Zunächst als Weihnachtsgeschenk für
fleißige Kinder in der mir anvertrauten Schul-
anstalt.

1. Heft, 224 S. 2. Heft, 264 S.

"Das Irrenhaus." (a)

"Regeln der Lebensklugheit für das weibliche
Geschlecht." (b)

Leipzig: Auf Kosten des Herausgebers, 1801.

N: Vol. LXIX, pt. 1, pp. 246-247. (E).

K: Vol. I, pt. 2, p. 86 a.

Ebert, Johann Jakob. (118)

Fabeln und Erzählungen für Kinder und junge
Leute beiderley Geschlechts.

261 S.

Leipzig: Seeger, 1798.

N: Vol. LXII, pt. 2, pp. 470-471. (E).

K: Vol. I, pt. 2, p. 91 a.

Engel, Johann Jakob.   (119)
    Der Fürstenspiegel.
    308 S.
    Berlin: Unger, 1798.
    N̲: Vol. XLVII, pt. 1, pp. 246-253; Vol. LXXXVII,
    pt. 1, p. 185. (Staatswissenschaft).
    K̲: Vol. I, pt. 2, p. 126 b.

—————————.   (120)
    Lorenz Stark, ein Charaktergemälde.
    3 Bogen.
    Berlin: Mylius, 1798.
    N̲: Vol. LXXXVII, pt. 1, pp. 190-191. (VS).
    K̲: Vol. III, Romane, p. 36 b.

—————————.   (121)
    Der Philosoph für die Welt.
    3 Theile.
        "Tobias Witt."   (a)
        "Die Bienenkörbe."   (b)
        "Die Curmethoden."   (c)
        "Elizabeth Hill."   (d)
        "Das Zaubermahl."   (e)
        "Fragment eines Gastmahls."   (f)
        "Das Irrenhaus."   (g)
        "Joseph Timm."   (h)
    Berlin: Mylius, 1775-1800.
    N̲: Vol. LIX, pt. 1, pp. 261-165. (VS).
    K̲: Vol. I, pt. 2, p. 126 b.

Engel, Lucian.   (122)
    Gemälde des menschlichen Herzens, in Rücksicht
    auf Moralität und Menschenkunde.
    1. Bändchen, 21½ Bogen.
    Berlin: Belitz, 1801.

N: Vol. LXXV, pt. 2, pp. 390-392. (R).
K: Vol. I, pt. 2, p. 126 b.

Engel, Moritz.   (123)
   Glück der Häuslichkeit.
   1 ½ Bogen.
   Leipzig: in Commission bey Linke, 1801
   N: Vol. LVIII, pt.1, pp. 166-168. (VS).
   K: Vol. I, pt. 2, p. 127 a.

_____.   (124)
   Für jugendliche Seelenveredlung in Fabeln, Er-
   zählungen und Denksprüchen.
   298 S.
   Leipzig: Link, 1801.
   N: Vol. LXXX, pt. 2, pp. 513-514. (E).
   K: Vol. II, pt. 4, p. 139 a.

Engelhardt, Karl August.   (125)
   Erdmann, eine Bildungsgeschichte.
   1. Band, XXXII ⊬ 279 S. 2. Band, 312 S. 3. Band,
   360 S.
   Leipzig: Crusius, 1801.
   N: Vol. LXXVI, pt. 2, pp. 455-457. (E).
   K: Vol. III, Romane, p. 87 a.

Engelhardt, Karl August, und Merkel, Johann.   (126)
   Neuer Kinderfreund.
   7. und 8. Band, 404 S.
   Leipzig: Barth, 1795-1796. (E).
   N: Vol. XXXII, pt. 2, pp. 397-398. (E).
   K: Vol. I, pt. 2, p. 129 b.

56

[Essich, Johann Gottfried.]   (127)
    Die gute Christine. Oder eine Geschichte für
Dienstbothen, auch für Eltern und Herrschaften.
13 Bogen.
Augsburg: Stage, 1793.
N: Vol. IX, pt. 1, p. 206. (VS).
K: Vol. I, pt. 2, p. 164 a.

[_____.]   (128)
    Die gute Christine, die Zweite. Eine Geschichte
für bürgerliche Mädchen, welche gute Weiber werden wollen; und ihre Mütter, die gute Weiber seyn
sollen.
520 S.
Leipzig: Stagesche Buchhandlung, 1802.
N: Vol. CI, pt. 2, pp. 453-459. (VS).
K: Vol. I, pt. 2, p. 164 a.

[_____.]   (129)
    Karl, Lenore und Klara, Christinens und Phillipps
gute und glückliche Kinder. Eine Geschichte für
Familien überhaupt, und für Waisen ins besondere;
zu einer unterhaltenden und nützlichen Lektüre,
besonders auch für Lehrjungen und jüngere reisende Professionisten und Handwerksgesellen.
1. Bändchen, 274 S. 2. Bändchen, 198 S.
Leipzig: Stagesche Buchhandlung, 1803.
N: Vol. LXXXIX, pt. 2, p. 307. (VS).
K: Vol. I, pt. 2, p. 164 a.

Evers, August Friedrich Christoph.   (130)
    Moralische Erzählungen.
1. Band, 20½ Bogen.
Schwerin: Bärensprung, 1802; Leipzig: Wienbrack,
1802.

<u>N</u>: Vol. XCI, pt. 2, pp. 345=347. (R).
<u>K</u>: Vol. III, Romane, p. 39 b.

Faber, Johann Heinrich.   (131)
    <u>Louise, oder der Sieg weiblicher Tugend im Con-
    traste zwoer Schwestern.</u>
    2 Bändchen, 29 Bogen.
    Frankfurt und Leipzig: Pech, 1792.
<u>N</u>: Vol. III, pt. 2, p. 566. (R).
<u>K</u>: Vol. III, Romane, p. 89 a.

Feldhahn, Charlotte.   (132)
    <u>Der Schatz in der Waldburg. Eine moralische No-
    velle für Töchter aus höhern Ständen.</u>
    88 S.
    Bayreuth: Lübecks Erben, 1798.
<u>N</u>: Vol. XLVI, pt. 2, p. 553. (VS).
<u>K</u>: Vol. III, Romane, p. 121 a.

Felswagen, L. F., und Hemper, K. F.   (133)
    <u>Die Familie Hellwig. Ein belehrendes und unter-
    haltendes Lesebuch für Deutschlands Söhne und
    Töchter.</u>
    VIII ≠ 178 S.
    Leipzig: Schädel, 1804.
<u>N</u>: Vol. XC, pt. 1, p. 264; Vol. C, pt. 2, pp. 381-
    382. (R).
<u>K</u>: Vol. I, pt. 2, p. 202 a.

Fischer, Gottlob Nathan Eus.   (134)
    <u>Gustav oder der Pädagog. Eine Geschichte für
    Kinder um sie über den Werth der Dinge zu be-
    lehren</u>. <u>K</u>: <u>Gustav oder der Papagey</u>.
    270 S.
    Leipzig: Leo, 1795.

<u>N</u>: Vol. XXVIII, Suppl. I, pp. 543-544. (E).
<u>K</u>: Vol. I, pt. 2, p. 220 b.

Fischer, Heinrich, Ludwig.   (135)
    <u>Bauernphilosophie, oder Belehrungen über man-</u>
    <u>cherley Gegenstände des Aberglaubens und ande-</u>
    <u>re nützliche Kenntnisse.</u>
    1. Bändchen, 232 S.
    Leipzig: Roch und Compagnie, 1800.
<u>N</u>: Vol. LXVII, pt. 1, p. 118. (VS).
<u>K</u>: Vol. I, pt. 1, p. 161 a.

Fischer, Karoline Augusti, née Venturini.   (136)
    <u>Gustavs Verirrungen. Ein Roman.</u>
    Leipzig: Gräff, 1801.
<u>N</u>: Vol. LXX, pt. 1, pp. 71-72. (R).
<u>K</u>: Vol. III, Romane, p. 58 a.

[_____.]   (137)
    <u>Vierzehn Tage in Paris.</u>
    11 Bogen
    Leipzig: Gräff, 1801.
<u>N</u>: Vol. LXX, pt. 1, p. 72. (R).
<u>K</u>: Vol. III, Romane, p.138 a.

Follenius, Ernst Friedrich.   (138)
    <u>Franz Damm, oder der Glückliche durch sich</u>
    <u>selbst.</u>
    1. Theil, VI / 386 S. 2. Theil, 447 S. 3. Theil,
    364 S. 4. Theil, 428 S.
    Leipzig: Barth, 1799-1801.
<u>N</u>: Vol. L, pt. 1, pp. 110-112; Vol. LXI, pt. 1,
    p. 98; Vol. LXXVI, pt. 1, p. 107. (R).
<u>K</u>: Vol. III, Romane, p. 43 b.

[_____.]   (139)

    <u>Die Milchbrüder, Ferdinand und Ernst, oder Ge-</u>
<u>schichte zweyer Freunde, aus den Papieren der-</u>
<u>selben gezogen</u>.
3 Theile.
Berlin und Stettin: Fr. Nicolai, 1798-1799.
<u>N</u>: Vol. XLIII, pt. 1, p. 47; Vol. XLVII, pt. 1,
pp. 117-118; Vol. L, pt. 1, p. 112. (R).
<u>K</u>: Vol. III, Romane, p. 95 a.

Frank, Wilhelm.   (140)

    <u>Emilie im vierfachen Stande. Als Kind, Jungfrau</u>,
<u>Gattinn und Mutter</u>.
1. Band, 180 S., 2. Band, 336 S.
Leipzig: Seeger, 1802.
<u>N</u>: Vol. LXXIV, pt. 1, pp. 266-268; Vol. LXXXIII,
pt. 2, pp. 541-542. (VS).
<u>K</u>: Vol. III, Romane, p. 38 a.

Franke.   (141)

    <u>Die Winterabende am Kamin</u>.
1. Bändchen.
    "Die belohnte Tugend."   (a)
    "Die Hochzeit, wie wenige gefeyert werden." (b)
    "Der Abend."   (c)
Eisenach: Wittekind, 1801.
<u>N</u>: Vol. LXXII, pt. 2, pp. 363-364. (R).
<u>K</u>: Vol. III, Romane, p. 44 b.

Freyer, Justus.   (142)

    <u>Eduard Humber, oder die Folgen allzurascher</u>
<u>Handlungen</u>.
1. Band, 24 Bogen; 2. Band, 26 Bogen.
Berlin: Nicolai, 1803.

N: Vol. XCIV, pt. 2, p. 496. (R)
K: Vol. III, Romane, p. 45 b.

Friedrich, J. P.   (143)
       Glaubwürdige Prophezeihungen in Beyspielen zur
       Beruhigung, Warnung und Unterhaltung.
       232 S.
       Halle: Buchhandlung des Waisenhauses, 1794.
       N: Vol. XIX, pt. 1, pp. 265-266. (VS).
       K: Not listed.

Fröbing, Johann Christoph.   (144)
       Georg Treumann und seine Familie und Freunde.
       Eine dialogisierte Geschichte.
       216 S.
       Hannover: Ritscher, 1796.
       N: Vol. XXXIII, pt. 2, p. 405. (VS).
       K: Vol. III, Romane, p. 46 a.

_____.   (145)

       Gespenster- und Hexenbüchlein. Ein Geschenk
       für seine bisherigen Leser.
       170 S.
       Hannover: Gebrüder Hahn, 1798.
       N: Vol. XL, pt. 1, pp. 274-275. (VS).
       K: Vol. I, pt. 2, p. 276 a.

_____.   (146)

       Heinrich Dornfelden, oder die Erbschaft. Ein Le-
       sebuch fürs Volk.
       369 S.
       Göttingen: Dieterich, 1797.
       N: Vol. XXXIX, pt. 1, p. 275. (VS).
       K: Vol. I, pt. 2, p. 276 a.

_____·   (147)

Der Menschenbeobachter. Ein Lesebuch für alle
Stände.
10 Bogen.
   "Thorheit eines Seifensieders."   (a)
   "Abergläubische Thorheiten und Verirrungen der
   Gespensterfurcht."   (b)
   "Süß Oppenheimer, Beherrscher seines Fürsten
   und Tyrann eines ganzen Volkes."   (c)
   "Carl Janvier, Mörder und Fresser seines Wohl-
   thäters."   (d)
   Bremen: Witmanns, 1796.
N: Vol. XXXIII, pt. 2, p. 406. (VS).
K: Vol. I, pt. 2, p. 276 b.

_____·   (148)

Wilhelm Ehrenpreis und Karoline Sebastiani; oder
der Spiegel für Ehegatten und die es werden wollen.
1. Band, 406 S.
Lemgo: Meyer, 1800.
N: Vol. LXVIII, Suppl. II, p. 722. (VS).
K: Vol. I, pt. 2, p. 103 a.

_____·   (149)

Calender für das Volk. Auf das Jahr 1805.
192 S.
Hannover: Gebrüder Hahn, 1805.
N: Vol. CIII, pt. 1, p. 167. (VS).
K: Vol. I, pt. 2, p. 276a.

Frömmichen, Sophie.   (150)
   Emilie von Wilmar, oder Belohnung der Menschen-
   freundlichkeit.
   2. Band.

62

Braunschweig: Schulbuchhandlung, 1798.

N: Vol. XLIII, pt. 2, pp. 319-320. (R).

K: Vol. III, Romane, p. 36 b.

_____.   (151)

Lida. Ein Geschenk für die erwachsene Jugend.
328 S.
Braunschweig: Schulbuchhandlung, 1801.

N: Vol. LVII, pt. 1, pp. 256-258. (VS).

K: Vol. II, pt. 3, p. 546 b.

Funke, Carl Philip.   (152)

Neues Elementarbuch zum Gebrauche bey dem Privatunterrichte.
1. Theil, 2. Hälfte, welche noch einige angenehme und nützliche Leseübungen enthält. Auch
unter dem Titel: Neue Bilderfibel zum Privat-
gebrauch in Familien.
2. Theil, welcher einen Sittenspiegel für die
Jugend enthält. Auch unter dem Titel Sittenspiegel für die Jugend. Neues Elementarbuch.
310 S.
3. Theil, 1. Hälfte, VIII / 198 S. welche eine Vorbereitung zur Naturgeschichte enthält.
Berlin: Voß, 1797-1804.

N: Vol. XLII, pt. 2, pp. 530-531; Vol. XCII, pt. 1,
pp. 198-202. (E).

K: Vol. I, pt. 2, p. 285 a.

_____.   (153)

Lesebuch zum Gebrauch in Töchterschulen, nebst
einem Anhange von Liedern für Mädchen zur Unterhaltung in den Arbeitsstunden.
182 S.
Berlin: Voß, 1801.

<u>N</u>: Vol. LXXX, pt. 2, pp. 489-490. (E).

<u>K</u>: Vol. I, pt. 2, p. 285 b.

Geissler, Johann Friedrich von.   (154)

   <u>Geschichten für Kinder, zur Besserung und Be-</u>
   <u>förderung eines rechtschaffenen Lebenswandels</u>.
   168 S.

   "Freue dich, aber mit Vorsicht."   (a)
   "Ehrlichkeit bringt Segen."   (b)
   "Selbstbeherrschung."   (c)
   "Edelmuth im niedern Stande."   (d)
   "Wer ist mein Nächster?"   (e)
   "Dankbegierde und Großmuth."   (f)
   "Reichthum allein macht nicht glücklich."   (g)
   "Tollkühnheit."   (h)
   "Der Leichtsinnige auf schlimmen Wegen."   (i)
   "Frohsinn im Wohlthun."   (j)
   "Wer andern wohlthut, bereitet sich selbst
     das schönste Fest."   (k)
   "Gerechtigkeit und Billigkeit."   (l)
   "Dankbarkeit eines Bedienten."   (m)
   "Die gute Tochter."   (n)
   "Nicht das Wissen, sondern das Thun ist die
     Hauptsache der Religion."   (o)
   "Mache die nicht entbehrlichen Dinge zum Be-
     dürfnis."   (p)
   "Die Furcht läßt oft falsch sehen."   (q)
   "Strafe der Näscherey."   (r)

   Bayreuth: Lübecks Erben, 1802.

   <u>N</u>: Vol. LXXXIII, pt. 1, pp. 108-110. (VS).

   <u>K</u>: Vol. I, pt. 2, p. 360 b.

Glatz, Jakob.   (155)

   <u>Familiengemälde und Erzählungen für die Jugend</u>.
   1. Bändchen, XII ⫽ 179 S. 2. Bändchen, 182 S.
   Gotha: Perthes, 1799.

64

N: Vol. LXVIII, pt. 1, pp. 223-224. (VS).
K: Vol. I, pt. 2, p. 287 b.

_____. (156)

Moralische Gemälde für die gebildete Jugend.
1. und 2. Heft.
   "Der Leichtsinnige." (a)
Leipzig: Voß und Comp., 1803.
N: Vol. XCVIII, pt. 1, pp. 84-89. (E).
K: Vol. I, pt. 2, p. 387 b.

_____. (157)

Iduna, ein moralisches Unterhaltungsbuch für
die weibliche Jugend.
1. Band, 269 S. 2. Band, 263 S.
Frankfurt a.M.: Fr. Wilmans, 1803.
N: Vol. LXXXV, pt. 2, pp. 548-550. (E).
K: Vol. I, pt. 2, p. 387 b.

_____. (158)

Der zufriedene Jakob und sein Sohn.
296 S.
Leipzig: Fleischer, 1799.
N: Vol. LXVIII, Suppl. 2, pp. 705-706. (VS).
K: Vol. I, pt. 2, p. 387 a.

_____. (159)

Jacob Stille's Erzählungsbuch, oder kleine Bibliothek für Kinder, die das Lesen angefangen haben
und sich gern etwas erzählen lassen.
4 Bändchen.
Altona: Hammerich, 1802-1804.
N: Vol. CII, pt. 1, pp. 70-72. (E).
K: Vol. III, pt. 5, p. 335 b.

_____.   (160)

Kleine Romane für die Jugend.

1. Bändchen.

"Eduard Wallstedt, oder die Rückkehr zum Guten."(a)

"Wilhelm, der Findling."   (b)

2. Bändchen, 18 Bogen.

"Rosamunde!'Wer Unrecht duldet, findet zuletzt

noch Errettung.'"   (c)

Altona: Hammerich,

<u>N</u>: Vol. LXXIX, pt. 1, pp. 86-88; Vol. LXXXI, pt. 2,

pp. 536-537. (R).

<u>K</u>: Vol. I, pt. 2, p. 388 a.

_____.   (161)

Taschenbuch für die deutsche Jugend. Auf das
Jahr 1804.

268 S.

"Hannchen, oder die verkannte Unschuld."   (a)

"Die Drehorgel."   (b)

"Karl Eckrodt, eine Erzählung zum Beleg der

Sirachschen Bemerkung: 'Der schändet sich

selbst, der seine Mutter verachtet.'"   (c)

"Philip, oder schreckliche Verfolgung der Ver-

zärtelung und Spielsucht."   (d)

Fürth: Bureau für Litteratur, [1805].

<u>N</u>: Vol. XCV, pt. 2, pp. 515-516. (E).

<u>K</u>: not listed.

_____.   (162)

Unterhaltungsbuch der kleinen Familie von Grünthal (;) oder Erzählungen für die zartere Jugend.
Auch als Lesebuch in den Lehrstunden zu gebrau-
chen.

3. Bändchen, 310 S.

"Philip Rothmann, oder die traurigen Folgen

des Zorns."   (a)
Leipzig: Fleischer, 1801.
N: Vol. LXXV, pt. 2, p. 546. (E).
K: Vol. I, pt. 2, p. 388 b.

_____.   (163)

Vater Traumann. Ein Lesebuch zunächst für Bürgerschulen. Auch bey dem Privatunterrichte
brauchbar. Seitenstück zu Thiemens Gutmann.
17 Bogen.
Schnepfenthal: Buchhandlung der Erziehungsanstalt, 1803.
N: Vol. XCI, pt. 2, pp. 442-443. (E).
K: Vol. III, pt. 5, p. 388 b.

Grätzmann, D. Fr.   (164)
Albert und Henriette, oder nur Liebe für die
Gottheit, Tugend und Kunst erwirbt uns die höch-
ste Bildung. Ein Lese- und Erziehungsbuch für
Kinder, und alle, die das edle Geschäfft der
Erziehung betreiben.
238 S.
Leipzig: von Kleefeld, 1804.
N: Vol. XCVII, pt. 2, pp. 473-476. (E).
K: Vol. I, pt. 2, p. 395 b.

Gruber, J. G.   (165)
Adolph Freyherr von Knigge; über den Umgang mit
Menschen. Im Auszuge für die Jugend, mit einer
durchgängigen Beyspielsammlung.
272 S.
Leipzig: Hartknoch, 1801.
N: Vol. LXXIV, pt. 2, pp. 466-467. (VS).
K: Vol. II, pt. 3, p. 369 a.

Gruber, Johann Gottfried.   (166)
     Die Hölle auf Erden in der Geschichte der Fa-
     milie Fredini. Gegen Salzmanns Himmel auf Erden.
     373 S.
     Leipzig: Kummer, 1800.
  N: Vol. LXIII, pt. 2, pp. 614-615. (VS).
  K: Vol. III, Romane, p. 66 a.

Grüner, Christian Siegmund.   (167)
     Der Märtyrer der Wahrheit: eine charakteristisch-
     romantische Geschichte.
     216 S.
     Leipzig: Meißner, 1799.
  N: Vol. XXII, pt. 1, pp. 186-187; Vol. LIV, pt. 2,
     pp. 365-363. (VS), (R).
  K: Vol. III, Romane, p. 92 b.

Gürnth, Christine Dorothea.   (168)
     Oeconomisch-moralischer Hausbedarf für Mädchen
     von reiferm Alter und angehende Gattinnen.
     2 Bände.
     Leipzig: Supprian, 1799.
  N: Vol. XLII, pt. 1, pp. 277-278; Vol. LIV, pt. 1,
     p. 190. (E).
  K: Vol. III, pt. 5, p. 64 b.

Gutmann, Adam.   (169)
     Waldheim, oder seltsame und lehrreiche Ge-
     schichte, so sich mit der Grafschaft Waldheim
     zugetragen. Für den Bürger und Bauersmann.
     6½ Bogen.
     München: Lentner, 1792.
  N: Vol. II, pt. 1, p. 78. (VS).
  K: Vol. III, pt. 6, p. 142 a.

H., J. P. (170)

    <u>Angenehme Unterhaltungen und Spaziergänge eines</u>
    <u>Erziehers mit seinem Zöglinge. Ein Lesebuch für</u>
    <u>reifere Knaben.</u>
    179 S.
    Wien: Camesina, 1803.
<u>N</u>: Vol. LXXXV, pt. 2, pp. 538-539. (E).
<u>K</u>: Vol. III, pt. 6, p. 17 a.

Haken, Johann Christian Ludwig. (171)

    <u>Amarenthen (Xeranthemum Annum L. T.)</u>.
    1. Sammlung, 302 S.
      "Weibertreue mit Belegen." (a)
    2. Sammlung, 365 S. 3. Sammlung, 382 S.
    Magdeburg: Keil, 1802-1804.
<u>N</u>: Vol. LXXIII, pt. 1, pp. 65-66; Vol. LXXXIX, pt. 1,
    pp. 14-15; Vol. XCIV, pt. 1, p. 135. (R).
<u>K</u>: Vol. III, Romane, p. 8 a.

Halm, Karl. (172)

    <u>Die Familie Bendheim.</u>
    2. Theil, VIII ≠ 422 S.
    Berlin: Momser, 1805.
<u>N</u>: Vol. C, pt. 2, pp. 380-381. (R).
<u>K</u>: Vol. II, pt. 3, p. 14 b.

[Hammersdörfer, Carl.] (173)

    <u>Timon der Zweyte, Leben und Meinungen eines</u>
    <u>wohlwollenden Menschenfeindes</u>.
    34½ Bogen.
    Leipzig: Hamann, 1792. <u>K</u>: 1798.
<u>N</u>: Vol. II, pt. 2, p. 540. (R).
<u>K</u>: Vol. III, Romane, p. 140 a.

Hatzel, Adam Heinrich. (174)

Georg Reinhards, eines deutschen Bauers, Le-
bensgeschichte.
252 S.
Heilbronn a. Neckar und Rotheburg o.d. Tauber:
Claß, 1796.
N: Vol. XXXIII, pt. 1, p. 206. (VS).
K: Vol. II, pt. 3, p. 58 b.

Haubold, J. S. G. (175)

Moralische Maximen, erläutert in auserlesenen
Erzählungen und leichtfaßlichen Gesprächen. Ein
Lesebuch für alle Stände, und vorzüglich für die
Jugend.
XVI ≠ 224 S.
Gotha: Ettinger, 1802.
N: Vol. LXXXII, pt. 1, pp. 253-255. (VS).
K: Vol. II, pt. 3, p. 60 a.

Hauenschild, Christian August. (176)

Immerwährender Calender der gesunden Vernunft,
oder Handbuch zur Erklärung des Calenders auf
alle Jahre.
208 S.
Weißenfels: Friedrich Severin, 1792.
N: Vol. XX, pt. 1, p. 275. (VS).
K: Vol. II, pt. 3, p. 297 b.

[Heinsius, T. H.] (177)

Ehrmanns ländliche Freuden.
288 S.
Bayreuth: Lübecks Erben, 1793.
N: Vol. X, pt. 2, pp. 553-554. (VS).
K: Vol. I, pt. 2, p. 104 b.

Henning, August. (178)
 Sittliche Gemälde. ⌐
 1. Band, 321 S.
  "Geschichte zweyer Selbstmörder." (a)
  "Zwölf Briefe eines Greises an seinen Sohn." (b)
  "Drei Erzählungen." (c)
 Neustrelitz: Michaelis, 1798.
N̲: Vol. XLIX, pt. 1, pp. 117-119. (VS).
K̲: Vol. II, pt. 3, p. 105 a.

Hermes, Johann Tim. (179)
 Verheimlichung und Eil; oder Lottchen und ihrer
 Nachbarn Geschichte.
 1. Theil, 496 S. 2.Theil, 466 S.
 Berlin: Braun, 1802; Leipzig: Nauck, 1802.
N̲: Vol. LXXV, pt. 1, pp. 76-81. (R).
K̲: Vol. III, Romane, p. 68 b.

Herrmann, Friedrich. (180)
 Eduard Bernau, eine Geschichte aus welcher Kin-
 der Menschen kennen lernen sollen.
 1. Theil, 188 S. 2. Theil, 267 S.
 Warschau: Wilke, 1797.
N̲: Vol. XXXVIII, pt. 1, p. 94; Vol. XLI, pt. 1,
 pp. 58-59. (R).
K̲: Vol. III, Romane, p. 16 a.

_____. (181)
 Moralische Erzählungen für Kinder von acht bis
 zwölf Jahren.
 VIII ⫻ 144 S.
 2. verbesserte und vermehrte Auflage; Warschau:
 Wilke, 1798.
N̲: Vol. LV, pt. 2, pp. 427-428. (E).
K̲: Vol. II, pt. 3, p. 114 b.

_____.

Moralische Kinderbibliothek (,) oder die menschlichen Pflichten (,) in Erzählungen für die er-
wachsnere Jugend.
1. Theil, XVI ≠ 486 S. 2. Theil, XVI ≠ 463 S.
3. Theil, VIII ≠ 557 S.
Lübben: Gotsch, 1802, 1804.

N: Vol. LXXXI, pt. 2, pp. 537-540. Vol. XCIX, pt. 2,
pp. 433-438. (E).

K: Vol. II, pt. 3, p. 114 b.

Heusinger, Johann Heinrich Gottlieb.   (183)

Erzählungen.
13 Bogen.
Jena: Voigtische Buchhandlung, 1804.

N: Vol. CI, pt. 1, pp. 67-69. (R).

K: Vol. III, Romane, p. 63 a.

_____.   (184)

Die Familie Wertheim.
2. - 4. Theil.
Gotha: Perthes, 1798-1799.

N: Vol. LII, pt. 2, p. 464; Vol. LXIV, pt. 1,
pp. 255-256. (E).

K: Vol. II, pt. 3, p. 134 a.

Hihrdt.   (185)

Barthel Most, oder Leben und Abentheuer eines
Pädagogen neuerer Zeit. Von ihm selbst aufgezeich-
net.
XII ≠ 444 S.
Magdeburg: Creutz, 1796.

N: Vol. XXIX, pt. 1, pp. 233-235. (R).

K: Vol. III, Romane, p. 13 a.

Hildebrandt, Johann Andreas Christoph.   (186)
    <u>Amalie Waldenfels, eine Unterhaltung für er-</u>
    <u>wachsene Töchter</u>.
    17½ Bogen.
    Halberstadt: Greß, 1804.
<u>N</u>: Vol. XCVIII, pt. 2, pp. 466-468. (E).
<u>K</u>: Vol. III, pt. 6, p. 141 b.

<u>   </u>.   (187)
    <u>Augusta du Port, oder Geschichte einer Unglück-</u>
    <u>lichen. Ein Gegenstück zu Friedrich Brack</u>.
    1. Theil, 14 Bogen; 2. Theil, 244 S.
    Berlin: Langhoff, 1798.
<u>N</u>: Vol. XLV, pt. 1, p. 36; Vol. XLVI, pt. 1, p. 62.
    (R).
<u>K</u>: Vol. III, Romane, p. 63 b.

Hirzel, Johann Caspar.   (188)
    <u>Auserlesene Schriften zur Beförderung der Land-</u>
    <u>wirthschaft und der häuslichen und bürgerlichen</u>
    <u>Wohlfahrth. D</u>arin: Die Wirthschaft eines phi-
    losophischen Bauern.
    1. Band, 495 S. 2. Band, 562 S.
    Zürich: Orell und Comp., 1792.
<u>N</u>: Vol. VIII, pt. 2, pp. 405-409. (VS).
<u>K</u>: Vol. II, pt. 3, p. 153 a.

Horrer, George Adam.   (189)
    <u>Der Schullehrer oder gemeinnütziges Handbuch</u>
    <u>für Schullehrer und Freunde der Schulen</u>.
    2. Heft, 8 Bogen.
        "Mittel, Aufmerksamkeit in dem Kindern zu er-
        wecken und das Nachdenken zu befördern."   (a)
        "Kathegorische Unterhaltung über die Ruhr."   (b)
        "Kurze Nachricht von einer verdorbenen Dorf-

schule, und durch welche Mittel sie der neue
Lehrer gebessert hat." (c)
Leipzig: Brockhaus, 1801.
N: Vol. LXXV, pt. 2, p. 547. (E).
K: Vol. II, pt. 3, p. 196 a.

Huber, Joseph J. (190)
Isider, Bauer zu Ried. Eine Geschichte für das
Landvolk, wie auch für unsre Bürger in Städten.
1. Theil, 24 Bogen. 2. Theil, 25 Bogen.
München: Lentner, 1797.
N: Vol. XXXVI, pt. 2, p. 486. (VS).
K: Vol. II, pt. 3, p. 203 b.

[Jacobs, Friedrich Wilhelm.] (191)
Allwin und Theodor. Ein Lesebuch für Kinder.
167 S.
Leipzig: Dyck, 1802.
N: Vol. CII, pt. 1, pp. 70-72. (E).
K: Vol. I, pt. 1, p. 46 a.

Jemehr, T. S. See Hermes, Joh. Tim.

Jünger, J. F. (192)
Wilhelmine. Eine Geschichte in zwey Theilen.
1. Theil, 246 S. 2. Theil, 323 S.
Berlin: Lagarde, 1796. K: Leipzig: Köchly, 1795.
N: Vol. XXXI, pt. 1, p. 186. (R).
K: Vol. III, Romane, p. 71 a.

Käppel, Gottfried. (193)
Sittengemälde unsers Zeitalters.
1. Bändchen, IV / 136 S.
Leipzig: Sommer, 1795.

74

<u>N</u>: Vol. XIX, pt. 2, p. 400. (E).

<u>K</u>: Vol. III, pt. 5, p. 258 b.

Karrer, P. J.   (194)

    <u>Hilmar, der Rathgeber für junge Kaufleute; oder</u>
<u>moralisches Taschenbuch für Handlungszöglinge</u>.
272 S.

      "Moralisches Gemälde eines treuen Handlungs-
        diener."   (a)

    Augsburg: Stagesche Buchhandlung, 1800.

<u>N</u>: Vol. LXII, pt. 2, pp. 509-511. (Handlungswissen-
schaft).

<u>K</u>: Vol. II, pt. 3, p. 145 b.

Kellner, Georg Christoph.   (195)

    <u>Liebe auf den verschiedensten Stufen ihrer Rein-</u>
<u>heit und Würde</u>. Auch unter dem Titel <u>Die Launen</u>
<u>der Liebe</u>.
1. Theil, 207 S. 2. Theil, 215 S.

    Leipzig: Lüschler, 1802.

<u>N</u>: Vol. XCII, pt. 1, pp. 90-91. (R).

<u>K</u>: Vol. III, Romane, p. 81 b.

[Kerndörffer, Heinrich August.]   (196)

    <u>Anton, oder der Knabe und der Jüngling wie er</u>
<u>seyn sollte</u>.
2 Bändchen, 144 S., 211 S.

    Leipzig: Lincke, 1800.

<u>N</u>: Vol. LXVIII, pt. 1, pp. 107-108. (R).

<u>K</u>: Vol. I, pt. 1, p. 82 b.

——————————.   (197)

    <u>Bekenntnisse eines glücklichen Vaters. Ein Weih-</u>
<u>nachtsgeschenk für gute Söhne</u>.
8 Bogen.

Frankfurt und Leipzig, 1796.

N: Vol. XXIV, pt. 1, pp. 103-104. (E).

K: Vol. I, pt. 1, p. 195 b.

—————————.   (198)

Darstellungen aus der Menschenwelt. Zur Beför-
derung eines frohen und weisen Lebensgenusses.
VI ≠ 288 S.
Leipzig: Jacobäer, 1798.

N: Vol. XLI, pt. 2, pp. 547-549. (VS).

K: Vol. II, pt. 3, p. 330 a.

[—————————.]   (199)

Moralische Gemälde aus der Ehe. Zur Beförderung
häuslicher Freuden und ehelicher Glückseligkeit.
300 S.
Leipzig: Linke, 1797.

N: Vol. XXXIV, pt. 1, pp. 167-169. (R).

K: Vol. II, pt. 3, p. 330 a.

[—————————.]   (200)

Kleines Taschenbuch zur Bildung und Veredlung
der Jugend.
Leipzig: Linke, 1801.

N: Vol. LIX, pt. 1, pp. 223-224. (E).

K: Vol. III, pt. 5, p. 298 a.

—————————.   (201)

Wanderungen eines Missmüthigen in die Gefilde
ländlicher Zufriedenheit.
VIII ≠ 204 S.
Leipzig: Jacobäer, 1798.

N: Vol. XLV, pt. 1, p. 206. (VS).

K: Vol. III, Romane, p. 148 b.

Kleine, F. A.   (202)

Eli, oder wie dürfen Kinder nicht erzogen werden?
Ein nützliches Lehr- und Exempelbuch für Ältern
und Erzieher.
XXIV ╱ 488 S.
Leipzig: Barth, 1800.
N: Vol. LXIV, pt. 1, pp. 255-260. (E).
K: Vol. I, pt. 2, p. 118 a.

_____.   (203)

Geschichte einer Volksschulreform, zur dienli-
chen Nachricht für Menschen, welche Lust haben,
ihre geringern Brüder zu beglücken.
9½ Bogen.
Frankfurt und Leipzig: Platvort, 1794.
N: Vol. XVI, pt. 2, p. 475. (E).
K: Vol. I, pt. 2, p. 368 a.

_____.   (204)

Wallmonts Ruhestunden in seiner ländlichen Hütte.
1. Bändchen, 224 S. 2. Bändchen, 446 S.
Leipzig: Platvort, 1798.
N: Vol. XLV, pt. 2, pp. 548-549. (VS).
K: Vol. III, Romane, p. 148 a.

Klinger, Johann Siegmund.   (205)

Anleitung zur Belehrung der Jugend über die Er-
haltung des Lebens und der Gesundheit. In socra-
tischen Gesprächen mit vielen Beyspielen, welche auch bei der Erklärung des Gesundheitscate-
chismus gebraucht werden können.
222 S.
Hof: Grau, 1797.
N: Vol. XXXVI, pt. 1, pp. 61-62. (VS).
K: Vol. II, pt. 3, p. 359 a.

Knigge, Freyherr Adolf von.   (206)
    Geschichte des Amtraths Gutmann.
    374 S.
    Hannover: Ritscher, 1794.
    N̲: Vol. XVI, pt. 1, pp. 55-57. (R).
    K̲: Vol. III, Romane, p. 74 b.

Köhnke, M. C.   (207)
    Erzählungen zum Nutzen und Vergnügen für junge
    Kinder. Nebst einem Anhange von Fabeln und Lie-
    dern.
    20 Bogen.
    Berlin: Frölich, 1803.
    N̲: Vol. XCI, pt. 2, pp. 443-444. (E).
    K̲: Vol. II, pt. 3, p. 384 b.

_____.   (208)

    Nützliches und angenehmes Lesebuch für die mit-
    lere und wißbegierige Jugend besonders beym Pri-
    vatunterrichte zu gebrauchen.
    362 S.
        "Der Knabe mit der Nachtigal."   (a)
        "Die ungleichen Brüder."   (b)
        "Der Dank mit dem bloßen Munde ist noch kein
         Dank."   (c)
        "Die Rechthaberey."   (d)
        "Schuster, bleib bey deinem Leisten."   (e)
        "Ein gutes Handwerk hat einen goldenen Boden."(f)
    Braunschweig: Culemann, 1802.
    N̲: Vol. LXXXII, pt. 1, p. 256. (VS).
    K̲: Vol. II, pt. 3, p. 384 b.

Kramer, Carl Siegmund.   (209)
    Kleine Erzählungen und Sittengemälde.
        "Sieg der Natur."   (a)

"Marie Arnold."   (b)

"Wilhelm Ehrmann."   (c)

Halberstadt: Groß d. J., 1797.

N̲: Vol. XXXVII, pt. 2, p. 362. (VS).

K̲: Vol. III, Romane, p. 38 b.

Krämer, Johann Georg.   (210)

Jakob Ehrenmann, oder die Schule zu Wiesenfeld.
Eine Geschichte fürs Volk auf dem Lande, wie
auch in unsern Städten und zunächst für junge
Leute.

381 S.

Leipzig und Augsburg, 1802.

N̲: Vol. LXXVII, pt. 1, pp. 233-236. (E).

K̲: Vol. II, pt. 3, p. 407 a.

Kraus, Ulrich.   (211)

Klostergeschichten für Jünglinge und Mädchen.

315 S.

"Anton und Therese."   (a)

"Amalie Bergheim."   (b)

"August Wintersee."   (c)

"Klement Weicher."   (d)

"Christian Ehrenberg."   (e)

"Nepomuck und Wilhelmine."   (f)

"Wolfgang und Mariane."   (g)

"Eleonore."   (h)

"Karl und Louise."   (i)

"Ferdinand und Franziska."   (j)

Freyburg, 1796.

N̲: Vol. XXXII, pt. 1, pp. 159-160. (R).

K̲: Vol. III, Romane, p. 74 b.

Krons, W. [Kraus, Ulrich.]   (212)
    Neue Klostergeschichten.
    256 S.
      "Die Ruinen."   (a)
      "Das Freudenmädchen, oder schreckliches Bei-
      spiel der Klostertyrannei."   (b)
    Frankfurt: Diez, 1799.
  N: Vol. L, pt. 1, pp. 106-108. (R).
  K: Vol. III, Romane, p. 74 b.

Kroymann, J. und Möller, J. C.   (213)
    Der Jugendfreund.
    1. Band, 1. Abtheilung, 11 Bogen. 1. Band, 2. Ab-
    theilung, 12 Bogen.
    Altona: Hammerich, 1801.
  N: Vol. LXXI, pt. 2, p. 518; Vol. LXXV, pt. 1, p.
    192. (E).
  K: Vol. II, pt. 3, p. 429 a.

Kügelgen, Kasper Jacob.   (214)
    Die Leiden des jungen Werthers Huber, oder die
    schrecklichen Folgen der Onanie, eine wahre Ge-
    schichte zur Warnung und Beherzigung.
    129 S.
    Hamburg: Harold Jr., 1805.
  N: Vol. C, pt. 2, p. 467. (E).
  K: Vol. II, pt. 3, p. 438.

    ——————————————.   (215)

    Lesebuch.
    128 S.
      "Die Geschichte des jungen Robert Saulier,
      eines Emigranten."   (a)
    Andernach: Lassaulx und Heckmann, 1805.

N: Vol. CIV, pt. 2, pp. 354-355. (E).

K: Vol. II, pt. 3, p. 438 a.

Kühne, Christian Friedrich Gottlob.   (216)

  Emilie von Wallenthal, oder das Leben einer

  deutschen Buhlerinn.

  1. Theil, 13 Bogen. 2. Theil, 15 Bogen.

  Leipzig: von Kleefeld, 1801.

N: Vol. LXXI, pt. 2, pp. 365-366. (R).

K: Vol. III, Romane, p. 147 b.

L., F. R.   (217)

  Moralische Chrestomathie für Jünglinge und Jung-

  frauen, zur Bildung des Herzens, in Erzählungen

  Beyspielen, moralischen Aufsätzen und morali-

  schen Poesien. Zum Gebrauch in und außer Schu-

  len.

  16 Bogen.

   "Der gute Sohn."   (a)

   "Die tugendhafte Rache."   (b)

   "Die kindliche Liebe."   (c)

   "Der rechtschaffende Sohn."   (d)

   "Joel und Geman."   (e)

   "Phanuel."   (f)

   "Phanor und Diana."   (g)

   "Der gebesserte Sohn."   (h)

  Celle: Schulze dem jüngern, 1797.

N: Vol. XL, pt. 1, pp. 188-190. (E).

K: Vol. I, pt. 1, p. 439 a.

Labowsky, Alexander von.   (218)

  Moralische Schilderungen aus dem menschlichen Le-

  ben.

  104 S.

"Sophron und Philarete."   (a)
    Bayreuth: Lübecks Erben, 1793.
<u>N</u>: Vol. XXII, pt. 1, pp. 277-278. (VS).
<u>K</u>: Vol. II, pt. 3, p. 454 b.

Lafontaine, August.   (219)
    <u>Moralische Erzählungen</u>.
    1. Band, 24 Bogen.
        "Liebe und Tugend."   (a)
    2. Band, 24 Bogen.
        "Idda von Tokenburg, oder die Stärke der Ein-
        bildungskraft."   (b)
    3. Band, 24 Bogen.
        "Das Nadelöhr."   (c)
        "Die Versöhnung, eine wahre Familienscene." (d)
    4. Band, 4 Bogen.
        "Die Strafe im Alter, oder die Folgen des
        Leichtsinns."   (e)
        "Väterliche Gewalt."   (f)
    5. Band, 5 Bogen.
        "Die gefährliche Probe."   (g)
        "Liebe und Dankbarkeit."   (h)
        "Die Stärke des Vorurtheils."   (i)
        "Verbrechen aus Leichtsinn."   (j)
        "Der Hochmuth."   (k)
    Berlin: Voßsche Buchhandlung, 1794-1800.
<u>N</u>: Vol. XIV, pt. 2, pp. 501-503; Vol. XX, pt. 2,
    pp. 390-394; Vol. XXX, pt. 1, pp. 258-260;
    Vol. XLII, pt. 2, pp. 357-361; Vol. LXI, pt. 2,
    pp. 315-316. (R).
<u>K</u>: Vol. III, Romane, p. 76 a.

_____.   (220)

    <u>Kleine Romane und moralische Erzählungen</u>.
    1. und 2. Theil.

"Liebe und Tugend." (a)

3. Theil, 18 Bogen.

"Idda von Toggenburg, oder die Stärke der Ei-

fersucht." (b)

"Der edelste Mann." (c)

4. Theil, 18 Bogen.

"Verbrechen aus Leichtsinn." (d)

"Die gefährliche Probe." (e)

" Liebe und Dankbarkeit." (f)

"Die Stärke des Vorurtheils." (g)

5. Theil, 17 Bogen.

"Die Strafe im Alter oder die Folgen des

Leichtsinns." (h)

"Die Versöhnung." (i)

6. Theil, 17 Bogen.

"Die väterliche Gewalt." (j)

"Die Rache." (k)

7. Theil, 278 S.

"Der Hochmuth." (l)

"Die Wirkungen der selbstsüchtigen Grundsätze."(m)

"Die Stärke des Gewissens." (n)

"Verbrechen und Strafen." (o)

Berlin: Sander: 1799-1801.

<u>N</u>: Vol. LII, pt. 1, p. 48; Vol. LVI, pt. 2, pp. 377-
378; Vol. LIX, pt. 1, pp. 100-103. (R).

<u>K</u>: Vol. III, Romane, p. 76 b.

_____. (221)

<u>Leben eines Landpredigers</u>.

2 Bände, 9 Bogen.

Berlin: Sander, 1801.

<u>N</u>: Vol. LXX, pt. 2, pp. 348=352. (R).

<u>K</u>: Vol. III, Romane, p. 78 a.

Langbein, A. J. C.   (222)

   <u>Feyerabende</u>.

   3. Band.

     "Mariane Richard."   (a)

     "Achmet und Valide."   (b)

     "Das Damenpferd."   (c)

   Leipzig: Breitkopf und Härtel, 1798.

<u>N</u>: Vol. XLVII, pt. 1, pp. 39-40. (R).

<u>K</u>: Vol. III, Romane, p. 79 a.

Laodes, Friedrich.   (223)

   <u>Erzählungen aus dem Reiche der Wirklichkeit</u>

   <u>und der Phantasie</u>.

   1. Band, 27 Bogen.

   Koburg und Leipzig: Sinner, 1800.

<u>N</u>: Vol. LXVI, pt. 2, pp. 354-355. (R).

<u>K</u>: Vol. III, Romane, p. 79 b.

LaRoche, Sophie.   (224)

   <u>Briefe von Lina als Mädchen. Ein Buch für junge</u>

   <u>Frauenzimmer, die ihren Verstand bilden wollen</u>.

   1. Band, 266 S. 3. Band, 240 S.

   2. Band, 16½ Bogen. Auch unter dem Titel <u>Briefe</u>

   <u>an Lina als Mutter. Ein Buch für junge Frauen-</u>

   <u>zimmer, die ihren Verstand bilden wollen</u>.

   Leipzig: Gräff, 1795-1797.

<u>N</u>: Vol. XXVII, pt. 1, p. 206; Vol. XXXIX, pt. 1,

   pp. 125-126. (VS).

_____.   (225)

   <u>Liebe Hütten</u>.

   1. Theil, 394 S. 2. Theil, 414 S.

   Leipzig: Gräff, 1803.

<u>N</u>: Vol. LXXXVIII, pt. 2, pp. 387-388. (R).

<u>K</u>: Vol. III, Romane, p. 79 b.

Laukhard, Friedrich Christian.   (226)

    <u>Friedrich Christian Laukhards Leben und Schick-</u>
    <u>sale zur Warnung für Eltern und studirende Jüng-</u>
    <u>linge. Ein Beytrag zur Charakteristik der Univer-</u>
    <u>sitäten in Deutschland.</u>
    1. Theil, 396 S. 2. Theil, 512 S.
    Halle: Michaelis und Bispink, 1792.
  <u>N</u>: Vol. IV, pt. 2, pp. 462-465. (VS).
  <u>K</u>: Vol. II, pt. 3, p. 486 a.

Laun, Friedrich. See Schulze, Friedrich A.

[Lehotzky, Martin.]   (227)

    <u>Moral in Beyspielen für Frauenzimmer edler Er-</u>
    <u>ziehung.</u>
    3. Theil, 252 S.
      "Seltener und Korde, oder die glücklich be-
      siegte Eifersucht."   (a)
      "Beate und ihre Töchter."   (b)
      "Lotte und Emilie, Beatens Töchter."   (c)
      "Die Waldorfsche Familie, oder die Folgen der
      Verzärtelung."   (d)
    Leipzig: Pottische Buchhandlung, 1795.
  <u>N</u>: Vol. XXVIII, Suppl. 4, pp. 537-538. (E).
  <u>K</u>: Vol. II, pt. 4, p. 139 a.

Lenke, F. R.   (228)

    <u>Moralisch-romantische Dichtungen für Deutsch-</u>
    <u>lands Jünglinge und Mädchen in den gesittetern</u>
    <u>Ständen.</u>
    335 S.
    Leipzig: Reinicke, 1795.
  <u>N</u>: Vol. XXIV, pt. 1, p. 115. (VS).
  <u>K</u>: Vol. I, pt. 1, p. 81 a.

Leo, Josef Christoph Otto.   (229)
   Das glückliche Dorf in sittlich- politisch-
   und landwirthschaftlicher Hinsicht betrachtet,
   und in einem nachahmungswürdigen Beyspiele dar-
   gestellt.
   XII ≠ 332 S.
   Leipzig: Kleefeld, 1804.
N: Vol. XCVIII, pt. 1, pp. 235-238. (Haushaltungs-
   wissenschaft).
K: Vol. II, pt. 3, p. 523 b.

Lindemann, August. [K: Lang.]   (230)
   Menschenwerth und Menschenglück. In Gemälden
   aus dem häuslichen Leben.
   300 S.
   Altona: Hammerich, 1799.
N: Vol. LIV, pt. 2, p. 371. (VS).
K: Vol. III, Romane, p. 87 a.

_____.   (231)
   Taschenbuch für weisen und frohen Lebensgenuß.
   12½ Bogen.
       "Fritz Kronthal, oder das glückliche Alter." (a)
   Altona: Hammerich, 1802.
N: Vol. LXXIII, pt. 2, pp. 512-514. (VS).
K: Vol. II, pt. 3, p. 559 a.

Lohmann, Johanna Friederike.   (232)
   Claudine Lahn, oder Bescheidenheit und Schön-
   heit behält den Preis.
   1. Theil, 296 S. 2. Theil, 414 S.
   Leipzig: Jacobäer, 1802-1803.
N: Vol. LXXXVII, pt. 1, pp. 39-41. (R).
K: Vol. III, Romane, p. 79 a.

86

Löhr, J. A. C.   (233)

    <u>Der Weihnachtsabend in der Familie Thalberg.</u>
    <u>Für Kinder.</u>
    133 S.
    Leipzig: Fleischer d.J., 1805.
  <u>N</u>: Vol. CI, pt. 2, pp. 383-387. (E).
  <u>K</u>: Vol. II, pt. 3, p. 582 b.

Lossius, Kaspar Friedrich.   (234)

    <u>Gumal und Lina. Eine Geschichte für Kinder, zum</u>
    <u>Unterricht und Vergnügen, besonders um ihnen die</u>
    <u>ersten Religionskenntnisse beyzubringen.</u>
    1. Theil; 2..Theil, 364 S. / ½ Bogen Vorrede;
    3. Theil, 287 S.
    Gotha: Perthes, 1797-1800.
  <u>N</u>: Vol. XLV, pt. 1, pp. 197-198; Vol. L, pt. 1,
    pp. 246-247; Vol. LVIII, pt. 2, pp. 499-500;
    Vol. LXXXV, pt. 1, p. 209. (E).
  <u>K</u>: Vol. II, pt. 3, p. 590 b.

Loßius, Rudolph Christoph.   (235)

    <u>Meister Liebreich, ein nützliches Lesebuch für</u>
    <u>Volksschulen und bürgerliche Familien.</u>
    1. Theil, 262 S. 2. Theil, 276 S. 3. Theil, 220S.
    Gotha: Perthes, 1800-1801.
  <u>N</u>: Vol. LXIV, pt. 2, pp. 499-500; Vol. LXXIX, pt. 1,
    p. 224. (E).
  <u>K</u>: Vol. II, pt. 3, p. 590 b.

_____.   (236)

    <u>Dramatische Sprüchwörter zur angenehmen und nütz-</u>
    <u>lichen Unterhaltung für Kinder.</u>
    Auch unter dem Titel <u>Sittengemälde aus dem gemei-</u>
    <u>nen Leben zum belehrenden Unterrichte für Kinder.</u>
    2 Bändchen.

Gotha: Perthes, 1800.

N: Vol. LXVIII, pt. 1, p. 209. (E).

K: Vol. II, pt. 3, p. 590 b.

Lucius, Karl Friedrich.   (237)

    Fritz Rheinfeld der Sonderling.

    1. Theil, 280 S. 2. Theil, 418 S.

    Leipzig: Gabler, 1793.

N: Vol. XXVIII, pt. 2, pp. 343-358. (R).

K: Vol. III, Romane, p. 122 b.

_____.   (238)

    Neueste Novellenlese belehrend und vergnügend.

    1. Bändchen, 168 S.

      "Der edleste Mann."   (a)

    Leipzig: Grieshammer, 1796.

N: Vol. XXXVI, pt. 1, p. 164. (R).

K: Vol. II, pt. 4, p. 251 b.

Ludwig, Christine Sophie von.   (239)

    Moralische Erzählungen.

      "Die arme Familie."   (a)

      "Was vermag das Beyspiel nicht."   (b)

    Ronneburg und Leipzig: Schumann, 1802.

N: Vol. LXXIX, pt. 1, p. 91. (R).

K: Vol. III, Romane, p. 89 b.

_____.   (240)

    Die arme Familie. Zum Besten der Armen.

    Zwickau: Schumann, 1799.

N: Vol. LXVIII, Suppl. 1, pp. 704-705. (VS).

K: Vol. III, Romane, p. 89 b.

_____.   (241)

    Die Familie Hohenstamm: oder Geschichte edler

Menschen.
1. Theil, 430 S. 2. Theil, 460 S. 3. Theil,
446 S. 4. Theil, 496 S.
Leipzig: Gräff, 1793-1796.
N: Vol. X, pt. 2, pp. 483-484; Vol. XIX, pt. 2,
pp. 323-324; Vol. XXVIII, Suppl. 1, pp. 217-218;
Vol. XXIX, pt. 2, pp. 517-518; Vol. LXX, pt. 1,
pp. 72-73. (R).
K: Vol. III, Romane, p. 89 b.

[_____.]   (242)

Henriette, oder das Weib, wie es seyn kann.
Aus der Familie Hohenstamm.
422 S.
Leipzig: Gräff, 1800.
N: Vol. LXIII, pt. 1, pp. 141-143. (VS).
K: Vol. III, Romane, p. 89 b.

Ludwig, Johann.   (243)
Fragmente aus dem häuslichen Leben des Bürgers
Klugmann und des Landmanns Frölich. Oder über
die Glückseligkeit des Bürgers und Landmanns.
Ein unterhaltendes Lesebuch in den Winteraben-
den.
317 S.¨
Nürnberg: Raspesche Buchhandlung, 1799.
N: Vol. LXVIII, Suppl. 2, pp. 700-702. (VS).
K: Vol. I, pt. 2, p. 246 b.

[_____.]   (244)

Geschichte des Tobias Veiels, eines jungen
Schulmeisters. K: . . . ., oder über die Mittel,
durch welche sich ein Lehrer beliebt machen
kann.
131 S.

Nürnberg: Raspesche Buchhandlung, 1800.

N: Vol. LXVII, pt. 2, p. 502. (E).

K: Vol. I, pt. 2, p. 367 b.

Mauchart, Johann D.   (245)

Historisches Cabinet für Jünglinge und Mädchen.
Zur Beförderung einer zweckmäßigen Anwendung des
Jugendalters.
17½ Bogen.
   "Luciens Bekenntnisse, oder die erste Untreue."(a)
   " Gefahren des Tanzes--oder Pastor Brand und
   seine Familie."   (b)
Stuttgart: Metzler, 1796.

N: Vol. XXIX, pt. 2, pp. 312-313. (E).

K: Vol. II, pt. 4, p. 49 a.

_____.   (246)

Die Hesperiaden. Ein Magazin für jugentliche
Unterhaltung.
1. Stück, 224 S. 2. Stück, 181 S. 3. Stück.
3. Stück, 194 S. 7. Stück, 200 S. 8. Stück, 181S.
Schnepfenthal: Buchhandlung der Erziehungsanstalt,
1798-1803.

N: Vol. LXII, pt. 2, pp. 471-472; Vol. XCIII, pt. 1,
   pp. 179-181. (E).

K: Vol. II, pt. 3, p. 127 b.

Mehring, Daniel Gottlieb Gebh.   (247)

Der Philosoph im Walde, oder über Vaterlandsliebe und Bürgertreue. Ein philosophischer Roman.
1 Bogen Vorrede / 407 S.
Berlin: Himburg, 1796.

N: Vol. XXXII, pt. 1, pp. 89-91. (R).

K: Vol. III, Romane, p. 106 a.

90

Meißner, August Gottlieb.   (248)

    <u>Skizzen</u>.

    12. Sammlung.

      "Die ältere Ehefrau, vielleicht ein Beyspiel

      ohne Gleichen."   (a)

    Leipzig: Verlag der Dykschen Buchhandlung, 1796.

<u>N</u>: Vol. XXXI, pt. 1, pp. 187-189. (R).

<u>K</u>: Vol. III, Romane, p. 93 b.

_____.   (249)

    <u>Charakterzüge aus dem Leben edler Geschäftsmän-</u>
    <u>ner und berühmter Kaufleute. Zur Lehre und Nach-</u>
    <u>ahmung der merkentilischen Jugend</u>.

    9½ Bogen.

    Elberfeld: Büschler, 1805.

<u>N</u>: Vol. CIII, pt. 1, pp. 166-167. (VS).

<u>K</u>: Vol. II, pt. 4, p. 7С a.

Meyer, Ehregott.   (250)

    <u>Die Kunst sich glücklich als Kaufmann oder Fa-</u>
    <u>brikant zu etabliren, oder Belehrungen für junge</u>
    <u>Kaufleute und Fabrikanten, welche sich etabliren,</u>
    <u>etc. wollen</u>.

    XVI ╪ 530 S.

    Weimar: Gebr. Gädike, 1803.

<u>N</u>: Vol. LXXXVIII, pt. 1, pp. 259-261. (Handlungs-
wissenschaft).

<u>K</u>: Vol. II, pt. 4, p. 97 b.

Meynier, Louise.   (251)

    <u>Kleine dramatische Kinderromane zur Bildung und</u>
    <u>Veredlung des jugendlichen Herzens</u>.

    1. Bändchen, 22 Bogen.

      "Der Schein betrügt."   (a)

      "Böse Gesellschaft verdirbt gute Sitten."   (b)

"Die Artigkeit macht, daß man den Mangel der
      Schönheit nicht achtet."   (c)
" Was der Mensch werth ist, wiederfährt ihm." (d)
"Morgenstunde hat Gold im Munde."   (e)
"Jung gewohnt, alt gethan."   (f)
"Ist der Mann noch so fleißig, und die Frau
      liederlich, so geht alles hinter sich."   (g)
"Sprichwörter."   (h)
   Koburg: Simmer, 1802.
N: Vol. LXXIX, pt. 1, pp. 222-224. (E).
K: Vol. II, pt. 4, p. 103 b.

Mildorf, Ludwig.   (252)
   Gutmann (,) oder der aufrichtige Menschenfreund.
   Ein Lesebuch für Bürger und Landleute.
   1. und 2. Theil.
   Leipzig: Linke, 1799.
N: Vol. XLIX, pt. 1, pp. 265, 271. (VS).
K: Vol. II, pt. 3, p. 111 a.

Moll, Georg Philipp.   (253)
   Cornelia, oder Beyträge zur Beförderung der
   häuslichen Glückseligkeit.
   278 S.
     "Hipparinius, Sohn des Dion."   (a)
     "Über Strafen und Bessern in Rücksicht auf
     die Geschichte des Hipparinius."   (b)
     "Die Familie Harstig; ein Gemälde nach dem
     Leben."   (c)
   Tübingen: Heerbrandt, 1800.
N: Vol. LXII, pt. 2, p. 552. (VS).
K: Vol. II, pt. 4, p. 128 b.

Morus, P. C. W.   (254)
   Heinrich von Wild, oder die böse Tante und der

gute Onkel.

10½ Bogen.

Ansbach: Brügel, 1804.

N: Vol. XCV, pt. 2, pp. 341-342. (R).

K: Vol. III, Romane, p. 97 a.

Moser, Christoph Ferdinand und Wittich, Chr. Ferd.   (255)
Der Landschullehrer.

   1. Band, 1. Stück, 3 Bogen.

     "Die Martinsgans von 1796, oder Beyspiel mo-
     ralischer Schulzucht."   (a)

   3. Band, 1. Stück, 5 Bogen.

     "Die Schulzucht, wie sie nicht sein soll."   (b)

Ulm: Wohlersche Buchhandlung, 1796-1799.

N: Vol. XL, pt. 1, p. 58; Vol. LV, pt. 1, pp. 236-
237. (E).

K: Vol. II, pt. 4, p. 147 b.

[Müller, Ernst.]   (256)

Bilderbuch für die nachdenkende Jugend zur angenehmen und nützlichen Unterhaltung.

15 Bogen.

Leipzig: Voß und Leo, 1792.

N: Vol. VI, pt. 1, pp. 53-56. (E).

K: Vol. I, pt. 1, p. 270 a.

———————————.   (257)

Stumme Liebe. Ein häusliches Gemälde.

132 S.

Leipzig: Industrie Komtoir, 1804.

N: Vol. XCIV, pt. 1, pp. 92-93. (VS).

K: Vol. III, Romane, p. 97 b.

Müller, Gustav.   (258)

Gustav Reinwald, oder die geheime Geschichte

des Grafen von R. Eine moralische Erzählung.
1. Theil, 207 S. 1. Theil, 215 S.
Stuttgart: Erhard, 1801.
<u>N</u>: Vol. LXXI, pt. 2, pp. 353-357. (R).
<u>K</u>: Vol. III, Romane, p. 97 b.

M[üller], H[einrich].   (259)
<u>Traurige Folgen unbedachtsamer Verlobung. Eine
wahre Geschichte zur Warnung für Ältern, Jünglinge und Mädchen.</u>
278 S.
     "Wilhelm und Albertine."   (a)
Magdeburg: Bauer, 1800.
<u>N</u>: Vol. LX, pt. 2, pp. 358-359. (R).
<u>K</u>: Vol. III, Romane, p. 43 b.

_____.   (260)

<u>Selbstmord und Raserey, die Folgen der zärtlich-
sten Liebe. Ein Beytrag zur Erfahrungs-Seelenkun-
de.</u>
147 S.
Magdeburg: Bauer, 1798.
<u>N</u>: Vol. LIV, pt. 2, pp. 369-371. (VS).
<u>K</u>: Vol. III, Romane, p. 129 a.

Müller, Johann Gottwald.   (261)
<u>Ferdinand. Ein Original-Roman in vier Bänden.</u>
1. Band, 21¼ Bogen. 2. Band, 29 1/8 Bogen.
Altona: Hammerich, 1802.
<u>N</u>: Vol. CII, pt. 2, pp. 360-361. (R).
<u>K</u>: Vol. III, Romane, p. 41 b.

_____.   (262)

<u>Friedrich Brack, oder Geschichte eines Unglück-
lichen. Aus dessen eigenhändigen Papieren.</u>

1. Band, 312 S. 2. Band, 349 S. 3. Band, 381 S.
4. Band, 396 S.
Berlin und Stettin: Nicolai, 1793-1795.
N: Vol. IX, pt. 1, pp. 24-26; Vol. XII, pt. 1,
pp. 61-62; Vol. XX, pt. 1, pp. 223-225; Vol. XXVII,
pt. 2, pp. 298-302. (R).
K: Vol. III, Romane, p. 21 a.

_____.   (263)

Heinrich Boßhard, eines schweizerischen Landmannes,
Lebensgeschichte.
213 S.
Winterthur: Steiner, 1804.
N: Vol. C, pt. 2, pp. 425-428. (VS).
K: Vol. I, pt. 1, p. 321 a.

_____.   (264)

Selim der Glückliche, oder der Substitut des Ori-
muzd, eine morgenländische Geschichte.
1. Band, 292 S / 39 S. Vorrede. 2. Band, 336 S.,
3. Band, 340 S.
Berlin und Stettin: Nicolai, 1792.
N: Vol. II, pt. 1, pp. 99-115. (R).
K: Vol. III, Romane, p. 129 a.

Müller, K. L. Meth.   (265)
    Gustav Salden.
    23½ Bogen.
    Berlin: Unger, 1802.
N: Vol. LXXXVII, pt. 1, pp. 217-219. (R).
K: Vol. III, Romane, p. 98 b.

Münch, Johann Gottlieb.   (266)
    Züge aus dem Leben glücklicher Menschen.
    Leipzig: Gräff, 1795.

N: Vol. XXII, pt. 2, pp. 544-545. (VS).
K: Vol. III, Romane, p. 155 b.

[_____.]   (267)
    Züge aus dem Leben unglücklicher Menschen.
    1. Band, 14 Bogen.
      "Die arme Wittwe mit ihren fünf Kindern."   (a)
      "Moriz Weber."   (b)
      "Ein Seitenstück zu Moriz Weber."   (c)
      "Auch das kümmerlichste Brot läßt sich noch
      brechen, wenn ein Bruder neben uns verschmach-
      tet."   (d)
      "Eine Geschichte aus dem katholischen Deutsch-
      land."   (e)
    2. Band, 14 Bogen.
      "Das arme Bürgermädchen."   (f)
    Leipzig: Gräffsche Buchhandlung, 1793-1794.
N: Vol. XIII, pt. 1, p. 181; Vol. XVIII, pt. 2,
   pp. 338-341. (VS).

Naubert, B.   (268)
    Sitten und Launen der Grossen (Großen). Ein Ka-
    binet von Familienbildern.
    464 S.
    Leipzig: Weygandsche Buchhandlung, 1794.
N: Vol. XIX, pt. 2, pp. 403-404. (R).
K: Vol. III, Romane, p. 131 a.

[Niceus, Christian Friedrich.]   (269)
    Der Spottvogel unter Satanskindern.
      "Gespräche zwischen einem Juden, Schmuel, und
      einem Doktor Ehrmann über die Handlungsweise
      der Juden und Christen."   (a)
      "Ärztliche Besuche des Doktors Ehrmann, bey
      dem Kommerzienrathe Beil."   (b)

"Der Pfänderverleiher und Prinzessin Wohl-
lust, beyde Satanskinder."   (c)
"Briefe an den Kommerzienrath Beil, von dem
Rektor Klinz."   (d)
    Leipzig: Graffe, 1804.
N: Vol. CIII, pt. 1, pp. 224-225. (VS).
K: Vol. III, Romane, p. 134 a.

Nicolai, Friedrich.   (270)
    Vertraute Briefe von Adelheit B** an ihre
    Freundinn Julie S**.
    242 S.
    Berlin und Stettin: Nicolai, 1799.
N: Vol. LV, pt. 1, pp. 143-144. (R).
K: Vol. III, Romane, p. 22 a.

O., H. F. von.   (271)
    Karl Kronheim. Ein Beytrag zur Geschichte
    menschlicher Verirrungen und Besserung.
    16 Bogen.
    Leipzig: Supprian, 1798.
N: Vol. LXII, pt. 1, pp. 91-92. (R).
K: Vol. III, Romane, p. 76 b.

Oesfeld, Heinrich Gotthelf Friedrich.   (272)
    Sittenspiegel für Kinder.
    Altona und Leipzig: Kaven, 1798.
N: Vol. LII, pt. 1, pp. 196-198. (E).
K: Vol. III, pt. 5, p. 259 a.

Pahl, J. G.   (273)
    Handbibliothek für meine Tochter. Oder das Le-
    sebuch für das schöne Geschlecht.
    1. Bändchen, 401 S.

"Über die Lektüre der Frauenzimmer." (a)

"Die Hausmutter." (b)

"Zur Charakteristik der Weiber." (c)

2. Bändchen.

"Ein biographischer Beytrag zur Geschichte
des menschlichen Elends." (d)

"Winke über den Genuß sinnlicher Freuden." (e)

"Herzenserleichterungen eines Kammermädchens."(f)

"Weibliche Schönheit." (g)

Nördlingen: Beck, 1796-1797.

N̲: Vol. XXXIX, pt. 1, pp. 100-108; Vol. XLI, pt. 1,
pp. 165-169. (E).

K̲: Vol. II, pt. 4, p. 291 b.

Palm, Friedrich G. et al. (274)

Neuer Volkskalender, oder Beyträge zur nützlichen, lehrreichen und angenehmen Unterhaltung
für allerley Leser, zunächst für den Bürger und
Landmann.

Auf das Jahr 1793. 18 Bogen.

"Nachrichten von klugen und thörichten, nützlichen und schädlichen Handlungen." (a)

"Auswahl einiger deutscher Sprichwörter nebst
Beyspielen derselben." (b)

Auf das Jahr 1794. 18 Bogen

Auf das Jahr 1795. 17 Bogen.

"Gute Menschen." (c)

Auf das Jahr 1797. 284 S.

Auf das Jahr 1798. 266 S.

"Edle Charakterzüge aus der Volksklasse." (d)

"Vernachläßigte Erziehung in der ersten Kindheit." (e)

"Fehler der Eltern wodurch sie der Kinder Liebe und Achtung verscherzen." (f)

"Beschreibung einer gut eingerichteten Haus-
haltung, oder was der Wirth thun soll um ein
nützlicher,wohlhabender Bürger zu werden."   (g)
Auf das Jahr 1799. 273 S.
Auf das Jahr 1803. 166 S.
Auf das Jahr 1804. 210 S.
K: 1.-15.Jahrgang von G. F. Palm, I. E. Ewald, Kü-
ster, Fröbing, J. C. Rühlemann, K. F. Kutscher,
Stelzner und Petri.
Hannover: Gebrüder Hahn, 1793-1799. K: Hannover:
Hahn, 1793-1807.
N: Vol. IV, pt. 1, pp. 155-158; Vol. XIII, pt. 1,
pp. 273-274; Vol. XX, pt. 1, pp. 58-60; Vol. XXXI,
pt. 2, pp. 549-551; Vol. XXXVIII, pt. 2, p. 486;
Vol. XLIX, pt. 1, pp. 264-266; Vol. LXXXII, pt. 1,
p. 259; Vol. XCIX, pt. 1, pp. 119-120. (VS).
K: Vol. III, pt. 6, pp. 102 a - 102 b.

Panitz, G. H.   (275)
Der Volksfreund, ein Lesebuch für jeden braven
Bürger- und Landmann.
1. Bändchen, 238 S. 2. Bändchen, 414 S.
Görlitz: Hermsdorf, 1792-1794; Schleswig und Leip-
zig: Brie, 1792-1794.
N: Vol. XXI, pt. 1, p. 226; Vol. X, pt. 1, pp. 124-
126. (VS).
K: Vol. III, pt. 6, p. 102 a.

Pestalozzi, Heinrich.   (276)
Lienhard und Gertrud; ein Versuch die Grundsätze
der Volksbildung zu vereinfachen.
Ganz umgearbeitet; 3. Theil, 389 S.
Zürich und Leipzig: Ziegler und Söhne, 1792.
N: Vol. V, pt. 1, pp. 91-95. (R).
K: Vol. II, pt. 3, p. 554 b.

Pfaff, Heinrich Ludwig.   (277)
    Unterhaltendes Historienbuch für Bürger und Bau-
    ersleute.
    21½ Bogen.
    Gotha: Perthes, 1793.
    N̲: Vol. X, pt. 1, pp. 199-200. (VS).
    K̲: Vol. I, pt. 2, p. 329 b.

Plato, Christian K.   (278)
    Der Jugendfreund in angenehmen und lehrreichen
    Erzählungen für Lehrer und Kinder.
    4. Bändchen, 15 Bogen. 5. Bändchen, 15 Bogen.
    6. Bändchen.
    Auch unter dem Titel Nützliches Historienbuch für
    die lieben Bürger und Landleute zur Unterhaltung
    ihrer Familien in Abendstunden.
    3. Theil, 10 Bogen.
    Quedlinburg: Ernst, 1793-1797.
    N̲: Vol. XVI, pt. 1, pp. 276-277; Vol. XLI, pt. 1,
    pp. 173-174. (E).
    K̲: Vol. II, pt. 3, p. 280 a.

Pockels, Carl Friedrich.   (279)
    Neue Beyträge zur Bereicherung der Menschenkun-
    de überhaupt, und der Erfahrungsseelenlehre ins-
    besondere. Ein Buch für Gelehrte und Ungelehrte.
    212 S.
        "Züge eines unerhörten Geizes."   (a)
        "Briefe eines Selbstentleibers, kurz vor sei-
        nem Tode geschrieben."   (b)
        "Leben und Tod eines Selbstmörders, der bald
        Naturalist, bald Religionsschwärmer war."   (c)
        "Sonderbarer Widerspruch in der Seele eines
        vorsätzlichen Vater- und Muttermörders."   (d)

100

Hamburg: Hoffmann, 1798.

N: Vol. LI, pt. 1, pp. 274-275. (VS).

K: Vol. II, pt. 4, p. 367 b.

Ramann, Sylvester Jakob.   (280)

Neue Sammlung von Sprüchwörtern, zur Unterhaltung und Belehrung.

XVI ≠ 207 S.

"10 Jahre ein Kind, 20 Jahre ein Jüngling."   (a)

"Es hackt keine Krähe der andern ein Auge aus."(b)

"Wer bald giebt, giebt doppelt."   (c)

"Aufgeschoben ist nicht aufgehoben."   (d)

"Geradezu ist der Wahrheit Straße, und guter
Weg hat keine Krümme."   (e)

"Tugend und Handwerk sind der Kinder bestes
Erbteil."   (f)

Altenburg: Rink, 1801. K: Erfurt: Schnuphase,
1801.

N: Vol. LXXXII, pt. 2, pp. 537-539.(VS).

K: Vol. II, pt. 4, p. 425 b.

——————————.   (281)

Stephan oder der Handwerker, wie er seyn soll.
231 S.

Altenburg:Rink, 1802; Erfurt: Schnuphase, 1802.

N: Vol. LXXXII, pt. 2, p. 539. (VS).

K: Vol. III, Romane, p. 109 b.

——————————.   (282)

Moralischer Unterricht in Sprüchwörtern und Erzählungen erläutert für die Jugend.

3. Bändchen, 12½ Bogen.

Erfurt: Keyser, 1792.

Moralischer Unterricht in Sprichwörtern, durch
Beyspiele und Erzählungen erläutert für die Ju-

gend.

2. verbesserte Auflage; 1. Bändchen, XVI / 199 S.
5. Bändchen, 180 S. 6. Bändchen, 1800 S.
Erfurt: Keyser, 1792-1800.

<u>N</u>: Vol. II, pt. 1, pp. 309-310; Vol. XVIII, pt. 1,
p. 107; Vol. LXVIII, pt. 1, pp. 221-223. (E).

<u>K</u>: Vol. II, pt. 4, p. 425 b.

Ramdohr, Friedrich Wilhelm Basilius von.   (283)
<u>Moralische Erzählungen</u>.
2 Theile.
   "Usbeck."   (a)
   "Signora Avveduta."   (b)
   "Daphne und Phöbus."   (c)
   "Die neue Semele."   (d)
   "Die sonderbare Wirthschaft oder Ehe als Cicis-
   beatur."   (e)
   "Der schöne Geist von Pyrmont."   (f)
Leipzig: Dyk, 1799.

<u>N</u>: Vol. LXIV, pt. 2, pp. 362-368. (R).

<u>K</u>: Vol. II, pt. 4, p. 427 a.

Reepmann, Joseph.   (284)
<u>Ein rechtschaffenes Exempelbuch für unstudierte
Leute, welche bey müßigen Stunden eine unschuldi-
ge und nützliche Ergötzung suchen</u>.
2. Theil, 28 Bogen.
Augsburg: Wolfische Buchhandlung, 1797. <u>K</u>: 1792.

<u>N</u>: Vol. XXXVI, pt. 2, p. 406. (VS).

<u>K</u>: Vol. II, pt. 4, p. 451 b.

Reichlin, August Friedrich Freyherr von Meldegg.   (285)
<u>Die Menschheit in besonderen Zügen; in Briefen
eines reisenden Philosophen, zur Beförderung des
wahren Menschenglückes aufgesetzt und als Pendant</u>

zu Salzmanns Carl von Carlsberg zu betrachten.
Auch unter dem Titel <u>Eduard von Wallers Briefe</u>
<u>an seinen Freund, oder der reisende Philosoph</u>.
1. Bändchen, 240 S. 2. Bändchen, 223 S.
Leipzig: Böttger, 1795; <u>K</u>: Augsburg: Späth, 1791.
<u>N</u>: Vol. XXVIII, pt. 1, pp. 60-61. (VS).
<u>K</u>: Vol. III, pt. 6, p. 144 a.

[Richter, Carl Friedrich.]   (286)
   <u>Zöglinge meiner Phantasie</u>.
   239 S.
      "Folgen der Habsucht."   (a)
      "Mittel gegen Schwärmerei."   (b)
   Magdeburg: Keil, 1798.
   <u>N</u>: Vol. XLIII, pt. 1, p. 43. (R).
   <u>K</u>: Vol. III, Romane, p. 155 a.

Rochlitz, Friedrich.   (287)
   <u>Amaliens Freuden und Leiden als Jungfrau und</u>
   <u>Gattinn und Mutter. Ein Geschenk an alle mei-</u>
   <u>ne Schwestern, die die ersten mit mir theilen,</u>
   <u>und die zweiten vermeiden wollen</u>.
   354 S.
   Leipzig: Supprian, 1797.
   <u>N</u>: Vol. XXXII, pt. 1, pp. 204-205. (VS).
   <u>K</u>: Vol. II, pt. 4, p. 528 a.

_____.   (288)

   <u>Charaktere interessanter Menschen in moralischen</u>
   <u>Erzählungen zur Unterhaltung in einsamen ruhigen</u>
   <u>Stunden</u>.
   1. Theil, 468 S.
      "Die frühe Verbindung."   (a)
      "Die Landmädchen."   (b)
      "Nachbar Milner."   (c)

2. Theil, 392 S. 3. Theil, 392 S. 4. Theil, 328 S.
   "Die Verwandten." (d)
Züllichau und Freystadt: Darnmann, 1799-1803.

<u>N</u>: Vol. XLVII, pt. 2, p. 327; Vol. LI, pt. 2, p. 549;
Vol. LII, pt. 1, p. 165; Vol. LXXIX, pt. 1,
pp. 76-77; Vol. LXXXVII, pt. 1, pp. 54-55. (R).

<u>K</u>: Vol. II, pt. 4, p. 528 a; Vol. III, Romane,
p. 115 a.

[_____.] (289)

<u>Erfahrungen aus dem Tagebuch eines unbemerkten</u>
<u>Mannes, für Jünglinge und Mädchen aus feinern</u>
<u>Ständen.</u>
2 Theile.
   "Die fürstliche Geliebte." (a)
   "Der Weltdank." (b)
   "Der Wanderer." (c)
Leipzig: Jacobäer, 1796-1797.

<u>N</u>: Vol. XXIX, pt. 1, p. 126. (VS).

<u>K</u>: Vol. I, pt. 2, p. 142 b.

_____. (290)

<u>Erinnerungen zur Beförderung einer rechtmäßigen</u>
<u>Lebensklugheit. In Erzählungen und praktischen</u>
<u>Aufsätzen.</u>
1. Theil, 338 S.
   "Der Spieler. Erste Abtheilung." (a)
   "Meines Onkels Briefe an seinen männlichen
    Sohn über Weiblichkeit und männliche Bestim-
    mung." (b)
   "Die Stärke des Vorurtheils." (c)
2. Theil, 345 S.
   "Der Spieler. Zweyte Abtheilung." (a)
   "Ferdiners Hochzeitstag." (d)
   "Emiliens Heiratsgeschichte." (e)

3. Theil, 380 S.
   "Der Spieler. Dritte Abtheilung."   (a)
4. Theil, 341 S.
   "Kleine Gemälde."   (f)
   "Die verständige Wahl."   (g)
Züllichau und Freystadt: Darnmann, 1798-1800.

N: Vol. XLV, pt. 2, pp. 541-544; Vol. LI, pt. 2,
pp. 549=554; Vol. LXIII, pt. 1, pp. 301-303. (VS).

K: Vol. II, pt. 4, p. 528 a.

_____.   (291)

Familienleben.
1. Theil, VIII ≠ 328 S.
   "Schuldigkeit."   (a)
   "Gustav."   (b)
2. Theil, IV ≠ 372 S.
   "Lucin."   (c)
   "Wählerey."   (d)
   "Louis."   (e)
   "Leonore und ihre Mutter."   (f)
   "Grandison."   (g)
Frankfurt a.M.:Hermann d.J., 1801-1803.

N: Vol. LXXIII, pt. 1, pp. 66-69; Vol. LXXXVII,
pt. 1, pp. 51-54. (R).

K: Vol. III, Romane, p. 115 a.

_____.   (292)

Die Verwandten.
2 Theile.
Züllichau: Darnmann, 1802.

N: Vol. LXXIX, pt. 1, pp. 54-55. (R).

K: Vol. III, Romane, p. 115 a.

Röper, F. L.   (293)

    Versuche zur Beförderung wahrer Lebensweisheit.
    Auch unter dem Titel Schimpf und Ernst für Alt
    und Jung.
    6½ Bogen.
    Berlin: Maurer, 1801.
N: Vol. LXXVI, pt. 1, p. 272. (VS).
K: Vol. II, pt. 4, p. 540 a.

Sft., J. G.   (294)

    Kleine Geschichten für Kinder von sechs bis zehn
    Jahren, die gern etwas lesen, was ihnen verständ-
    lich, nützlich und angenehm ist.
    1. Theil, VIII ≠ 214 S. 2. Theil, 262 S. 3. Theil,
    236 S. 4. Theil, 278 S. 5. Theil, 242 S.
        "Die zwei unähnlichen Schwestern."   (a)
        "Vater Roderichs Unterhaltungen mit seinen En-
        keln."   (b)
    Leipzig: Fleischer d. J., 1792-1796.
N: Vol. II, pt. 2, pp. 617-618; Vol. VI, pt. 1,
    pp. 216-217; Vol. XVII, pt. 1, pp. 253-254;
    Vol. XXIV, pt. 2, pp. 374-377; Vol. XXX, pt. 1,
    pp. 50-52. (E).
K: not listed.

Salzmann, Christian Gotthilf.   (295)

    Conrad Kiefer, oder Anweisung zu einer vernünftigen
    Erziehung der Kinder. Ein Buch fürs Volk.
    268 S.
    Schnepfenthal: Buchhandlung der Erziehungsan-
    stalt, 1796.
N: Vol. XXIX, pt. 2, pp. 542-545. (VS).
K: Vol. III, pt. 5, p. 18 a.

_____.   (296)

Krebsbüchlein, oder Anweisung zu einer unver-
nünftigen Erziehung der Kinder.
3. Auflage.
Erfurt: Kayser, 1792.
N̲: Vol. VIII, pt. 1, pp. 32-34. (E).
K̲: Vol. III, pt. 5, p. 18 a.

_____.   (297)

Erster Unterricht in der Sittenlehre für Kinder
von acht bis zehn Jahren.
373 S.
Schnepfenthal: Buchhandlung der Erziehungsanstalt, 1803.
N̲: Vol. CII, pt. 1, pp. 71-78. (E).
K̲: Vol. III, pt. 5, p. 18 a.

Scherwinsky, F. D. E.   (298)

Moral in Beyspielen für Bürger und Landleute.
439 S.
Leipzig: Fleischer dem Jüngern, 1800.
N̲: Vol. LXVI, pt. 1, pp. 271-272. (VS).
K̲: Vol. III, pt. 5, p. 76 a.

Schilling, Gottfried.   (299)

Die Irrgänge des Lebens.
Auch unter dem Titel Felixens Abentheuer und Lieb-
schaften, eine Robinsonade.
1. Theil, 213 S.
Gera und Leipzig: Haller, 1802.
N̲: Vol. LXXIX, pt. 1, pp. 89-90. (R).
K̲: Vol. III, Romane, p. 41 b.

[Schilling, Gustav].   (300)

Clärchens Geständnisse. Ein Seitenstück zu Rös-

chens Geheimnissen.
1. Bändchen, 292 S. 2. Bändchen, 248 S. 3. Bändchen, 236 S.
Freyburg: Craz, 1799.
N̲: Vol. LIV, pt. 1, pp. 45-46; Vol. LXI, pt. 1,
pp. 98-99. (R).
K̲: Vol. III, Romane, p. 122 a.

_____.   (301)

Drako Dämon der Hölle.
270 S.
Weißenfels und Leipzig: Severin, 1798.
N̲: Vol. XLVI, pt. 1, pp. 98-99. (R).
K̲: Vol. III, Romane, p. 122 b.

_____.   (302)

Die gute Frau.
1. Theil, 237 S. 2. Theil, 246 S.
Pirna: Arnold, 1802.
N̲: Vol. LXXVII, pt. 2, pp. 309-311. (R).
K̲: Vol. III, Romane, p. 122 a.

_____.   (303)

Julius. Ein Gegenstück zu dem Guido von Sohnsdom. Auch unter dem (plagiirten) Titel August,
ein Gemälde aus dem achtzehnten Jahrhundert.
1. Theil, 286 S. 2. Theil, 272 S.
Freyburg: Craz, 1798.
N̲: Vol. XLVII, pt. 1, pp. 33-35; Vol. LXX, pt. 2,
pp. 354-356. (R).
K̲: Vol. III, Romane, p. 122 b.

_____.   (304)

Der Mann, wie er ist.
21 Bogen.

Pirna: Arnold, 1801.

N: Vol. LXXI, pt. 2, pp. 357-359. (R).

K: Vol. III, Romane, p. 122 b.

[_____.]   (305)

Röschens Geheimnisse.

1. Band, 275 S. 2. Band, 255 S.

Pirna: Arnoldsche Buchhandlung, 1798-1799.

N: Vol. XLVII, pt. 1, pp. 33-34; Vol. LI, pt. 2,
p. 336. (R).

K: Vol. III, Romane, p. 122 a.

_____.   (306)

Das Weib, wie es ist.

396 S.

Pirna: Arnold und Pinther, 1800.

N: Vol. LXIII, pt. 2, pp. 615-616. (VS).

K: Vol. III, Romane, p. 122 a.

Schink, Johann Friedrich.   (307)

Moralische Dichtungen.

1. Band, 358 S. 2. Band, 464 S.

Berlin und Stettin: Nicolai, 1799, 1800.

N: Vol. L, pt. 2, pp. 375-376. (R), Vol. LXI, p.102.

K: Not listed.

Schlez, Johann Ferdinand.   (308)

Geschichte des Dörfleins Traubenheim. Fürs Volk
und für Volksfreunde.

Letzte Hälfte.

Nürnberg: Grattenauer, 1792.

N: Vol. XXVIII, Suppl. 3, pp. 565-567. (E).

K: Vol. III, pt. 5, p. 95 a.

_____.

Gregorius Schlaghart und Lorenz Richard, oder
die Dorfschulen zu Langenhausen und Traubenheim.
Ein Erbauungsbuch für Landschullehrer.
1. Hälfte, 14 Bogen. Letzte Hälfte, 261 S.
Nürnberg: Felseckersche Buchhandlung, 1795.
N: Vol. XXIII, pt. 1, pp. 54-55; Vol. XXVIII,
Suppl. III, pp. 546-547. (E), (VS).
K: Vol. III, pt. 5, p. 95 b.

_____.

Fliegende Volksblätter, zur Verdrängung schädli-
cher oder doch geschmackloser Volkslesereyen.
2. Bändchen.
"Martens; oder wie wohl man sich bey der Ehr-
lichkeit befindet." (a)
"Der zufriedene Hausirer oder Recept gegen
die Unzufriedenheit." (b)
"Das Nachtquartier, oder Philipps Leiden und
Freuden." (c)
"Zwey ungleiche Schuhmacher." (d)
Bayreuth: Lübecks Hofbuchhandlung, 1800.
N: Vol. LXVII, pt. 1, pp. 116-117. (VS).
K: Vol. III, pt. 5, p. 95 b.

_____.

Kleine romantische Volksschriften. Ein Lesebuch
für Schulen.
1. Sammlung, 15 Bogen. 2. Sammlung, 16 Bogen.
2. vermehrte Ausgabe; Heilbronn: Claß, 1802.
N: Vol. LXXVI, pt. 2, pp. 532-534. (VS).
K: Vol. III, pt. 5, p. 95 b.

Schlüter, Friedrich.
Franz Bernhard (,) der Heilige genannt. Eine

<u>pragmatische Geschichte</u>.
1. Band, 352 S. 2. Band, 364 S. 3. Band, 18 Bogen.
Quedlinburg: Friedrich Joseph Ernst, 1794-1795.
<u>N</u>: Vol. XX, pt. 2, pp. 394-397; Vol. XXIV, pt. 2,
pp. 478-480; Vol. XXVII, pt. 2, p. 306. (R).
<u>K</u>: Vol. III, Romane, p. 44 b.

Schmerler, Johann Adam.   (313)
<u>Moralische Erzählungen und Schilderungen</u>.
1 Bändchen, 336 S.
Nürnberg: Pech, 1792.
<u>N</u>: Vol. V, pt. 2, pp. 549-550. (VS).
<u>K</u>: Vol. III, pt. 5, p. 104 b.

Schmiedtgen, Johann Gf. D.   (314)
<u>Anna, oder der Fallstrick der Ehre und des Reich-</u>
<u>thums. Ein Volksbuch. Besonders für den Bürger</u>
<u>und den Landmann; für den Herrendiener und Die-</u>
<u>nerinn</u>.
248 S.
Leipzig und Gera: Heinsius, 1796.
<u>N</u>: Vol. XXIX, pt. 2, pp. 484-485. (VS).
<u>K</u>: Vol. III, pt. 5, p. 123 a.

——————————.   (315)
<u>Dämmerungen. Für Deutschlands gute Töchter</u>.
371 S.
  "Benjamine, oder die Aster."   (a)
  "Der Widerspruch, oder die Bettlerfreude."   (b)
  "Das Gericht der Grünlinge. Ein ländliches
  Familiengemälde."   (c)
Leipzig: Leo, 1796.
<u>N</u>: Vol. XXXII, pt. 1, pp. 202=204. (VS).
<u>K</u>: Vol. III, Romane, p. 123 a.

_____. (316)

Das Haus derer von Gradnow, oder die Liebe nach der Ehe.
1. Theil, 300 S. 2. Theil, 272 S.
Leipzig: Fleischer, d.J., 1798.
N: Vol. LV, pt. 2, pp. 311-312. (R).
K: Vol. III, Romane, p. 123 b.

_____. (317)

Helene, oder so kommt man zu Ehren. Ein Volks-buch, als ein Gegenstück zu: Anna, oder der Fall-strick der Ehre und des Reichthums.
286 S.
Leipzig: Fleischer d.J., 1797.
N: Vol. XXXIX, pt. 2, p. 555. (VS).
K: Vol. III, pt. 5, p. 123 a.

Schnell, J. P. L. See Snell.

Schulze, Friedrich August. (318)

Die ganze Familie, wie sie seyn sollte; ein Ro-man wie er seyn kann.
220 S.
Dresden: Arnold, 1801.
N: Vol. LXXVI, pt. 1, p. 103. (R).
K: Vol. III, Romane, p. 80 b.

_____. (319)

Prinz Gelbschnabel. Ein Märchen aus Gottliebs Papieren.
18 Bogen.
Berlin: Sander, 1803. K: 1802.
N: Vol. LXXX, pt. 2, pp. 346-347. (R).
K: Vol. III, Romane, p. 80 b.

Schumann, August.   (320)
    <u>Gemälde nach Originalen äterer und neuerer Zeit</u>.
    223 S.
        "Friederike Werneck; traurige Folgen der Un-
        treue."   (a)
        "Die Freunde; ein wahres aber seltenes Bey-
        spiel wahrer Freundschaft unserer Zeit."   (b)
        "Trauung durch List."   (c)
    Liegnitz, 1794.
<u>N</u>: Vol. XVI, pt. 1, pp. 57-58. (R).
<u>K</u>: Not listed.

Schwarz, Ignaz.   (321)
    <u>Karl Stösels Kinderjahre. Ein Roman aus der</u>
    <u>wirklichen Welt</u>.
    268 S.
    Leipzig: Linke, 1798.
<u>N</u>: Vol. XLVII, pt. 1, pp. 116-117. (R).
<u>K</u>: Vol. III, Romane, p. 136 a.

Schwarz, Johann Wilhelm.   (322)
    <u>Erdenglück und Menschenwohl. Ein unterhaltendes</u>
    <u>Lesebuch für Kinder, die glücklich werden wollen</u>.
    18 Bogen.
    Leipzig: Hilscher, 1793.
<u>N</u>: Vol. VI, pt. 1, pp. 56-57. (E).
<u>K</u>: Not listed.

Sebas, Christian Ludwig.   (323)
    <u>Fernando, ein historischer Beytrag zur sittli-</u>
    <u>chen Charakteristik der Menschen</u>.
    3 Bände.
    Leipzig: Voß und Leo, 1793-1794.
<u>N</u>: Vol. XV, pt. 1, p. 51. (R).
<u>K</u>: Vol. III, Romane, p. 41 b.

Seidel, Carl August.   (324)

    <u>Anton, oder eins folgt aus dem andern. Eine Ge-
schichte zur Warnung und Belehrung für Kinder.</u>
    18 Bogen.
    Weißenfels: Severin, 1792.
  <u>N</u>: Vol. VI, pt. 1, pp. 215-216. (E).
  <u>K</u>: Vol. III, Romane, p. 128 b.

[Sintenis, Christian Friedrich].   (325)

    <u>Dialogen des Küsters Ehrentraut, mit den Honoratio-
ren seines Dorfes.</u>
    1. Theil.
    Berlin: Langhoff, 1796.
  <u>N</u>: Vol. XXIX, pt. 1, pp. 123-124. (VS).
  <u>K</u>: Vol. III, Romane, p. 31 a.

[_____].   (326)

    <u>Mütterlicher Rath an meine Tochter, wie sie die
glücklichste Gattin, Mutter und Hausfrau werden
könne.</u>
    385 S.
    Halle: Hendels Verlag, 1793.
  <u>N</u>: Vol. IX, pt. 1, pp. 116-119. (R).
  <u>K</u>: Vol. II, pt. 4, p. 432 b.

_____.   (327)

    <u>Richard Grimm, mit dem Beinamen Autodidakt; an-
sässig zu Grimsthal, wo die Sonderlinge zuhause
sind.</u>
    1. Theil, 374 S.2.Theil, 366 S.
    Zerbst: Füchsel, 1795-1797.
  <u>N</u>: Vol. XXIV, pt. 1, pp. 271-276. (R).
  <u>K</u>: Vol. III, Romane, p. 57 a.

Snell, Ludwig Imm. (328)

Ein nützliches Allerley zur Belustigung, Besserung, Belehrung und Warnung der unerfahrenen Jugend, auch für manche Alten gut.
1. Theil, 224 S. 2. Theil, 328 S.
Offenbach: Brede, 1800.
N: Vol. LXVIII, pt. 2, p. 328. (VS).
K: Vol. III, pt. 5, p. 265 a.

_____. (329)

Neue unterhaltende und lehrreiche Geschichten
für Kinder.
214 S.
    "Ungesalzene und dabei gefährliche Späße."   (a)
    "Gefahr der muthwilligen Ausgelassenheit."   (b)
    "Völlerei."   (c)
    "Ein Mörder, der sich selber bestraft."   (d)
    "Zur Vorsicht beym Scherzen."   (e)
    "Ehrlichkeit bey großer Armut."   (f)
Frankfurt a.M. und Bremen: Fr. Wilmans, 1796.
N: Vol. XXXIX, pt. 1, pp. 100, 108-109. (E).
K: Vol. III, pt. 5, p. 265 a.

_____. (330)

Sittenlehre in Beyspielen für Bürger und Land-
leute.
356 S.
Frankfurt a.M. und Bremen: Wilmans, 1795.
N: Vol. XXII, pt. 2, pp. 398-400. (VS).
K: Vol. III, pt. 5, p. 264 b.

_____. (331)

Sittenlehre für Kinder. Ein Lesebuch zum Gebrauch in deutschen Schulen.
14 Bogen.

Frankfurt a.M.: Wilmans, 1804.

<u>N</u>: Vol. XCIII, pt. 1, pp. 246-247. (E).

<u>K</u>: Vol. III, pt. 5, p. 264 b.

_____.   (332)

<u>Warnungen für die unerfahrne Jugend in Beyspie-</u>
<u>len meistens unkluger oder böser Menschen.</u>
264 S.

Lemgo: Meyersche Buchhandlung, 1800.

<u>N</u>: Vol. LXVII, pt. 2, pp. 501-502. (E).

<u>K</u>: Vol. III, pt. 5, p. 265 a.

Soldan, C. H.   (333)

<u>Neues allgemeines deutsches Lesebuch für Bürger</u>
<u>und Landschulen, und für den häuslichen Unter-</u>
<u>richt. Oder Materialien zur Übung des jugendli-</u>
<u>chen Verstandes und zur Beförderung der Morali-</u>
<u>tät und Religiosität.</u>
304 S.

Weissenfels: Severin, 1801.

<u>N</u>: Vol. LXXVII, pt. 2, pp. 543-544. (VS).

<u>K</u>: Vol. III, pt. 5, p. 267 b.

Spazier, Karl.   (334)

<u>Carl Pilgers Roman seines Lebens. Ein Beytrag</u>
<u>zur Erziehung und Kultur des Menschen.</u>
1. Theil, 393 S. 2. Theil, 402 S. 3. Theil, 378 S.
Berlin: Verlag der Akademischen Kunst- und Buchhandlung, 1792.

<u>N</u>: Vol. I, pt. 1, pp. 270-273; Vol. VII, pt. 2,
pp. 466-471; Vol. XXIX, pt. 1, pp. 54-59. (VS).

<u>K</u>: Vol. III, Romane, p. 107 a.

Spieß, Christian Heinrich.

<u>Die ganze Familie, wie sie seyn sollte.</u>

See Schulze, F. A.

Spieß, Christian Heinrich K.   (335)
    Meine Reisen durch die Höhlen des Unglücks und
    Gemächer des Jammers.
    1. Bändchen, 320 S. 2. Bändchen, 362 S. 3. Bänd-
    chen, 372 S. 4. Bändchen, 292 S.
    Leipzig: Leo, 1796-1798.
    N: Vol. XXXI, pt. 1, pp. 33-35; Vol. XL, pt. 1,
       pp. 137-139; Vol. XLVII, pt. 2, pp. 405-406. (R),
       (VS.)
    K: Vol. III, Romane, p. 133 b.

Starke, Gotthelf, Wilhelm Christoph.   (336)
    Gemälde aus dem häuslichen Leben und Erzählun-
    gen.
    1. Sammlung, 19½ Bogen. 2. Sammlung, 17½ Bogen.
    3. Sammlung, 19 Bogen.
       "Die armen Alten."   (a)
       "Das Rothkelchen."   (b)
       "Der Schatz."   (c)
    Berlin: Vieweg dem Ältern, 1793-1796.
    N: Vol. V, pt. 2, p. 353; Vol. XIX, pt. 2, p. 333;
       Vol. XXX, pt. 1, pp. 254-258. (R), (VS).
    K: Vol. III, pt. 5, p. 310 a.

Steinbeck, Christian Gottlieb.   (337)
    Der aufrichtige Kalendermann. Ein gar kuriöses
    und nützliches Buch. Für die Jugend und den ge-
    meinen Bürger und Bauersmann.
    3. Theil, 10½ Bogen.
    Leipzig: Fleischer d.J., 1804.
    N: Vol. XCVI, pt. 2, pp. 490-491. (VS).
    K: Vol. III, pt. 5, p. 319 b.

_____.   (338)

   Versuch eines Erziehungsbuchs für deutsche Bür-
   ger und Landleute.
   1. Bändchen, 11 Bogen.
   Gera: Expedition der Volkszeitung, 1796.
N: Vol. XXXIII, pt. 2, pp. 329-336. (E).
K: Vol. III, pt. 5, p. 320 a.

Stickl, Franz J.   (339)

   Gotthold, oder der christliche Leser im Buche
   der Natur. Ein Erbauungsbuch für den gemeinen
   Mann.
   1. und 2. Hälfte, 38 Bogen.
   München: Lentner, 1798.
N: Vol. XLVI, pt. 2, p. 556. (VS).
K: Vol. I, pt. 2, p. 408 b.

Streithorst, Johann.   (340)

   David Klaus. Ein Sittenbuch für gute Leute in
   allen Ständen.
   XXXVI / 188 S.
   Halberstadt: beym Verfasser und im Waisenhause,
   1796. K: Leipzig: Andrä, 1796.
N: Vol. XXXI, pt. 2, p. 551. (VS).
K: Vol. III, pt. 5, p. 352 a.

[Stutz, J. E.]   (341)

   Frohmanns und Oesterlings Familiengeschichte,
   für Eltern und Kinder.
   Breslau: Korn, 1793.
N: Vol. XII, pt. 1, pp. 56-58. (R).
K: Vol. III, Romane, p. 47 a.

[Thielau, Antoinette Wilhelmine von].   (342)
     Friederike Weiß und ihre Töchter.
     Berlin: Fröhlich, 1805.
   N: Vol. CI, pt. 2, p. 456. (VS).
   K: Vol. III, Romane, p. 149 b.

Trautvetter, Johann Valentin.   (343)
     Gespräche und Erzählungen über landwirtschaftli-
     che Gegenstände, besonders über die Viehzucht.
     Ein Lesebuch für die Jugend, wie auch zum Ge-
     brauche für (die) Lehrer derselben.
     XII / 230 S.
     Göttingen: Schröder, 1800.
   N: Vol. LXVIII, Suppl. 2, pp. 642-644. (Haushaltungs-
     wissenschaft).
   K: Vol. III, pt. 5, p. 467 a.

Tresenreuter, Sophie von.   (344)
     Häusliches Glück; oder die rechtschaffene Wittwe
     im Kreise ihrer Kinder.
     18 Bogen.
     Weißenfels und Leipzig, Severin, 1798.
   N: Vol. LXVIII, Suppl. 1, p. 202.(R).
   K: Vol. III, Romane, p. 55 a.

_____.   (345)
     Lotte Wahlstein, oder die glückliche Anwendung
     der Zufälle und Fähigkeiten.
     1. Band, 520 S. 2. Band, 510 S.
     Kopenhagen und Leipzig: Proft., 1791.
   N: Vol. XIV, pt. 2, pp. 482-484. (R).
   K: Vol. III, Romane, p. 147 a.

[Tzschucke, Carl Friedrich].   (346)
     Leben und Schicksale, auch seltsame Abentheuer

Eduard Isenflamms, eines relegirten Studenten.
232 S.
Berlin: Schöne, 1799.
N: Vol. XIV, pt. 1, pp. 43-44. (R).
K: Vol. III, Romane, p. 82 a.

[_____].   (347)
    Leben und Schicksale relegirter Studenten. Ein
    Spiegel menschlicher Leidenschaften.
    1. Bändchen, VIII ╪ 319 S. 2. Bändchen, 246 S.
    3. Bändchen, 231 S. 4. Bändchen, 232 S. 5. Bänd-
    chen, 247 S.
    Berlin: Öhmigke d.J., 1798-1801.
N: Vol. LIV, pt. 1, pp. 42-44; Vol. LXVII, pt. 1,
    pp. 27-29. (R).
K: Vol. III, Romane, p. 83 a.

Unger, Friederike Helene.   (348)
    Julchen Grünthal.
    2. durchaus veränderte und mit einem 2. Band ver-
    mehrte Ausgabe.
    4 ╪ 1 Bogen[!].
    Berlin: Unger, 1798.
N: Vol. XXXVIII, pt. 1, pp. 152-158. (R).
K: Vol. III, Romane, p. 142 a.

[Veillodter, Ludwig Christoph Carl].   (349)
    Lebensbeschreibungen merkwürdiger und berühmter
    Kaufleute.
    15 Bogen.
    Nürnberg, 1796.
N: Vol. XXIX, pt. 1, pp. 51-52. (Handlungswissen-
    schaft).
K: Vol. II, pt. 3, p. 498 b.

Villaume, P.   (350)
     Lesebuch für Bürger- und Landschulen.
     Auch unter dem Titel Lesebuch für Bürger-, Land-
     und Soldatenschulen.
     332 S.
     Hamburg: Villaume, 1801.
   N: Vol. LXXXIII, pt. 1, pp. 110-111. (VS).
   K: Vol. III, pt. 6, p. 82 a.

Voigt, Christian Friedrich Tr.   (351)
     Moritz und Auguste, oder die Kleinen, wie sie
     seyn sollten.
     324 S.
     Leipzig: Küchler, 1800.
   N: Vol. LXVIII, Suppl. 1, pt. 2, p. 540. (E).
   K: Vol. III, Romane, p. 97 a.

─────────────────.   (352)
     Robert, oder der Mann, wie er sein sollte. Ein
     Seitenstück zu Elisa, oder das Weib, wie es sein
     sollte.
     1. Theil, 19 Bogen. 2. Theil, 19 Bogen. 3. Band.
     Leipzig: Seeger, 1799-1802.
   N: Vol. LXII, pt. 1, pp. 75-76; Vol. LXIX, pt. 1,
     pp. 114-115; Vol. LXXXII, pt. 1, p. 77. (R).
   K: Vol. III, Romane, p. 114 a.

Volkmann, Friedrich.   (353)
     Auguste, oder die Würde des weiblichen Geschlechts.
     1. Theil, 246 S. 2. Theil.
     Hamburg und Mainz: Vollmer, 1800.
   N: Vol. XXIX, pt. 1, pp. 124-126; Vol. LXVI, pt. 1,
     pp. 53-54. (VS).
   K: Vol. III, Romane, p. 145 a.

Völter, Philipp Jacob.   (354)

Der neue Landschullehrer.
2. Band, 1. Stück. 3. Band, 1. ≠ 2. Stück.
Tübingen: Heerbrandt, 1803-1805.

N: Vol. XCIII, pt. 2, p. 487; Vol. XCVIII, pt. 2,
pp. 470-471; Vol. CIII, pt. 1, p. 60. (E).

K: Vol. III, pt. 6, p. 109 b.

Wächtler, Friedrich.   (355)

Darstellungen handelnder Menschen und ihrer
Schicksale.
XXII ≠ 352 S.
Weißenfels und Leipzig: Severin, 1793.

N: Vol. IX, pt. 2, pp. 400-401. (R).

K: Vol. III, Romane, p. 146 b.

Wagener, Samuel Christoph.   (356)

Moralische Anekdoten.
1. Theil, 300 S. 2. Theil, 276 S.
Berlin: Matzdorf, 1803-1804.

N: Vol. LXXIX, pt. 2, p. 552; Vol. XCVI, pt. 1,
p. 54. (VS).

K: Vol. III, pt. 6, p. 126 a.

─────────────.   (357)

Die Gespenster. Kurze Erzählungen aus dem Reiche
der Wahrheit.
1. Theil, 3½ Bogen. 2. Theil, 5 Bogen. 3. Theil,
4¼ Bogen.
Neue Gespenster.
1. Theil, 2. Theil.
Berlin: Maurer, 1797-1800.

N: Vol. XXXIV, pt. 1, pp. 119-122; Vol. XLIII, pt. 2,
pp. 543; Vol. LII, pt. 2, p. 404; Vol. LXXIV,
pt. 2, p. 340; Vol. LXXVI, pt. 2, p. 534. (VS).

K: Vol. III, Romane, p. 146 b.

Wagner, Aloys.   (358)

    <u>Wilhelm Freidwald, oder die braven Fröhlichhau-</u>

    <u>ser</u>.

    6½ Bogen.

    Offenbach: Weiß, 1792.

<u>N</u>: Vol. III, pt. 2, pp. 388-389. (VS).

<u>K</u>: Vol. III, Romane, p. 46 a.

Wagner, Ludwig.   (359)

    <u>Lehren der Weisheit und Tugend in auserlesenen</u>

    <u>Fabeln, Erzählungen und Liedern. Ein Buch für die</u>

    <u>Jugend</u>.

    3. vermehrte und verbesserte Auflage. Leipzig:

    Fleischer, d.J., 1798.

<u>N</u>: Vol. LII, pt. 1, p. 200. (E).

<u>K</u>: Vol. III, pt. 6, p. 128a.

Wahrmann, Tobias.   (360)

    Kleine Lesebibliothek für die wißbegierige Ju-

    gend.

    1. Bändchen, 12 Bogen. 2. Bändchen, 12 Bogen.

      "Die Reue kommt immer zu spät."   (a)

      "Die belohnte Ehrlichkeit."   (b)

      "Michel und Jakobine, eine Erzählung."   (c)

    3. Bändchen, 12 Bogen.

      "Die falsche Wahl."   (d)

      "Der Christbaum."   (e)

      "Der zerbrochene Krug."   (f)

      "Der Waise."   (g)

    4. Bändchen, 12 Bogen.

      "Folge der Verschwendung."   (h)

      "Der Vorwitz bestraft sich immer selbst."   (i)

      "Edelmuth eines Mohren."   (j)

    Breslau: Korn d.Ä., 1793-1795.

<u>N</u>: Vol. XIII, pt. 2, pp. 449-450; Vol. XV, pt. 1,

pp. 179-180; Vol. XXV, pt. 2, p. 331. (E).

K: Vol. III, pt. 6, p. 136 a.

Wallenrodt, Johanna, Isabella Eleonore.   (361)
    Adolph und Sidonie von Wappenkron.
    1. Theil, 433 S.
    Halle: Hendels Verlag, 1796.
    N: Vol. XXXV, pt. 1, p. 97. (R).
    K: Vol. III, Romane, p. 147 b.

_____.   (362)
    Theophrastus Grodmann, einer von den seltenen
    Erdensöhnen, ein Roman für Denker und Edle.
    1. Theil, 308 S.
    Leipzig: Böhme, 1794.
    N: Vol. XV, pt. 1, pp. 50-51.(R).
    K: Vol. III, Romane, p. 52 b.

Waller, Anton Chr. August Michaelis.   (363)
    Miscellaneen aus dem Gebiete der Phantasie für
    Freunde und Freundinnen unterhaltender Lektüre.
    8½ Bogen.
    Ronneberg: Liebhold, 1801; Leipzig: in Commission
    bey Fleischer, 1801.
    N: Vol. LXXV, pt. 2, pp. 399-400. (R).
    K: Vol. III, pt. 6, p. 143 b.

Wening, J. Adam.   (364)
    Leben, Reisen und Schicksale Georg Schweigharts
    eines Schlossers, ein Büchlein (Buch! Buch!) für
    Meister, Gesellen und Lehrjungen.
    2. ≠ 3. Bändchen zusammen 33 Bogen.
    Salzburg: Dyle, 1792.
    N: Vol. IV, pt. 2, pp. 598-599. (R).
    K: Vol. I, pt. 1, p. 497 a.

Will, Amalie.
  Meine Freuden und Leiden als Jungfrau und Gattinn.
  See Rochlitz, Friedrich

Wobeser, Wilhelmine Karoline von.   (365)
  Elisa, oder das Weib wie es seyn sollte.
  1. Theil, 328 S. 2. Theil, 138 S. Über den Um-
  gang der Weiber mit Männern.
  Leipzig: Gräff, 1795-1799.
  N: Vol. XXVI, pt. 1, p. 125; Vol. LIX, pt. 1,
  pp. 100-101. (VS).
  K: Vol. III, Romane, p. 35 b.

Wurmsamen, Athanasius.   (366)
  Ulrich Höllriegel. Kurzweilige und lehrreiche
  Geschichte eines Würtembergischen Magisters.
  14½ Bogen.
  Waldangelloch und Leipzig, 1801.
  N: Vol. LXXVI, pt. 1, pp. 100-101. (R).

Z., E. C.   (367)
  Moral in Beyspielen für die Jugend.
  XIV ≠ 291 S.
  Berlin: Felisch, 1799.
  N: Vol. XLIX, pt. 1, p. 264. (E).
  K: Vol. II, pt. 4, p. 139.

Zober, Karl.   (368)
  Der rechtschaffende Dienstbote.
  Berlin: Maurers B., 1798.
  N: Vol. XLVIII, pt. 2, pp. 395, 402. (VS).
  K: Vol. I, pt. 2, p. 46 a.

Anonymous.   (369)
   Launthal und Burks Jugendgeschichte.
   Augsburg: C. F. Bürgien [Bürglen?], 1795.
K: Not listed.

B., Ernst.   (370)
   Der Wechsel. Eine Morgenlektüre für geplagte
   Männer, deren Weiber gern ein X für ein U ma-
   chen.
   Leipzig: Joachim, 1800.
K: Vol. III, Romane, p. 18 b.

Herrmann, Fr.   (371)
   Die Familie Angely. Eine Geschichte aus den Zei-
   ten des französischen Revolutionskrieges.
   Lübben: Gotsch, 1804.
K: Vol. III, Romane, p. 74 b.

Knigge, Freyherr Adolf von.   (372)
   Geschichte des armen Herrn von Mildenburg.
   3 Theile.
   Hannover: Hahn, 1789-1797.
K: Vol. III, Romane, p. 74 b.

_____.   (373)
   Die Reise auf die Universität. Ein Seitenstück
   zu der Reise nach Braunschweig.
   Neuburg: Joachim, 1805.
K: Vol. III, Romane, p. 112 a.

Lafontaine, August.   (374)

    <u>Baron von Bergedorf oder das Prinzip der Tugend</u>.

    Leipzig: Sander, 1803.

<u>K</u>: Vol. III, Romane, p. 78 b.

Meynier, Johann Heinrich.   (375)

    <u>Kleine Geschichten zur Besserung und Veredlung</u>

    <u>jugendlicher Herzen</u>.

    Nürnberg: Fr. Campe, 1813.

<u>K</u>: Vol. II, pt. 4, p. 103 a.

Salzmann, Christian Gotthilf.   (376)

    <u>Moralisches Elementarbuch nebst einer Anleitung</u>

    <u>zum nützlichen Gebrauch desselben</u>.

    1. Theil, 412 S.

    Neue verbesserte Auflage; Leipzig: Siegfried

    Liebrecht Crusius, 1785.

<u>K</u>: Vol. III, pt. 5, p. 18 a.

_____.   (377)

    <u>Ernst Haberfeld, oder wie aus einem Bauern ein</u>

    <u>Freiherr wird</u>.

    Schnepfenthal: Buchhandlung der Erziehungsanstalt,

    1805.

<u>K</u>: Vol. III, pt. 5, p. 18 a.

_____.   (378)

    <u>Heinrich Glaskopf. Ein Unterhaltungsbuch für die</u>

    <u>Jugend</u>.

    Schnepfenthal: Buchhandlung der Erziehungsanstalt,

    1820 (published posthumously).

<u>K</u>: Vol. III, pt. 5, p. 18 a.

_____.   (379)

    Heinrich Gottschalk in seyner Familie, oder er-
    ster Religionsunterricht für Kinder von 10 bis
    12 Jahren.
    Schnepfenthal: Buchhandlung der Erziehungsanstalt,
    1804.
K: Vol. III, pt. 5, p. 18 a.

_____.   (380)

    Sebastian Kluge. Ein Volksbuch.
    Leipzig: W. Vogel, 1790.
K: Vol. III, pt. 5, p. 18 a.

_____.   (381)

    Simon Blaukohl.
    Schnepfenthal: Buchhandlung der Erziehungsanstalt,
    1806.
K: Vol. III, pt. 5, p. 18 a.

Schindler, Johann Carl Gottlob.   (382)
    Robert, oder der Mann, wie er nicht seyn sollte.
    Ein Gegenstück zu Robert, der Mann wie er seyn
    sollte.
    3 Theile.
    Leipzig: Schladebach, 1800-1802.
K: Vol. III, Romane, p. 114 a.

[Siede, Christian Friedrich].   (383)
    Raritäten aus Berlin und merkwürdige Geschichten
    einiger Berlinischen Freudenmädchen. Auch dem un-
    schuldigsten Mädchen lesbar.
    2. Theil.
    Berlin: Schöne, 1794.
K: Vol. III, Romane, p. 82 b.

Sintenis, Christian Friedrich.   (384)
    <u>Hallos des Zweyten glücklicher Abend</u>.
    Leipzig: Erich Fleischer, 1797.
  <u>K</u>: Vol. III, Romane, p. 58 b.

Wahl, S. W.   (385)
    <u>Adolphine</u>.
    Leipzig: Gräff, 1794.
  <u>K</u>: Vol. III, Romane, p. 5 a.

Wallenrodt, Johanna Isabella Eleonore.   (386)
    <u>Fritz, der Mann, wie er nicht seyn sollte; die</u>
    <u>Folgen einer üblen Erziehung</u>.
    2 Theile.
    Gera: Haller, 1800.
  <u>K</u>: Vol. III,Romane, p. 46 a.

Zschokke, Heinrich.   (387)
    <u>Die Brannteweinpest. Eine Trauergeschichte zur</u>
    <u>Warnung und Lehre für Reich und Arm, alt und jung</u>.
    Aarau: Sauerländer, 1837.

_____.   (388)

    <u>Das Goldmacherdorf. Eine anmuthige und wahrhafte</u>
    <u>Geschichte</u>.
    Aarau: Sauerländer, 1817.

_____.   (389)

    <u>Das Loch im Ärmel</u>.
    Aarau: Sauerländer, 1812.

_____.   (390)

    <u>Meister Jordan, oder Handwerk hat goldenen Bo-</u>
    <u>den. Ein Feyerabend-Büchlein für Lehrlinge, ver-</u>

ständige Gesellen und Meister.
Aarau: Sauerländer, 1845.

Number of Educational Novels published each year

between 1792 and 1805

__1792__: (5), (34), (38), (66), (71), (94), (96), (109),
(131), (164), (169), (176), (190), (226), (256),
(264), (274), (282), (294), (296), (308), (313),
(324), (334), (345), (358), (363), (114).
Total: 28 novels.

__1793__: (1), (16), (18), (28), (70), (85), (89), (93),
(99), (109), (113), (127), (177), (218), (237),
(241), (262), (267), (274), (277), (278), (282),
(294), (322), (326), (330), (341), (355), (360).
Total: 29 novels.

__1794__: (9), (11), (80), (81), (93), (98), (143), (203),
(206), (219), (241), (262), (268), (274), (275),
(278), (282), (294), (312), (320), (323), (334),
(336), (360), (362).
Total: 25 novels.

__1795__: (2), (17), (31), (42), (50), (56), (79), (88),
(112), (114), (126), (134), (167), (190), (219),
(224), (227), (228), (241), (262), (266), (274),
(278), (282), (285), (294), (309), (327), (330),
(360), (365).
Total: 31 novels.

__1796__: (3), (6), (8), (23), (26), (55), (68), (83), (91),
(111), (116), (126), (144), (147), (174), (192),
(197), (211), (219), (238), (241), (247), (248),
(273), (274), (278), (282), (289), (294), (295),
(314), (315), (325), (329), (334), (335), (336),

(338), (340), (349), (353).
Total: 41 novels.

1797: (33), (48), (60), (64), (78), (88), (97), (104),
(105), (107), (146), (152), (180), (190), (199),
(205), (209), (217), (219), (224), (234), (273),
(274), (278), (282), (284), (287), (317), (335),
(357).
Total: 30 novels.

1798: (9), (22), (44), (51), (54), (62), (86), (108),
(118), (119), (120), (132), (139), (145), (150),
(168), (178), (181), (184), (187), (198), (201),
(204), (219), (222), (234), (246), (260), (271),
(272), (274), (279), (282), (286), (290), (301),
(303), (305), (316), (321), (335), (339), (344),
(347), (348), (359), (368).
Total: 47 novels.

1799: (7), (41), (61), (65), (67), (82), (88), (110),
(138), (139), (152), (155), (158), (167), (168),
(174), (187), (212), (219), (220), (230), (240),
(243), (246), (252), (255), (270), (274), (282),
(283), (288), (290), (305), (307), (346), (347),
(352), (357), (367).
Total: 39 novels.

1800: (32), (39), (43), (45), (100), (101), (106),
(115), (121), (135), (138), (148), (162), (166),
(172), (189), (194), (196), (202), (219), (223),
(234), (235), (236), (242), (244), (246), (253),
(259), (282), (288), (290), (298), (306), (307),
(310), (328), (332), (343), (347), (351), (352),
(353), (357), (365).
Total: 45 novels.

1801: (21), (30), (35), (40), (53), (57), (58), (87),
(90), (95), (117), (122), (123), (124), (125),
(136), (137), (138), (141), (151), (153), (160),
(165), (189), (200), (213), (216), (219), (220),
(221), (246), (258), (280), (291), (293), (304),
(318), (333), (347), (350), (352), (363), (366).
Total: 43 novels.

1802: (15), (19), (27), (36), (47), (49), (69), (73),
(114), (128), (130), (140), (154), (159), (160),
(171), (175), (179), (182), (189), (191), (195),
(208), (210), (231), (232), (239), (246), (251),
(261), (265), (281), (288), (291), (299), (302),
(311), (252).
Total: 38 novels.

1803: (10), (13), (14), (20), (26), (37), (52), (72),
(102), (103), (129), (142), (157), (159), (163),
(170), (182), (207), (225), (246), (250), (274),
(291), (298), (319), (337), (356).
Total: 27 novels.

1804: (4), (24), (29), (46), (59), (63), (74), (77),
(84), (133), (152), (159), (161), (164), (171),
(182), (183), (186), (229), (254), (263), (257),
(269), (274), (331), (354), (356).
Total: 27 novels.

1805: (12), (92), (149), (171), (214), (215), (249),
(324).
Total: 8 novels.

CHAPTER II

THE CONTENTS

This chapter lists the characters, virtues and vices
of the novels of education. The reviewers of the <u>Neue All-</u>
<u>gemeine Deutsche Bibliothek</u> generally discuss virtues and
vices abstractly. We are rarely told of the methods by
which virtue is promoted and vice prevented. Twenty novels
appearing in the bibliography were therefore read for check-
ing the reliability of the reviews: (76), (85), (86), (119),
(120), (121), (211), (212), (224), (234), (235), (258),
(276), (295), (296), (308), (309), (337), (341) and (348).
It appeared from a careful reading that the abstractness of
the novels of education was itself partly responsible for
the rather general tenor of the reviews. The weakness of
characterization or the plot development does not give the
reviewer much scope beyond pointing out the educational
aims of the writers. Nevertheless all novels whose reviews
only mention the themes without any plot summaries have
also been included and are designated by "also."

To these plots given in the reviews I have added
major themes from those books listed separately in the bibliography [(369)-(390)] which I have read, but which were
not reviewed in the <u>Neue Allgemeine Deutsche Bibliothek</u>.

134

All themes have been tabulated in descending order of authority for the characters, in alphabetical order for virtues and vices. The content of the reviews will accordingly appear under several headings.

All quotations are taken from the Neue Allgemeine Deutsche Bibliothek. The reference can easily be verified as to volume, part and page by means of Chapter I, where under the respective number these data are found.

List of the Contents

A. Characters

Prince (Fürst)

Hermann is a good and just ruler in a story which a teacher tells his pupils (76d). Throughout history, thrifty, honest, generous, just and kind princes have helped their subjects dam the rivers, grow forests, build streets, schools, churches and hospitals; princes who preferred hunting, gambling and drinking left the reins of government in the hands of poor counsellors. They exploited the people. Such princes lost the respect of their subjects (119). Friendly princes make their subjects happy (237), careless princes bring poverty to their lands (178c). Prince Gustav rewards his Privy Counsellor Hallo with a village for eighty years of loyal service. Hallo sets a practical example of statesmanship for the Prince as he frees the serfs, allows them to plant their own fields, gives them a teacher, a pastor, a doctor and a mid-wife (384). An irresponsible prince seduces an innocent girl who has been educated by the French governess Latour. The girl is not avenged because her seducer is a prince (106).

> "Ein armer Knabe fängt ein Rothkelchen, will
> es verkaufen, und dafür sich und seiner Mutter
> Brod schaffen. Indem er sich diese Freude vor-
> stellt, reitet der Fürst vorrüber. Der Junge
> greift nach dem Hut, und läßt das Rothkelchen
> fliegen; er erhebt ein jämmerlich Geschrey; der

Fürst läßt nach der Ursache erkundigen, und verspricht seiner Mutter Wochengeld, und ihm Erziehung."(336b)

"Der Prinz Alfonso, der von seinem Erscheinen an bis auf den letzten Bogen eben nicht im besten Lichte erscheint, tritt plötzlich als ein ganz anderer Mensch auf, und wird etwas zu schnell bekehrt." (247)

"Hier ein Beweis, daß der Verf[asser] auch den Gang und die Kabalen des Hof- und Ministerlebens kennt und zu zeichnen versteht--über Staatseinrichtungen--Projectmacher--die Art und Weise, wie gutherzige Fürsten gemißbraucht werden--wie sie bey ihrem besten Willen, Gutes zu stiften, oft Unheil anrichten und, statt Seegen, Fluch erndten.--Über Steuer und Zinsfuß.--Über alle diese aufgedeckten Geheimnisse muß man den Verf[asser] selbst lesen, und Rec[ensent] versichert, man werde ihn mit Vergnügen lesen. Möchten diese Capitel doch manchen Fürsten zum Handbuch dienen." (262)

Sovereign (Landesherr, Obrigkeit)

A "Landesherr" listens attentively to Gertrud. She tells him of the drinking, debt and disease among the farmers of Bonnal. The selfish bailiff, who is also the innkeeper, encourages their drinking and gambling. The "Landesherr" dismisses the bailiff and encourages the pastor, a new schoolmaster and the only uncorrupted family to reform the other villagers. Soon Bonnal is a healthy, neat and properous village (276).

A "Landesherr" discovers the corruption of the bailiff Schlacker when he disguises himself and talks with the farmers. He dismisses Schlacker, appoints Wenner and builds a schoolhouse and a hospital. He is now respected and loved by the farmers (308). Another kind "Landesherr" builds not only a schoolhouse and a hospital, but also an **pharmacy** and establishes a general disaster fund (85). The "Adel" is weak, ludicrous, and prejudiced and hence dispensable (178c).

> "Die Pflichten und Rechte der Obrigkeiten und Unterthanen werden . . . auseinandergesetzt. Beyde Theile erhalten eine heilsame Lektion; der Verf[asser] will nicht bloß gehorsame Unterthanen, er will auch gewissenhafte und menschenfreundliche Obrigkeiten bilden." (169)

> "Der Verf[asser] stellt . . . einen jungen Landesherrn auf, der eben so edel denkt, wie der Pfarrherr, in der Gemeine die gute Jahreszeit über residirt, den Dorfpfarrer Ehrmann zu seinem Vertrauten macht, und auf der Stelle das alles ausführt, was der aufgeklärte Dorfgeistliche ihm schönes vorgepredigt hatte." (177)

Also (150).

Bailiff (<u>Vogt</u>)

Vogt Ehrlich hires a teacher, a pastor and a doctor, serves in elections and is the honest treasurer of the village (308). The selfish Vogt Schlacker is careless with the account books, can be bribed easily and permits drinking after ten o'clock (308). The bailiff of Bonnal is the innkeeper himself and lures the farmers to his inn and encourages gambling and drinking. The farmers are corrupted and in debt until squire Arner Arner appoints another bailiff (276).

Also (85), (86).

Teacher (<u>Lehrer</u>, <u>Dorfschulmeister</u>)

The teacher instructs the children in reading and

writing (309), (388) and teaches them the catechism (309).
He must be well-educated himself (244) in Schulmeisterseminaria (177), (390). Since he also learns from life itself he teaches his pupils Lebensweisheiten (276), (309),
(388). Many teachers do not know what or how to teach,
they have only memorized their catechism and cannot help
their pupils (309). The good teacher Richard Lorenz rea-
sons with his pupils (309). Another schoolmaster employs
Socratic dialogue (234) in order to teach Christian virtues (234), (282).

The good teacher does not lecture to his pupils (258),
(309), but sits among them and talks with them (186). Or he
walks with them through the fields and woods and tells them
about plants and animals (71). He becomes their friend
(388), (237). All children love and respect such a teacher (244). A good teacher educates his pupils through reason and play (309), the bad one flares up and relies on
punishment (43), (309).

> "In dieser Geschichte werden alle die Fehler,
> die gewöhnlich in Hinsicht des Lehrens began-
> gen werden, nebst ihren gemeinschädlichen Fol-
> gen, auf eine sehr eindringliche und belehren-
> de Art dargestellt." (255b)

> "Rector Misoteutus, ein ganzer Hebräer und
> Grieche, verstößt Fritz Rheinfeld auf gut jü-
> disch mit dem fürchterlichsten Fluche." (237)

Teacher Schlaghart thinks of his children as a nui-
sance, because they keep him from sleeping, drinking and
gossiping (309). Dissatisfied with himself because of his

145

failure, teacher Barthel Most seeks and finds the only
joy in drinking. He is betrayed by his wife, spoils his
own son, punishes his pupils cruelly and mistreats his
colleagues (8). An unimaginative teacher merely lets
his pupils copy and therefore is not bothered by them
(309).

To show the ill effects of prostitution a teacher
goes with older students first to a house of ill repute
and then to a hospital (334). A young teacher can show
an older teacher better methods (43) and improves a poor
schoolhouse: he puts the blackboard near the light, opens
the windows and tells pupils to come with clean clothes
and fingernails (189c).

> "Ein Lehrer redet [in diesem Buche] zwar vorn
> herein seine Klasse an, und giebt ihnen viel gu-
> te zur Lebensklugheit gehörige Moral vorweg.
> . . . Dann erzählt er ihnen die merkwürdigen Ge-
> schichten seiner ehemaligen Schüler. . . . Er be-
> handelt sie wie Leser. Die Geschichten selbst
> sind gut erzählt, und zeigen, an welchen Klip-
> pen (der Verführung und des Betruges) die Unbe-
> sonnenheit und Leichtgläubigkeit der Jünglinge
> scheitern kann, wie zuweilen Jugendfehler noch
> drückende Folgen sich in den spätern Jahren äus-
> sern, und wie sich doch diese Folgen durch an-
> haltende Rechtschaffenheit wieder heben lassen."
> (76a-d)

A teacher who wants to improve his school comes up
against the prejudice, narrowmindedness, laziness and
apathy of the parents, but can nevertheless educate their
children. He gains their respect because he talks and even
plays with them. While the parents only punish the chil-

146

dren, he shows them love (183c).

A still popular story, which was widely imitated,
has a schoolteacher for a hero. Zschokke's Das Goldmacherdorf (388) shows how a run-down village, inhabited by
drinkers, is changed into a clean and attractive place.
The teacher is neat, reads and works with his pupils and
sends untidy children home. On Sundays he walks with the
boys and the girls through fields and woods, tells them
about the moon, the sun, the animals and the seasons. Because he does not punish them his pupils love and respect
him and imitate his politeness and kindness. Their parents,
now seeing their neat children, are themselves ashamed and
mend their own clothes, wash themselves, stop drinking,
clean their homes and repair the streets.

> "Amalie Waldenfels ist eine sehr gebildete
> Wittwe eines rechtschaffenen Mannes, deren ganzer
> Reichtthum ein guter Ruf und häusliche Geschick-
> lichkeit ist. Da sie ihre beyden Töchter treff-
> lich erzieht: so erweckt dieß bey vielen Müttern
> ihrer Stadt den Wunsch, daß sie eine Art Erziehungs-
> anstalt errichten, und neben den ihrigen auch frem-
> den Töchtern nützlich werden möchte--und dieß ge-
> schah. Amalie sitzt nun unter ihren Schülerinnen,
> und sucht sie bey ihren weiblichen Arbeiten durch
> moralische Belehrungen sowohl als wissenswerthe
> Kenntnisse zu unterhalten: und dieß thut sie ent-
> weder selbst, oder durch die ältern ihrer Zöglin-
> ge, die, vorher dazu vorbereitet, eine Unterre-
> dung auf die Bahn bringen, oder etwas nützliches
> vorlesen." (186)

Also (89), (202).

See also Classroom, Private Tutor.

Pastor (<u>Pfarrer</u>, <u>Pfarrherr</u>, <u>Landgeistlicher</u>, <u>Prediger</u>)

The good pastor reforms a village. He selects a competent teacher, preaches sermons which the farmers understand and visits their homes (85), (237), (308). Pastor Heilmann speaks clearly, thinks and listens patiently to the farmers (308), pastor Ruhe walks erect and smiles (179), and pastor Helfrich visits the hospital and the poorhouse frequently (313).

The pastor must be well-educated, yet he should talk to the people in their simple language (198). A pastor who uses Greek and Latin in his sermons cannot be understood (308), (388). Pastor Nimmsweg can write and speak Latin, yet "ein Dutzend Trulliber vereinigt dieses Scheusal in sich." (179)

A helpful pastor advises a father in raising his son (295), educates a foundling (160b) and visits families frequently so that he can settle arguments between husbands and wives (295) and neighbors (179). He helps a boy who is afraid of darkness and witches (376); he scolds a soldier for his bad manners and makes him give up drinking (378).

> "Prediger Froland [unternimmt] im ersten Theile dieser Schrift auf Befehl seines Landesfürsten, dem sein entworfener Plan zur Verbesserung der Volksschulen in die Hände gekommen war, eine Reise durch das Land, um die Schulen zu untersuchen. . . . Wie er den Zustand derselben gefunden, wird von jedem Ort kurz berichtet und der Prediger sowohl, wie der Schulmeister charakterisirt. Im 2ten Theile folgt des Predigers Plan, wie Volksschulen

verbessert werden können. Nach einigen zweckmäßigen Betrachtungen über die Wohlfahrt in den
niedern Ständen, und über die Schulen, welche
vorhanden sind, werden die Vorschläge bekannt
gemacht, um eine Lehrerpflanzschule anzulegen."
(203).

"Der Verf. läßt seinen Dorfpfarrer Ehrmann
völlig zweckmäßig erziehen und studiren. Der
junge Landesherr, . . . der eben so edel denkt
[wie Ehrmann], macht diesen zu seinem Vertrau-
ten. Daß es jenem [Ehrmann] nunmehr sehr leicht
werden mußte, auch aus seiner Gemeine zu machen,
was er will, ergiebt sich von selbst. Worin
übrigens alle diese Verbesserungen bestehn, die
anfänglich in seinem Dorfe, und sodann im ganzen
Lande bewerkstelligt werden, läßt eben so ge-
schwind sich errathen. Anschaffung einer Dorf-
armencasse, Einführung besserer Gesangbücher,
und eines simplern Gottesdiensts überhaupt,
Schulmeisterseminaria, zweckmäßige Bürgerschulen, Anstalten zur Verhütung übereilter Beerdi-
gungen, für das platte Land besoldete Ärzte, Le-
segesellschaften, und was alles der gutgemein-
ten Dinge mehr sind." (177)

"Der Prediger zu Nachterstedt bey Halberstadt,
ein Mann, dem es nicht an guten Kenntnissen fehlte,
hatte sich die Grille in den Kopf gesetzt, seinen
Bauernjungen--Griechisch, Hebräisch, die Algebra,
Logik und Dogmatik beyzubringen, wobey er zugleich
eine Art von Militärdienst unter ihnen errichtet
hatte. Vor der Pfarrwohnung stand ein Schilder-
haus, und die Knaben mußten täglich vom Herrn
Pastor loci die--Parole holen."(334)

Also (83).

Private Tutor (Hofmeister, Hauslehrer)

A young tutor who has completed his studies at the

university gains confidence and experience in his tempo-

rary position. Then he is employed as a schoolmaster (308).

In order to teach well, he must have a good education him-

self. Then he marries the daughter of his Principal (34).

Hofmeister Launthal avoids Basedow's methods of teaching.
He tells his pupils stories, walks with them and punishes
them only "mit den Augen." He is part of the family and
travels with the boys. Launthal teaches them so well that
they pass the hard examinations and will not curse, drink
or gamble at their university (369). An employer tells
the tutor that his children have to learn how to read,
write and paint and trusts the Hofmeister without observing
him. The good Hauslehrer does not punish but explains to
the pupils where they have erred (258).

> "Alles dreht sich um einen jungen brutalen,
> aber dennoch gutmüthigen Russen herum, der eine
> besondere Leidenschaft für Tabakspfeifen und
> alte schmutzige Strümpfe hat. Ihn von diesen lä-
> cherlichen und ekelhaften Gegenständen abzuziehn,
> ihm zu gleicher Zeit wieder Liebe zu seiner ihm
> so sehr gehässigen Mutter einzuflößen; das ist
> das Problem, welches hier aufgelöst werden soll.
> Wie das der Verfasser oder sein Hofmeister ange-
> fangen hat, mag man in dem Buche selbst nachle-
> sen." (59)

Scholar (Gelehrter)

A famous scholar is a good father, yet he is unaware
of the real state of affairs:

> "Die Mutter ahndete zwar oft etwas [von dem
> unglücklichen Liebesverständnis ihrer Tochter
> zu einem adligen Herrn], aber der Vater [ein
> Rektor] ließ sich nicht in seinen Theorien irre
> machen, er sah vielmehr in allem . . . den noth-
> wendigen Fortgang seiner schon vor der Geburt
> der Kinder entworfenen Erziehungstheorie." (288d)

A scholar can be deluded easily (295). A pastor warns a father not to send his son to the university, because the

son's real interest is farming, not books (295).

> "Wie Gelehrte schon als Studenten den Grund
> zu ihrem glücklichen oder unglücklichen Leben
> legen, . . . von dem ist in dieser Schrift ei-
> ne gutgemeinte, aber nur flüchtig hingeworfene
> Darstellung, ohne sonderliche Anordnung, Aus-
> wahl und Präcision des Ausdrucks und der Gedanken."
> (218)

Merchant (<u>Kaufmann</u>)

A father teaches his adopted son the ethics of a merchant (389). A youth wants to be a merchant in spite of
his father's warnings. He is educated only by a greedy
shopkeeper, remains a servant and dies as a day laborer
(360d). A poor cabin-boy is diligent, orderly and careful; he becomes a successful merchant (219f).

The rich merchant Weichlich buys a big house, an expensive carriage, and has many servants. His children are
driven in the carriage, carried to their rooms and they
never get out into the open. Their bodies weaken, for
they drink coffee instead of milk, wine and beer instead
of water, eat cake instead of bread and spicy soups instead of vegetables. One dies at twelve, the other is
always sick (296).

Biographies of successful merchants, Barthol, Wel-
ser, L.C.Montaußier, Glover, Manduit (349), Hickert, Bal-
labene, Thurneisen, Graf Fries, Graf Schimmelmann, Burda-
les, Fadebeck, Tschepke, Schedal, Rindenschwender (249),
Hasenclever (249), (40) and others (194) illustrate the

ethics and thoughful decisions of good merchants. One merchant chooses a faithful wife and loyal friends. His business is a success (250).

A charitable merchant likes to help poor families who do not squander their money, but spend it with great care on simple clothes and food (120), (389).

> "Vater Hilmar unterrichtet seinen Sohn, aus historischen Beyspielen, warnt ihn für jeder gefährlichen Klippe, an der er scheitern könne, wenn er sich seinen Erinnerungen und Lehren nicht folgesam unterwerfe." (194)

Craftsman (Handwerker, Handwerksleute)

> "Tugend und Handwerk sind der Kinder bestes Erbtheil." (281)

> "Ein guter Handwerker hat einen goldenen Boden." (208f)

> "Schuster, bleib bey deinem Leisten." (208e)

A journeyman wants to become a locksmith. He helps a farmer plow his fields, saves a drowning child, talks with the mayors, pastors, apothecaries and doctors, and observes their churches, stores and homes. He rises early, does not drink and likes to walk (364).

Zschokke's novel Meister Jordan oder Handwerk hat goldenen Boden is the biography of an artisan. After his thrifty father, a carpet salesman, dies, Jonas Jordan is educated by his father friend and becomes a diligent tinsmith. He is very industrious, marries a thrifty and faithful wife and moves to the center of the town of Altenheim. The count buys a shield from him, recognizes his talents and selects him as court tinsmith. Jonas' son Veit attends the Gymnasium while he is an apprentice to his father and later goes to the university. He travels through Europe, is a consultant to a successful Parisian merchant, does not drink and play cards and withstands the lure of prostitutes. When he returns to Altenheim, Jonas and Veit build a school in which men learn trades so well that they are sought after throughout the land (390).

> "Handwerksleute werden schon als Lehrburschen durch schlechte Gesellschaft verdorben." (218)

> "Der erste Theil dieses nützlichen Taschenbuches enthält eine Anweisung für reisende Handwerksgesellen, wie sie geschickte, gute und glückliche Menschen werden und mit Vortheil ihre Wanderschaft zubringen können; der andere ein Hand- und Hülfsbüchlein für Handwerker, Hausväter und Handelsleute." (74)

> "Daß diese Erzählungen zur Absicht haben, Handwerksleuten von der Mittelsorte eine nützliche Leserey zu verschaffen, hat Rec[ensent] eben gesagt, und muß noch hinzufügen, daß, wer aus dieser Classe auf das Buch fällt, sich allerdings wird belehren können. . . . Kinderzucht, häusliche Ordnung, und Sitteneinfalt sind übrigens die Gegenstände, deren Wichtigkeit anschaulicher zu machen, der Verf[asser] eine Reihe aus dem gemeinen Leben geschöpfter Vorfälle weiter ausmalt, und überall mit den nöthigen Nutzanwendungen begleitet." (112)

Also (129).

Physician (Arzt)

A doctor from Würzburg cures suspicious farmers of their disease and their beliefs in quacks (308). Doctor

Süß gives his weak patient Schlaff sedatives and Doctor
Mark prescribes restoratives for patient Quöch whose pulse
is slow. Both patients die. Doctor Sinn cures his patient
Hemm with a few carefully selected medicines, tells him
to sleep much and to breath deeply (121c). Abaka, a young
and brilliant doctor, cures the sultan. He receives many
presents as well as the trust and friendship of the ruler.
Other doctors do not envy him, but love and respect him
because he remains modest (75).

Student (Student, Universitätsjüngling)

Tobias Plump enters a university. On the first evening in the strange town he loses his way. A "kind" girl
offers him wine, food and lodging, but in the morning
she presents him with a bill for "entertainment." After
this experience he never listens to strange girls (373).
The student Burk plans to marry a girl from his village.
He thinks often of her, falls behind in his studies and
has to spend an additional year at the university (369).
Eduard Isenflamm seduces several girls and fights many
bloody duels before he is finally expelled from the university (346). An irresponsible student throws dice and
loses. He is so thankful to his friend who pays his debts
that he stops this reckless habit (156a).

> "Der Vater ertheilt Fritz Rheinfeld in sei-
> nem Briefe zur Einrichtung seiner Studien die vor-
> trefflichsten Regeln. . . . Jeder junge Theologe
> mag sie mit Ernst beherzigen, und er wird Segen
> davon einärndten." (237)

154

"Thierische Ausschweifungen der sinnlichen
Wohllust, Verführungen, Saufgelage, Empörungen,
Duelle, Mord, Ehebruch, Relegationen folgen un-
aufhörlich auf einander." (347)

"[Dieses ist das] Gemälde eines unglücklichen
Jünglings, der mit einem gefühlvollen, unverdor-
benen Herzen in seinem achtzehnten Jahre die akademische Laufbahn ohne Führer antrat, in eine geheime Verbindung hineingezogen, und dadurch zu
allen Arten von Ausschweifungen verleitet wurde,
bis er sein schändliches Leben mit dem Selbstmorde eindigte, und den Tod seines tiefgebeugten Vaters beschleunigte." (82)

Servant (<u>Bedienter</u>, <u>Hausangestellter</u>, <u>Gesinde</u>)

A man wants to be employed as a servant. When he ap-
plies for a position he praises the house and the furniture,
the pictures and the wine; he degrades himself and flatters
the lord with empty words, he boasts to other servants about
his former success and his high positions. He does not receive the post (235). Pfuhl, a gardener, is happy because
he is healthy, does his work diligently and conscientiously
and sends his children to school. He does not worry about
the future, for he trusts his master to provide him with
food and lodging when he will be too old to work (235). Robert and Elise allow their servants to be masters for a
while; they soon realize that it is difficult to be a good
master (318).

"Gute und böse Eigenschaften der weiblichen
Dienstbothen werden in Beyspielen dargestellt."
(47)

"Der edle Müllerknecht, Johann Rehkater, erhielt
aus Dankbarkeit seinem Meister den einzigen Sohn."
(150m)

"Die Absicht des Vf. ist, in dieser Schrift
für Dienstbothen an dem Beyspiel Christinens
von einer christlichen Denkungsart, und von
den Pflichten in ihrem Beruf zu belehren, und
sie vor einer schlechten Denkungs- und Handlungsart zu warnen. . . . Zuerst macht der Vf.
seine Leser mit Christinens Eltern, mit ihren
häuslichen Tugenden, ihrem häuslichen Glücke,
und ihrer Kinderzucht bekannt; als dann läßt er
die Christine selbst in Dienste treten, beglei-
tet sie von einem Dienst in den andern, und er-
greift da die Gelegenheiten seinen Lesern nicht
nur gar viele gute Lehren über ihre Pflichten
zu geben; sondern ihnen auch an dem Beyspiele
Christinens zu zeigen, wie sie diese Lehren,
in den mannichfaltigen Verhältnissen, worinn
sie gerathen, anwenden können." (127)

"Der rechtschaffene Dienstbote verdient von
Herrschaften als ein wohlthätiges Geschenk für
ihr Gesinde gekauft zu werden." (368)

Burgher (Bürger)

Robert is an honest burgher (352); another man is patriotic (247); another has a neat and orderly household (243).

"Nützliche, kluge, schädliche und thörichte
Handlungen ermuntern andere Bürger das Thörichte zu vermeiden und das Nützliche nachzuahmen."
(274g)

"Bürger Klugmann begeht viele Fehler, aber
lernt von diesen." (243)

"Der Verf[asser] . . . stellt einen Mann auf,
der, ausser der reinen und strengen Moralität
die er mit dem Weibe gemein hat, Besonnenheit,
Sinn für Pflicht und Beruf, Entschlossenheit,
Treue, Freymüthigkeit und Festigkeit in sich
vereinigte, und zwar ein Ideal, aber doch kein
für die wirkliche Welt unerreichbares, bilde.
. . . Der Mann, wie er seyn sollte, ist im
Grunde nichts anders, als ein ehrlicher Bürger
deren es hoffentlich in der Welt noch recht viele giebt." (352)

Farmer (<u>Bauer</u>, <u>Landmann</u>, <u>Landleute</u>)

   Farmers are taught reading and writing; they are
told to clean their homes and streets, to grow better
woods and to protect themselves from harmful animals and
lightning. Their teachers are a "Vogt" (308), a "Landesherr" (276), a doctor (387), and a privy councellor (384).
A schoolmaster invites thirty-two lazy and dirty farmers
to visit him at midnight and teaches them the secret of
"making gold": the farmers now plow their fields, stop
drinking, mend holes in their clothes and save their money. Soon the farmers are prosperous and have indeed learned
the art of "making gold" (388). The farmers of Traubenheim
envy the clean house and the clothes of their pastor. They
stop drinking, plow and plant diligently and save their
money (308). Some farmers are ashamed of their dirty homes
and imitate their children whose teacher told them to come
to school with combed hair and clean hands. They must also
brush their shoes before entering a house (276). Other
farmers trust their pastor who talks about matters that
interest them instead of bringing up Kant. They consult a
doctor, not a quack, and do not stand under trees when rain
falls and lightning strikes (210).

   Wilhelm Friedwald tells the farmers of Fröhlichhausen about the disorder and immorality which has reigned
in France since the Revolution (358). Jacob Ehrenmann

talks with the farmers about church customs, secret societies, holidays, schools, quackery and prognostications
(210).

Erdmann Hülfreich describes the household of his
wife (15). A farmer raises his son to become a polite,
neat and thrifty adult; his neighbors imitate him (295).

Kleinjogg, whose real name was Jacob Guyer (40),
showed his neighbors that industry and work can lead to
happiness. He kept only as much land as he could manage,
forbade drinking on his farm so that his children would
not be influenced, and persuaded his neighbors to prohibit
inns and useless amusements in the village. Yet he could
not read (188).

Wilhelm Denker visits Jacob Guyer (Kleinjogg). He
develops his own farm upon Jacob's advice (86).

> "Die Lebensgeschichte Siegfried Habermanns,
> eines guten Landmanns in Mahrendorf hat diesel-
> be Tendenz, als die Geschichte Sebastian Kluge
> von Salzmann. Sie soll den Landmann belehren,
> wie er durch Arbeit und Fleiß und durch ein gu-
> tes vernünftiges Betragen sich selbst ein ver-
> gnügtes Leben und ein ruhiges Alter bereiten
> kann. Zu dem Ende erzählt denn dieser Habermann
> in der Schenke den jungen Leuten, die sich um
> ihn versammeln und ihm so gerne zuhören, alles
> was ihm in seinem Leben begegnet ist; wobey
> denn freylich allerhand gute Lehren vorkommen,
> die dem Landmanne sehr nützlich werden könnten,
> wenn er sie ausübte. . . . Das Resultat, welches
> aus dieser Erzählung fließen soll, ist dieß: daß
> ein gutdenkender, verständiger und kluger Mann
> in einem Dorfe viel Gutes stiften kann, wenn er
> will." (46)

> "Die Unterhaltungen sind eigentlich die Er-
> ziehungsgeschichte einer Bauernfamilie in einem

Brandenburgischen Dorfe aus den Zeiten Friedrich
des Einzigen eingekleidet. Der Vater Fröhlich,
der Schulmeister Güte, ein Hauslehrer und ein
Förster des Ortes sind die Hauptpersonen: und
häusliche Erziehung, Lectionen, Prüfungen, Gespräche, Besuche, Spaziergänge, mit eingerück-
ten, höchst alltäglichen Sentenzen und Sitten-
sprüchen, Liedern, biblischen Sprüchen, Räthseln,
Predigtauszügen und Unterredungen über Hexerey,
Feldbau, Thiere, u.s.w. machen den Inhalt aus."
(71)

    "Die Bauern des Dorfes Heidenau, denen es zu
wohl geht, werden aufrührerisch, organisiren
sich durch ihren Schulzen, und einem aus Paris
kommenden Schneider, begehen im Freyheitstaumel
eine Menge Ausschweifungen, und werden durchs
Militär zur Ordnung gebracht." (108)

    "Diese Schrift hat überdem das Gute, was man
bey so wenig Schriften fürs Volk antrifft, daß
sie bloß für eine bestimmte Gegend, nämlich für
die Schleßwig Holsteinische Lande geschrieben
sind, auch daß sie gute Verbesserungen der Land-
wirthschaft und mancherley Tugenden und gute
Handlungen durch Beyspiele in einzelnen kurzen
Geschichten zu empfehlen sucht." (275)

    "Der aufgeklärte Bauer Georg Reinhard . . .
verbessert erstlich sein angeerbtes väterliches
Gütchen und seine Feldwirthschaft, und seyn Beyspiel würkt nachher auch auf seine Mitnachbarn,
so daß im ganzen Dorfe der Landbau zu größrer
Vollkommenheit gedeiht. Der Kleebau, die Verbesserung der Äcker und Wiesen, und die Stallfütte-
rung wird eingeführt, und die Brache beschränkt.
Da Reinhard durch sein Benehmen sich die allgemeine Achtung und das Vertrauen seines Orts erwirbt, erhält er auch den nöthigen Einfluß, die
Dorfpolizei zu verbessern, eine Menge alter Vorurtheile zu besiegen, und sonst viel Gutes zu
stiften." (174)

    "[Timon der Zweyte], ein Mensch, dem es in
der großen Welt auf keine Weise hat glücken wollen, sucht einen einsamen Aufenthalt, und flieht
den Umgang mit Menschen. Er geräth endlich in
ein Dorf, wo er gute Leute antrifft, und sich
mit diesen Menschen wieder aussöhnt. Daselbst
nun bauet er ein Haus, wo er gute Leute antrifft,

bleibt dort, und stiftet nicht nur unter den
Landleuten, sondern auch in der benachbarten
Residenz und am Hofe viel Gutes." (173)

"Die Geschichte geht immer innerhalb der
Sphäre des Landmanns fort; . . . dabey werden
überall so faßliche Lehren über Landökonomie,
Kinderzucht, und ein christliches Verhalten
im Umgange mit den Nebenmenschen, und in den
Geschäften dieses Lebens eingestreut, daß,
wenn dieses Buch auch würklich von dem Land-
manne und dem Städter gelesen wird, . . . Zer-
störung mannichfaltiger Vorurtheile und Ver-
breitung weiser und christlicher Grundsätze
unter dem Landvolke, gewiß bey vielen erreicht
wird." (190)

Class (Stand)

"Man ist doch etwas seinem Stande schuldig."
(84b)

Adolph und Sidonie von Wappenkron wrongly believe
that their noble birth alone should give them position
and honor. They will not understand that true nobility
is not inherited. True nobility is, however, the result
of constant self-development (361). Some poorly educated
women only want to marry in order to ascend into a higher
estate (316).

Every useful estate and profession is to be honored
(97). It is wise to choose "Stände, die ihren Mann nähren."
(315c) Members of a low class do noble deeds (154d), (274d).
Some, however, are prejudiced and rude (17).

"Ein gutes Handwerk hat einen goldenen Boden." (390), (208f)

"Schuster, bleib bey deinem Leisten." (208e)

Husband (<u>Ehemann</u>, <u>Gatte</u>)

Robert loves his wife, warns her of quacks, shares her worries and plays with the children (352). Milner, an attractive and well-educated man makes his wife happy. This assures a peaceful marriage (288c). Moritz, a carpenter, allows his passions to rule him. Only when bankrupt, he realizes that social conventions are necessary, marries and leads a moral life (304). The first duty of a good husband is to his wife. He talks with her, raises their children and keeps her happy with an occasional gift (274g). Creating such happiness makes a man truly noble (238a). The just and tolerant husband becomes his wife's confessor (98b).

A husband learns that his wife has offered her charms to a student for 100 thalers. He invites the student for dinner, returns the money to him and gives his wife eight groschen "for her trouble." (383)

The bad husband beats his wife often, drinks, spends money foolishly, does not come home for days and makes his wife miserable. He sleeps with other women, neglects his children, breaks the windows and has a bad temper (382). Fritz, who has had a poor upbringing, is disloyal, does not work, beats his wife mercilessly and never accepts the good woman's advice (386).

A husband is industrious and thrifty and loves his wife. But she is a spendthrift, hires too many servants,

sleeps late, does no housework, uses much make-up and
buys expensive clothes. His industry is in vain (251g).
A quarrelsome wife makes her husband's life miserable
(92). A selfish husband often argues with his wife until an accident happens. A monk cures him (291d). The
son of a rich man is spoiled and disobedient, while his
nephew is liked by the townspeople for his politeness.
The man is so weak that he listens to his jealous wife
and throws the poor nephew out of his home (138).

> "[Friedrich Bracks] Unstern führt ihn auf
> die Eisbahn des Ehestandes. So ist dieser vierte
> Band das beste Handbuch für jeden Ehestandskan-
> didaten, der Lust hat ex aliis sumere exemplum
> sibi, durch anderer Schaden klug zu werden. Die
> Heyraths- und Ehestandsgeschichte Bracks ist so
> sehr aus der Natur und dem Laufe der Welt gleich-
> sam herausgegriffen und mit so treffenden Zügen
> dargestellt, daß gewiß mancher Leser nicht um-
> hin kann, an sich selbst und an seine gemachten
> Erfahrungen, oder doch an Menschen um sich und
> neben sich zu denken." (262)

Wife (Eheweib, Gatte)

> "Denk' dir ein Weib im reinsten Jugendlich[t]
> Nach einem Urbild von dort oben,
> Aus Rosenglut und Lilienschnee gewoben;
> Gieb ihrem Bau das feinste Gleichgewicht;
> Ein stilles Lächeln schweb' auf ihrem Angesicht,
> Und jeder Reiz, von Majestät erhoben,
> Erweck' und schreck' sogleich die lüsterne Begier:
> Denk Alles das, du hast den Schatten kaum von ihr."
> (49)

Elisa obeys her mother: she renounces the intelligent
and virtuous man whom she loves and marries a selfish and
cold man. Nevertheless, Elisa respects him and treats him
so tenderly that he honors her. Although tempted by other

men, she never strays from the path of virtue. In a letter
which Elisa opens, her husband's mistress begs him for
3000 thalers. Elisa sells her jewelry and brings the money
to the mistress, so that her husband will not need to go
into debt. He is so surprised by her virtuous act, that
he finally learns to love her. They move to the country
and there she raises her children (365).

Antoinette marries a spoiled, careless and unprincipled gambler. Through her love and dedication she cures
him from his vice (69).

An aunt writes letters to her niece. She advises her
that she should read good novels, wash herself frequently,
prepare good meals, obey her husband and keep the house
clean so that her husband will always love her (224). Henriette, reared and educated by her father, becomes a moral
and loyal wife while her friend Auguste, whose parents did
not attend to her upbringing, becomes an unprincipled harlot (242). The good wife never interferes with her husband's
concerns (295), (377), but loves, honors and obeys him (377),
(390). If her husband is a drinker, she can reform him as
well as the entire village (276).

> "Unaufhörlich und unbegrenzt plagt August sei-
> ne äußerst vorsichtige und nachgebende Louise
> erst als Verlobte, dann als Gattinn, durch boden-
> lose Eifersucht, und durch, bald absichtlich
> scheinbare, bald wirkliche Untreue. . . . Aber
> Louise bekehrt ihren August, nachdem er sie ge-
> nug gequält hat und bessert noch ein sauberes
> Ehepaar dazu, das mit unserm August ein treffli-
> ches Kleeblatt, sich wechselseitig zu verderben,

bildete." (49)

"Der Schluß [dieses Buches] macht ein treff-
liches Beyspiel von dem Einfluß einer vernünftigen und gebildeten Frau auf die Beruhigung eines
Mannes, bey den Widerwärtigkeiten dieses Lebens."
(186)

"Signora Avveduta [ist] . . . die lebhaft und
interessant erzählte Geschichte einer zwiefachen
übereilten und widrig ausgefallenen Eheverbin-
dung, und die Lehre enthält, nur den Gatten zu
wählen, der noch dann gefallen wird, wenn man
ihn nicht bloß ein paar Tage lang gesehen, oder
nur ein paar Abende gehört hatte." (283b)

"[Der Verfasser] berührt und deckt die fein-
sten Nüancen ihrer Gefühle, und den verschleier-
ten Hintergrund ihres Characters mit eben so
viel Wahrheit als Delikatesse auf, und giebt dadurch dem andern Geschlechte Winke, Lehren und
Warnungen, die nicht genug beherzigt werden können. In dem Gemälde der Emma ist das feurig liebende, gutmüthige, aber zugleich schwache und
eitle junge Weib fast in allen Zügen eines so
komponirten Charakters richtig geschildert. Die
sinnlich-listige Sophie erscheint hier als das
Original eines verführerischen, leidenschaftli-
chen Weibes, deren Grundsätze weit jenseits der
zarten Sittenlehre des bessern Geschlechts liegen, Emmas Mutter ist ein großer und edler weib-
licher Charakter, in dem sich feste und helle
Vernunft mit reiner Weiblichkeit und liebenswürdiger Herzensgüte paart." (306)

"In [diesem] Abschnitt finet man: Ein Mittel
gegen Langeweile mancher, insonderheit angehen-
der, junger Eheweiber.--Vom frühen Aufstehen.--
. . . Von der Veränderlichkeit der ehelichen Liebe, die bey Philipp und seiner Christine nicht
Statt fand.--Etwas von der Kunst Christinens, ihren
Mann bey guter Laune zu erhalten.--Das liebenswür-
dige Weib; oder etwas von Christinens Vorzügen,
in Ansehung des Äußerlichen." (128)

"'Sind ein paar Personen beyderley Geschlechts
gesund beysammen, was läßt sich anders denken,
als ein Promoviren in patrem et matrem, wie dein
seliger Vater immer sagte; denn bloß Betens und
Schlafens halber wird das Bette nicht besucht.'
(p. 54). 'Gleichwohl schläft er bey ihr, und wie

man durchgängig behauptet, so gern, daß er kaum
die gesetzte Bettglocke erwarten kann.' (S. 62)"
(326)

Also (18a), (140), (166a).

Housewife (Hausfrau)

A married woman does not only have responsibilities
to her husband; she must also take care of the household.
When Lina is fifteen years old, her parents die and her
aunt Sophie sends her twenty-four letters in which she
teaches her the duties of a good housewife: the pleasant
arrangement of furniture, the importance of order in the
kitchen, thrift in the purchasing of food and care in the
hiring of servants. Since books are expensive, it is better
to borrow than to buy them. Only moral books should be read
(224). A thrifty wife buys grain and bakes bread herself
(371).

Erdmann Hülfreich describes the neat household of
his wife (15). A wealthy woman has more time and can help
in the households of poor people (157). In spite of many
misfortunes, the housewife Maria Weinerin does not despair
(45).

In order to keep her servants happy, Julie Wolmar
dances with them on festive occasions (37d). Henriette,
during a trip, changes roles with her servants: she becomes their servant while they are her master and mistress
(318).

An unvirtuous girl turns into a thrifty and loyal
housewife after smallpox cures her of her sins (300). Another housewife becomes an adulteress after she has squan-
dered her husband's money and hired so many servants that
he had to borrow money (98a). One woman believes she is a
poetess and neglects her duties in the house (186).

> "'[Nachdem alle schlafen gegangen waren] sah
> ich erst nach allem, nach Küche, Speisekammer, Stal-
> len und Hausthür, und dann legte ich mich, merke
> wohl, Liebe, wenn weibliche Umstände mich nicht zu-
> rückhielten, denn unter solchen hielt ich es für un-
> schicklich, neben meinen Mann.'" (326)

Also (128), (282a), (304), (376).

Parents (Ältern)

When Conrad is only five months old, his parents talk
to him as he watches them. They let him walk only when he
is ready and do not force him; they do not aid him with a
walking fence. When he is three years old, they point out
the farm animals, the woods, the meadows, the flowers, the
fields, the flies on the windows, the leaves and the stars
in order to develop his powers of observation and attention.
Obedience is not enforced with a cane, but with understanding. One day Conrad tears a doll away from his cousin so
that she cries. His father takes one of Conrad's toys away
from him. He cries and pities the girl. He will not again
hurt others. When Conrad gropes for a dangerous pair of
scissors his parents show him a picture book. This draws
his attention away from the scissors. Stories of bad and

good people teach him to dislike mean and violent acts and to prefer kind and gentle deeds which please other people (295).

Gutmann raises his children on a trip through Europe. They learn many things at an early age (111).

A polite ghost reminds parents who have neglected their children's upbringing of their duties and responsibilities to them (78a). Parents permit their son to choose bad friends. They can no longer control him (20).

> "Wenn das kleine Magaretchen von seinem Vater
> wegen seines Eigensinns war gezüchtigt worden,
> so lief es allemal bei die Mutter und verklagte
> den Vater. Diese bedauerte es, sagte auch wohl:
> das ist ein böser Vater, das arme Kind so zu
> schlagen! Da, Margaretehen, hast du einen Pfen-
> nig, gehe hin und hole dir eine Semmel. Ist's
> Wunder, wenn Margaretchen gegen den bösen Vater
> Abneigung bekam?" (296)

> "Aus väterlicher Liebe ließ Meister Liebe in
> sein Schlafzimmer seines Söhnleins Bett aufstel-
> len, auch dann noch, da es zwölf Jahre alt war.
>   Wenn er dann mit seinem Friederikchen in das
> Schlafzimmer kam, so fing er, wie Eheleute zu
> tun pflegen, an zu scherzen; das Scherzen wurde
> immer lebhafter und wurde am Ende Ernst.
>   . . . Der Sohn aber hatte nicht geschlafen,
> horchte erst den Liebkosungen des Vaters zu,
> dann richtete er sich leise empor und sahe auch
> zu, ohne daß die Eltern es bemerkten.
>   Da nun Heinrich der Meinung war, daß er sich
> nach seinem Vater bilden müsse, suchte er bei
> Lottchen in Ausübung zu bringen, was ihn der lie-
> be Vater gelehrt hatte. Im dreizehnten Jahre war
> er schon ein Mann, im achtzehnten Vater, im vier-
> undzwanzigsten Greis, im dreißigsten war seine
> Rolle zu Ende." (296)

Other instructions and examples show parents how to develop "virtues"; one father laughs as his son pulls off

the wings of a living fly, another one tells his daughter
to hate those who do not believe, for God hates them also.
Lottchen tells her mother that she has an upset stomach,
for she wants to taste wine. Her mother gives her the wine.
Lottchen is thus rewarded for her lying (296).

The greatest joy for parents is a good child who
through their care becomes a useful burgher (251f). Parents
advise their grown-up children in the choice of a spouse,
for a trusting child will always ask the parents (220i),
(237), (295); a daughter whose parents have forced her into marrying an unloved nobleman commits suicide (116).

> "Es soll inzwischen dieses Buch eben das seyn,
> und würken für sein [des Verfassers] Publikum, was
> Herrn Salzmann's sonst so genanntes Krebsbüchlein
> für die gebildeten Stände gewürkt hat. . . . Es
> enthält 16 Gespräche, worin nach gerade gezeigt
> wird und gezeigt werden soll: wie und wodurch vie-
> le Eltern die Liebe, das Vertrauen, die Achtung
> ihrer Kinder verlieren; wie sie selbst den Grund
> dazu legen, daß Kinder gegen ihre Geschwister
> feindselig, gegen ihren Nebenmenschen lieblos,
> rachgierig, neidisch und schadenfroh werden; wie
> die Eltern daran Schuld sind, daß ihre Kinder
> Hang zur Grausamkeit, zum Lügen und Verläumden,
> zum Naschen und Entwenden, zur Gefräßigkeit, zum
> Trotz und Eigensinn bekommen; wie und wodurch die
> Eltern ihre Kinder furchtsam vor Gespenstern, un-
> brauchbar für die Welt, und wie sie ihnen die Re-
> ligion verhaßt machen." (338)

Also (258), (376).

See also father, mother, upbringing, education.

Father (Vater)

A father is stern and serious. He advises his son how
to lead "ein nützliches Leben." He does not spank him (120).

A good father plays with his young son on the floor and talks to him even though the infant does not yet speak. He shows him the fields and is his companion (295). Later he guides him thoughtfully and gives him some money to teach him how to be thrifty (295), (389). Another father writes seventeen letters to his son who is about to leave his house. In these he discusses causes and effects, duties as a citizen and human being, conduct among people, and warns his son of the dangers of the world (197). The reward of a good father is a grateful son. Such a son will rescue him from bankruptcy, even though he has to leave his own position and the girl he loves (389).

A selfish father wants to marry his son Johns to the daughter of a rich but bad man. The son disobeys and runs away (219f).

Heinrich's father does not send his son to work. As he thus is useless at home, he is taken away to become a soldier (378).

> "In zwölf Briefen eines Greises an seinen Sohn giebt es über Freund und Feinde, Lebensweisheit, Seelengröße, Gefühl, Selbsttäuschung, Festigkeit des Charakters, Menschenerziehung u. s.w. manches unstreitig Brauchbares zu lesen." (178b)

> "Ein reiches Frauenzimmer, welches durch die Härte ihres Vaters einem edlen Jüngling entzogen, und mit Gewalt an einen Nichtswürdigen verheyrathet worden war, verfiel nach dessen bald erfolgtem Tode in den traurigsten Zustand der Menschenscheu und Menschenfeindlichkeit." (239)

Mother (<u>Mutter</u>)

An old woman is neglected by her children because she
spoiled them in their youth. They do not respect her and
do not care for their mother when she is old (296). Another old woman who gave careful advice to her daughter
later is rewarded by her love and respect (326). Gräfin
von B., who lives only for her two daughters, presents them
with a great treasure when they enter the world: good warnings and advice (132).

> "Ein junger Felsen, ein Freund des verstorbe-
> nen Sohnes des Verf[assers] erzählt seine und
> seines Freundes Hütten=Geschichte, die gewiß
> Mütter und Töchter interessiren wird, wenn sie
> nicht schon durch die Lektüre der bloß auf die
> Phantasie berechneten, und daher so schädlichen
> Moderomane verdorben sind." (225)

> "Wir lernen Christine [die erst ein Dienst-
> mädchen war] in dieser Schrift kennen als Braut,
> als Gattinn eines guten Mannes, als Mutter. . .
> 'Christine gab durchaus nicht zu, daß sich,
> selbst ihre jüngern Kinder, voreinander nackend
> auskleideten. Sie lehrte auch ihre kleinen Mäd-
> chen und Jungen gewisse Theile ihres Körpers
> schamhaft zu verdecken; und noch genauer nahm
> sie es in diesem Punkte bey ihren schon erwachse-
> nen Töchtern, die es auch gewiß nie gewagt hät-
> ten, um der Mode willen, oder aus einem verbuhl-
> ten Wesen sich auf unanständige Art, wie es oft,
> und zwar durch Verführung und böses Beyspiel
> mancher Mütter selbst geschieht, zu entblößen.
> Wer schamhaft ist, sagte Christine oft, ist vor
> vieler Verführung zur Wollust gesichert.'" (128)

> "Der zweyte Band beginnt mit dem Berufe der
> Mutter, und zunächst mit den bekannten Vorschrif-
> ten für Schwangere, worunter die der möglichsten
> Leidenschaftslosigkeit ganz vorzüglich dringend
> empfohlen wird. [In dem Buche wird] manches her-
> gebrachte unter schwangeren Frauen und in den
> Wochenstuben herrschende Vorurtheil nach seiner

Schädlichkeit und Armseligkeit aufgedeckt." (13)

Also (97a), (140), (353), (376).

See also parents, father, upbringing, education.

Children (Kinder)

A boy runs for a while, sweats, drinks cold water and dies (205); another one drinks from a swampy pond and later vomits five living frogs (9). A boy climbs a tree, slips and falls to his death (308). A little girl promises not to nibble sweets anymore. If she does, she will spank herself (282).

> "Eine gute Handlung wird immer wieder vergolten." (80)

> "Alle Erzählungen und Fabeln, welche in diesem Buche enthalten sind, zielen durch Warnungen und gute Beyspiele auf Verbesserung des jugendlichen Herzens, auf wirkliche Belehrung ab." (118)

Also (94), (170), (219d), (272), (331), (230), (328).

See also son, daughter.

Son (Sohn)

A good son helps his father when he is young. When he grows up he makes his father happy and becomes a successful merchant (158). Konrad Eck is so grateful to his father that he wants to rescue him when he is lost in India (389). Another grateful son helps his parents when they are poor (336a). The righteous son searches for his missing father, finds him on a galley and begs for his freedom (217a). A well brought-up son likes his sister whom he advises and

helps (3). He asks his father (295) or his mother (101)
about the character and the habits of girls before he
chooses a wife. Anton, a good son, helps his parents
clean the house and is careful not to tear his trousers
when he plays (196).

Also (95).

See also children.

Daughter (Tochter)

A wise daughter listens to the advice of her parents
(326) or her aunt (224). She improves her personal conduct,
manners, and appearance; she also selects her books with
care. She becomes a good wife (140), (287). A young woman
teaches the daughter of her friends to sew, knit, mend,
wash, cook, clean their homes and suggests activities to
keep them from being bored. She also tells them how to
retain their natural beauty through sufficient sleep, frequent washing and fresh air (186). An aunt warns a young
girl from reading violent and immoral novels and suggests
that she should read Wieland's Oberon, Wetzel's Herrmann
und Ulrike, Langbein's Schwänke, Cramer's Wacker, Schilling's Guido von Sohnsdom and the novels of Lafontaine
(224).

> "Der Geist, der hier erscheint, soll vor Wei-
> berstolz und vor Vernachläßigung der Pflichten,
> der Ehrfurcht und kindlichen Liebe warnen, und
> --bessern. . . . Die Todten kehren aus den Grä-
> bern wieder, um unsere Töchter zu überzeugen,

daß es schändlich sey, wenn sie beym Vater die
Mutter verläumden und stolz von dieser die
Schleppe sich nachtragen lassen!!!" (78a)

See also children.

Bride (Braut)

On the day of the wedding a bride greets her husband
with a smile and is very clean (377). She wears her mother's
bridal dress and thereby saves much money (388).

> "Der erste Theil der Briefe an Lilla enthält
> Maximen der Klugheit und Besonnenheit, welche
> der Braut vorgeschrieben werden, verdient aller-
> dings ernste Beherzigung. Liebe und Hochachtung
> müsse die Verlobte zum Manne hinziehen,--ächte
> und wahre Liebe; also nicht bloß jenes Glühen
> der Leidenschaft, wodurch nur die sogenannten
> Affektionsheyrathen zu entstehen pflegten. Wenn
> die Flamme auf beyden Seiten gleich hoch auflodert-
> te: so stehe die Liebe in großer Gefahr, von der
> gemeinschaftlichen Hitze allzufrühe verzehrt zu
> werden." (13)

Also (128).

Innocent Maiden (Jungfrau)

An ambitious mother sends her pious and virtuous
daughter to a boarding school in Berlin. The provincial
girl adapts herself to bad ways of the city where she is
surrounded by people like free-thinkers and French govern-
esses. She becomes an irresponsible and vain harlot (348).
Careless Minchen also leads an unvirtuous life (54a). Innocent princess Auguste is educated by her governess in
the pleasant surroundings of nature, far away from the
court. She remains a virtuous girl (353). Louise, in con-

173

trast to her two sisters, does not become an adulteress (131).

Mariane is brought up by a French governess who arouses the innocent girl's passions and emotions. A French prince tempts and seduces Mariane (106).

A young and handsome man charms Lucin, but her reason and self-control save her (291c).

> "Der Verf[asser] führt eine reine, unbefange-
> ne, jungfräuliche Unschuld in den Wirbel der gro-
> ßen Welt, und läßt sie da sinken, wo man es am
> wenigsten befürchtete." (300)

> "[In diesem Buche] ist Klarheit in der Zeich-
> nung der menschlichen Lagen, worinn ein junges
> durch die Barbareyen des französischen Revolu-
> tionskrieges in die weite Welt gestoßenes, sich
> selbst überlaßenes Mädchen kommen konnte. . . .
> Röschen sinkt von der hohen Stufe jungfräuli-
> cher Unschuld bis zur Koketten, und bald bis zur
> Ehebrecherinn herab." (305)

> "Was einige Menschenklassen, in Hinsicht auf
> ihre Glückseligkeit, für Umwege nehmen, . . .
> woran die Unschuld und reine Herzensgüte der Frau-
> enzimmer scheitern . . . von dem . . . ist diese
> Schrift eine gutgemeinte, aber nur flüchtig hin-
> geworfene Darstellung." (218)

> "Das Landmädchen [ist] eine Warnung für jun-
> ge unschuldige Mädchen vor den gefährlichen Net-
> zen reiner Wohllüstlinge." (288b)

> "Benjamine . . . stellt die . . . Folgen solcher
> Maßregeln, welche man zur Rettung weiblicher Ehre,
> dem Anschein nach klug und vortheilhaft, wählte,
> dar." (315a)

Also (383).

Bachelor (Jungeselle)

Fritz Rheinfeld selects a bride not merely for her

beauty or her money, as his friends do, but for her sincerity and good sense. Such a choice results in a happy marriage (237). A rich man tries to find a wife, but because he is too particular, he does not succeed (291d). Robert courts a woman. Respect and love forbid him to dishonor her before they are married (352).

> "Nachbar Milner [ist] eine anziehende Geschichte eines sittlich und physisch gut gebildeten Mannes, der durch mancherley Schicksale zur wahren Lebenswahrheit und in den sichern Hafen eines ruhigen Lebensglückes geführt worden ist." (288c)

> "Der schöne Geist von Pyrmont [stellt] eine zwiefache unangenehme Vereitelung seiner Erwartungen einer Heyrath mit Personen von adliger Abkunft [dar]. [Die hier dargestellten] eitlen Künstler, belletristischen Damen und ihre Koketterien sind überall zu Hause." (283f)

B. **Home, Family and School**

Upbringing (**Kindererziehung**)

In order to live a happy and fruitful life one must have first enjoyed a good upbringing in the home of one's parents (172). To learn about good and bad people the children must listen to true and invented stories, so that they can choose a character they themselves would like (295). Isidor, a farmer, tells his children stories about ambitious and lazy people (190). A father allows his son to think for himself and gives him at an early age a small allowance to teach him how to save and spend money wisely; he points out and corrects the mistakes his son makes. This well brought-up son becomes a famous scholar (288d).

When a pastor celebrates his birthday, a three month old child is left with him. The pastor raises Wilhelm, the foundling (160b).

A schoolmaster brings up the neglected children of the farmers, corrects their manners and improves their habits. They start to wear clean clothes and imitate his neat handwriting; he rewards them with love (309). Farmer Ferdinand Ehrenfels' upbringing is described (22). The cunning Gustav Reinwald can do whatever he wants: steal from the cooky jar, stay up as late as he pleases and sew his aunt's skirt to the chair only because his parents do not agree on how to punish him (258). A stupid mother boasts about her son to her visitors, overdresses him, but fails to let him play with other boys (316).

Karl is obstinate, because his parents' visitors stay so long that he cannot do his homework. He is bored with school, because his teacher only has him memorize the catechism (202). Several children are brought up by a French governess who is careless and lacks herself a proper education and refinement (268). A father neglects to arouse his son's industry. When the boy grows up he is weak and careless (69), (274e). Another father takes his son along plowing and lets him try his hand (114). Adam Gutmann in the days of the Revolution brings his children up well despite anarchy and the immorality of the French (206). Adults become either useful or useless citizens according to their good or poor upbringing (6). A traveling philosopher spends 150,000 thalers on his trip and writes letters to a friend with comments on the upbringing of children (285). An old man writes his son about the same topic (178b).

Gumal and Lina are black children of hostile African chieftains. Pedro, the helper of a missionary, shows the children how to use tools and they learn to cultivate their own little gardens in the wilderness. The children are amazed at the growth of the plants. The old missionary discovers their interest and teaches them that this growth as well as the course of the moon and the sun and their own existence are the work of God. One day Gumal loses his way but finds home in the end. He learns that it was God who protected him. Through his trust in Him he was able to remain calm and therefore could orient himself and find his way back. Lina learns to cook and mend and is happy to work for Gumal, Pedro and the old missionary, while the boy learns how to hunt, plant, harvest, and build furniture for Lina. After many years the happy children are married by the old man (234).

> "Es ist hier von verschiedenen Fehlern in der Erziehung und von der Art, sie zu verbessern, die Rede." (253b)

> "Auch hat der Verf[asser] in dieser Geschichte mehrere Personen aufgestellt, die durch ihre Erziehung entweder gut oder böse geworden sind." (6)

"'Bezahlet die Kinder durchaus nicht für eine Pflicht, ihr ziehet sonst Söldlinge für alle ihre Pflichten, Söldlinge für jede Tugend.'" (287)

"Des Vaters [Fritz Rheinfelds] Erziehungsweise mag leicht den Grund zu Fritzens sonderbarem Charakter gelegt haben: sie war etwas sonderbar: Seine Kinder erst mit der Natur, und dann mit dem Herrn derselben bekannt zu machen; ihnen eher zu sagen, wer der fromme Gellert war, als die erbaulichen Kourtisanerien des heidnischen Zeus erzählen; sie eher lehren, daß es grausam sey, ein Thier zu martern, oder zu tödten, als sie von dem dreyerley Tode der Hebräer, dem zeitlichen, geistlichen und ewigen zu unterrichten; ihnen lieber die pädagogischen Spaziergänge als den Himmelsweg in die Hand zu geben. Solche Sonderbarkeiten, deren der Vater so manche zeigte, und die ihm weder Salzmann noch dessen Krebsbüchlein damals schon konnten eingeflößt haben, mögen wohl unstreitig zu der verkehrten Bildung seines Charakters sehr viel beygetragen haben." (237)

"Weiterhin wird dieses pädagogische Alltagsprodukt etwas lehrreicher und unterhaltender; in sofern darin manche nützliche, obgleich schon tausendmal gesagte Maximen und Verhaltungsregeln zur weiblichen Erziehung vorgetragen, und die Fehler derselben vorzüglich unter dem Einflusse schwacher Mütter gerügt werden." (140)

"Fernando ist die Geschichte eines Wüstlings, der vor seiner schwachen Mutter von frühester Jugend an verzogen wird, und sich in der Folge aller moralischen Gebrechen und Ausschweifungen überläßt, die nur irgend eine übermüthige Denkungsart, und der unersättliche Hang zu sinnlichen Vergnügen hervorbringen können." (323)

Also (21a), (71), (219d), (320a).

See also parents, father, mother, education.

Education (Erziehung)

Gustav Rheinwald's poor upbringing is corrected by his uncle and later in the university (258). Carl Pilger

178

describes the poor education received at the Dessau Phil-
antropinum of Basedow and Wolke (334). Princess Auguste's
education takes place in the pleasant surrounding of nature, far away from the court. Thus the seeds of goodness
blossom in her (353). Only love for the divine, for virtue
and art, illustrated by events in pastor Frommfried's home,
leads to real education (<u>Bildung</u>) (164). A poor education
fosters the desire of vain women to rise to a higher class
(316).

"<u>Hipparinus, Sohn des Dion</u>, stellt die Wirkungen übertriebener Strenge gegen einen jungen
Wüstling, der jedoch nicht alles Gefühl für das
Gute ertödtet hat, in dramatischer Form dar."
(253a)

"Ysop kommt auf eine öffentliche Schule. . . .
Dieses giebt dem Verf[asser] Anlaß, sein Bekennt-
nis über Erziehung einzuschalten, zu deren Grundsatz er annimmt, Kinder durch Furcht zum Gehorsam zu gewöhnen, und nicht zu frühe Herren und
Männer aus ihnen zu machen, die Strenge der Für-
stenschulen, deren Zögling er war, zu rechtfer-
tigen, und gegen die Weichlichkeit der modernen
Erziehung in (und ausser) den Philanthropinen zu
eifern, wodurch Kinder für alle künftige Verhältnisse verwahrloset würden." (109)

"Es ist . . . die Märtyrergeschichte eines
Mönchs, der gelernt hatte, weiter zu sehen, als
seine hochwürdigen Obern und Confrates, aber nicht
gelernt hatte, daß ein Mönchskloster nicht der Ort
sey, wo man sein Übergewicht von Geistesbildung
fühlen und andern merken lassen dürfe. . . . Die
Erzählung, wie Armin zu dieser Bildung, die gewiß schief war, kam, giebt dem Verfasser, der,
wie mehrere Stellen beweisen, selbst ein Katholik
ist, Gelegenheit, gegen verkehrte Erziehung zu eifern." (5)

". . . die Moral, die der Verf[asser] durch
seine Wilhelmine lehren wollte, daß nämlich Über-

bildung und Verfeinerung zu mancherley Unheil
führe, das keine Kultur aufwägen kann, ist
achtenswerth." (73)

"Die Verf[asserin] hat . . . Personen auf
den Schauplatz geführt, die durch die Erziehung gut oder schlecht gebildet wurden. . . .
Sie hat [die Charaktere] fast alle zu gut oder
zu böse geschildert." (6)

"Die folgenden Maximen über Erziehung . . .
sind nicht neu, aber immer sehr wichtig, wenn
das Hauswesen einen regelmäßigen Gang gehen
soll." (287)

"Der Verf[asser] konnte bey der vernachläßig-
ten Erziehung, bey dem ausschweifenden Leben, das
er als Student, als Kandidat des Predigeramtes,
als Pfarrvicarius, und endlich sogar noch als Pri-
vatlehrer in Halle führte, woran vorzüglich ein
unbegreiflicher Leichtsinn, und aufs höchste ge-
stiegene Neigung zum Trunke Schuld war, nirgends
anders Rettung finden, als in einer gänzlichen
Veränderung aller seiner Verhältnisse,--im Sol-
datenstande." (226)

Also (21a), (125), (315a), (321).

See also parents, father, mother, upbringing.

Domesticity (Häuslichkeit, Hauswesen)

Meister Liebreich balances duty and pleasure in his

home in such a way that no one is overworked and shirks

his responsibilities. When their work is done, father, mo-

ther, son, daughter and the servants relax and tell each

other stories or observe the sky, the garden or a storm

(235). A mother tells her daughter who is about to be

married how to bring harmony, happiness and satisfaction

to her husband and into her home and how to keep it thus

(326). An aunt can do this also (224). Letters among four

180

members of the same family in which each one asks questions about his domestic duties are answered by the others (241). A very poor family can have as happy a home (224) as a wealthy one (111), (235).

Gustav Mehrwelt searches for happiness in a foolish way: he keeps the company of scholars and courtiers, he desires honor and love, he writes poetry and joins the freemasons. He finally finds happiness right at home, far away from the glitter of the world (33).

> "Die Nutzen der Häuslichkeit werden ins Licht gestellt." (294a)

> "Die Aufsätze haben alle den Zweck, Religiosität, Gewissenhaftigkeit, Vaterlandsliebe, Arbeitsamkeit, Ordnungsliebe, Reinlichkeit und andere häusliche Tugenden, als Verbesserungsmittel des häuslichen Wohlstandes und der bürgerlichen Glückseligkeit anschaulich zu machen." (311)

> "In eine angenehme Geschichte eingekleidet, werden hier nur wichtige moralische Lehren, die auf Beförderung der Arbeitsamkeit, Genügsamkeit und ächter häuslicher Glückseligkeit abzielen, vorgetragen." (31)

> "Dieser Mann von warmem Herzen spricht auf diesen wenigen Bogen von überaus vielen Dingen, hauptsächlich von dem Unwesen der Haushaltungen: 'Die Mutter klagte über Philippinens Ungehorsam. Zur Strafe erlaubt ihr der Vater zum Mittagessen nur Brodt und Wasser. Um die zwölfte Stunde traf er sie mit einem Topf Suppe beym Feuer an. Mann. Warum bekömmt Philippine wider mein Verbot, gekochte Speisen? Frau. Wenn sie Wasser trinken darf, so ist es gleichwohl, ob sie es kalt trinkt, oder warme Suppe davon macht.'" (91)

> "Glück der Häuslichkeit enthält gutgemeintes, aber unpoetisches, schleppendes und Langeweile erregendes Gemälde der häuslichen Glückselikeit." (123)

Also (168), (198), (206), (336c).

Village (Dorf)

The industrious and diligent farmers transform their dirty and unsightly village into a pleasant stopping place for travelers and eventually become rich (308), (388). Through better planned sowing the fields yield richer crops (46), (174). Herr von Mildenheim rebuilds his village after a hailstorm has destroyed much of it. He sets up a disaster fund and distributes the land evenly among the farmers (85).

> "Die erste Abtheilung schildert den Zustand des glücklichen Dorfs in sittlicher Hinsicht durch ehrerbietige Achtung und praktische Anseh-ung der Religion. . . . Die zweckmäßige Anwen-dung der gleichzeitig vorgeschriebenen Regeln, nach welchen die Jugend der Landleute erzogen und in Kirchen und Schulen Unterricht erhalten sollen, sind, nach Rochowscher Art, mit Hinsicht der Rheinländer lokal eingerichtet und verdie-nen allenthalben Nachahmnng." (229)

See also Farmer.

Monastery (Kloster)

Ernst is a good pupil and desires to continue his education in a monastery even though he loves Therese. Monks had told him that the monastic life is one of scho-larly devotion. After a short while he escapes from the un-bearable burden of monastic life: the stultifying singing of the Hours, the loneliness of a "life of imprisonment," the performance of the menial and meaningless tasks and the

hypocrisy of the monks' vows of chastity. He becomes a
soldier. One day he finds virtuous Therese in a house of
ill repute and buys her from her unsatisfied owner for
twenty thalers. Unable to provide for her, he takes her
to a convent, but visits her twice a week until she is
pregnant. Punished for her sin, Therese is chained to the
wall in the rat-infested dungeon where she bears her child
and dies. Ernst finds her and commits suicide by running
against a wall till his brain spurts from its cracked
skull (212b).

Wilhelm frees Julie from a convent. Her father had
forced her to take the vow of chastity. The couple lives
in an old ruin until found by farmers. Before these can
capture Julie, the lovers leap to their death so that their
brains are spattered along the rocky slope (212a).

Anton and Therese have vowed eternal love, but her
father forces her to become a nun, as she has refused to
marry a nobleman. Anton enters the convent in disguise and
escapes with Therese. She falls from a high wall, dies and
Anton--again--crashes his head against the wall (211a).

> "Es ist nichts mehr und nichts weniger, als
> --die Märtyrergeschichte eines Mönchs. . . .
> Von der Unvorsichtigkeit der gröbsten Art ist
> der Held dieser Geschichte, Armin--ein Mönch
> und doch in der Kutte ein erklärter Verächter
> und Gegner alles Mönchsthums und der ganzen
> Priesterschaft, gar nicht frey zu sprechen.
> Auch war das Ende vom Liede, Verfolgung der
> ärgsten Art von Seiten der Mönche wegen Ketze-
> rey, Kerker, Flucht, unstätiges hin und her
> treiben, wieder erhaschen, abermaliger Kerker

und endlich der Tod." (5)

Also (211b-j).

Classroom (<u>Schulzimmer</u>)

Gregorius Schlaghart lives in the same room in which
he teaches. His wife and children constantly disturb him
and his pupils. Because door and windows are seldom opened,
the students become drowsy and inattentive. Many instruments
for punishment compensate for the lack of seats, the poor
light and a broken blackboard (309). Richard Lorenz' school
has separate houses for his family and his pupils. The classroom is ventilated, and has many seats and tables, books,
chalk and a large blackboard (309). Pastor Froland visits
the schools of the land and tells the teachers how to improve on the arrangement of furniture, on ventilation and
the light in the classrooms (203). A new teacher improves
the school to which he has been assigned (189c).

> "Über Erziehung fand jedoch Recensent aller-
> dings etwas Neues, nämlich einen Vorschlag, Schulen
> im Freyen anzulegen, und auf gut peripatetisch un-
> ter Gottes freyem Himmel zu lehren. Auf manche
> Schulgebäude mag freylich passen, was der Verfas-
> ser dagegen sagt; aber sollte es denn nicht auch
> in diesem Puncte schon hie und da seit den Jah-
> ren, da man in unserer Pädagogik zu verbessern an-
> gefangen hat, besser geworden seyn? oder doch wirk-
> lich besser werden? Die Schwierigkeiten, die mit
> den Schulen im Freyen bey uns verbunden seyn wür-
> den, sind wirklich größer, als die der Verfasser
> sich dachte. Uns dünkt, daß es, ehe wir die Schul-
> gebäude niederreißen, doch besser sey, den Mittel-
> weg einzuschlagen--sie zu verbessern." (247)

> "[Jacob Ehrenmann] dringt auf die Nothwendig-
> keit des Unterrichts im Lesen und Schreiben, . . .

und zeigt auf die schlechte Einrichtung der Schulhäuser." (210)

See also Teacher.

Love (Liebe)

A virtuous girl loves a man so much that she loses her good judgement and is seduced (219h). Love does not have to be consummated and proven by physical union (72).

A man loses the faith and love of a woman because he puts her to cruel and excentric tests (7c). A man who loves his wife treats her gently and with understanding (37c). A girl loves a student who wants to marry her. But he only takes advantage of her and leaves her. She dies of grief and shame; he lives in bitter remorse (267f). Because love blinds inexperienced young men, Conrad Kiefer relies upon the better judgement of his father and only marries the girl of whom his father approves (295).

Love heals: it cures a man from habitual gambling (290a) and a count from seeing ghosts (48).

> "Fünf weibliche sehr verschiedene Charaktere bringen bey Gustav eben soviel Nüancen der Liebe hervor. . . . Das Ganze ist nicht nur auf Unterhaltung, sondern auf wirklichen Nutzen berechnet." (136)

> "Die Erzählung soll die Gewalt, die Launen, Eigenschaften und Folgen der ersten Liebe darstellen, wobey der Verf[asser] unstreitig die Absicht auf eine sehr lehrreiche, aus dem Innern der Natur jener Leidenschaft herausgehobene Weise erreicht hat. . . . [Hierin] ist die Rede von dem Unterschiede zwischen verliebt seyn und lieben: 'Ersteres ist Reiz, letzteres Wohlgefallen; jenes gründet sich auf Sinnlichkeit

und Vergnügen, dieses auf Achtung und Wohlgefallen; jenes hat mehr Leidenschaft; ist aber eben um deßwillen flüchtiger--eine Gluth, die durch sich selber verzehrt wird:dieses hat mehr Ruhe, ist aber um deßwillen bleibender,--eine Flamme, die durch sich selbst immer neue Nahrung erhält; jenes wird entzündet durch äußere Vorzüge des Mannes oder Weibes, dieses wird erweckt durch Vorzüge--äußere und innere des Menschen; jenes verzehrt das Gemüth in eine beständige Berauschung, dieses leitet es in ein besonderes Wohlseyn; vom Genuß des ersten mag sich das Herz des Tugendhaften selten Rechenschaft ablegen, auf den Genuß des zweyten blicket er immer mit Zufriedenheit und Selbstbilligung.'" (290f)

"In den drey letzten [Abschnitten], ist eine getrennte, getäuschte und wieder erwachende Geschlechtsliebe der Inhalt der Scene; aber mit so vieler Behutsamkeit, daß es dem ohnerachtet eine für Kinder nicht nur unschädliche, sondern auch lehrreiche Lektüre bleibt." (251h)

Also (210a), (290e).

See also <u>Bachelor</u>, <u>Innocent Maiden</u>.

Wedding (<u>Hochzeit</u>)

Weddings should be modest. Few people are to be invited, a large wedding costs too much (235), (295). The most important part of a wedding is a virtuous bride (141b). Amtsrath Gutmann does not choose the future wives or husbands of his children, he advises and persuades them as to the choice of their spouses and the arrangement of the weddings (206). A mother tells her daughter what to expect on the first wedding night: "'Gleichwohl schläft er bey dir, und wie man durchgängig behauptet, so gern, daß er kaum die gesetzte Bettglocke erwarten kann.'" (326)

A wise widow gives her six children in marriage. All of them are happy (344).

Also (290d).

See also Bride, Marriage.

Marriage (Ehe)

A boy and a girl marry too early and are therefore later very unhappy with each other (12f), (259a). Two persons should only marry if they still like one another several days after they have first met (283e). Since a husband's wealth and a wife's beauty are fleeting things, they do not result in a happy marriage. The wife becomes old and the husband loses his fortune. They then will dislike each other (316). Fritz Rheinfeld loves his wife because she is a moral woman, not merely because she is beautiful and rich. This assures him of a happy marriage (237). Wilhelmine loves a man of good appearance, but lets reason control her desires. She only marries him after she has convinced herself of his good character and honest intentions (192). A young couple, sweetly in love, marry happily and set a better example for others than the immoral descriptions found in many novels (257).

Being of a higher class does not determine the happiness of a marriage. A farmer can be happily married (304), so can a husband and wife from different classes (316). But a woman who only marries in order to get into a higher

estate makes herself and her husband unhappy (316). A
marriage is good when husband and wife live simply and
understand one another (10), (241). But a quarrelsome
couple (146) or a spendthrift and an adulterous wife (36b)
promise a short marriage. Albert and Karoline are not sat-
isfied with their marriage because she is too sentimental
and he does not understand her (290g). In order to better
their marriage, Wilhelm Ehrenpreis and Karoline Sebastiani
discuss their problems and differences (148). A traveler
writes to his friend Carl about his views on marriage and
suggests improvements (285).

> "Die frühe Verbindung [ist] eine wohl zu be-
> herzigende Warnung für junge Leute, sich vor
> frühen Liebeserklärungen zu hüten." (288a)

> "Dieser Roman ist ein eben so belehrendes
> als unterhaltendes Ehestandsgemälde, in wel-
> chen vielen Ehemännern und ihren Hälften ein
> trefflicher Spiegel vorgehalten wird." (304)

Also (36a), (206).

C. Virtues and other good examples

Caution (Vorsicht)

A boy, even though teased by friends, does not climb
a tree, because the branches would not hold him and he
might fall down (308). Accidents and misfortunes can be
avoided (312).

> "Zur Vorsicht beym Scherzen." (329e)

> "Freue dich, aber mit Vorsicht." (154a)

Cleanliness (<u>Sauberkeit</u>, <u>Reinlichkeit</u>)

When the farmers wash their children and themselves and keep their houses clean, fewer are sick (388). Children who come to school with dirty hands and faces are sent back home by their teachers (309), (388).

> "Die Geschichten haben alle den Zweck . . .
> Ordnungsliebe, Reinlichkeit und andere häusli-
> che Tugenden, als Verbesserungsmittel des häus-
> lichen Wohlstandes und der bürgerlichen Glück-
> seligkeit anschaulich zu machen." (311)

See also <u>Neatness</u>.

Dignity (<u>Würde</u>)

A father always warns his disobedient children, but never punishes them; they lose respect for him, defy and deride him (296). Gregorius Schlaghart, a teacher, imitates the dignified walk and intonation of the pastor, but gains no respect from the villagers, because he drinks and curses with the farmers in the evenings (309).

> "Menschenwürde und noch andere Gegenstände
> von nicht geringerm Belage sind es, worüber
> Herr K. [der Verfasser] seine Leser zu erbauen
> sich angelegen seyn ließ." (198)

Consideration, Charity, Kindness (<u>Liebenswürdigkeit</u>, <u>Edel-
muth</u>)

Vater Traumann helps his sick neighbor even though he has enough work with his own fields (163). When a neighbor dies, Isidor consoles his widow and helps her run her household (190). A boy helps a girl with her chores on the farm although he would rather play with his friends (294b). Meister Liebreich pays the rent for an old woman who is suffering from gout, because her "righteous" landlord cannot relieve her of her "duty" to pay. It would be unjust to the other tenants (235). A kind farmer gives a homeless widow with five children a place to work (267a). A beggar as well as a rich person can be charitable: a weaver asks for two pennies after he has lost everything in a fire; after he receives them he gives them to a farmer for taking another poor man to town (267d). David Klaus, the son of a shepherd, becomes a reader in the poorhouse and donates his savings and his books to the orphanage (340). To be merely virtuous without modesty and consideration of the judgement of others is not enough (219c). In spite of her own poverty Anna helps the poor (375).

"Wer bald giebt, giebt doppelt." (280c)

"Schön sind die Beyspiele des Edelmuths, . . . da sie nicht Ideale sind, sondern aus dem Reiche der Wirklichkeit stammen." (3)

"Andern wohlthun, ist der beste Dank gegen Gott, und die süßeste Freude." (154k)

"Der Aufsatz Durch Wohlthun macht man Undankbare enthält überaus viel Lehrreiches und verräth eine große Bekanntschaft mit dem menschlichen Herzen." (114)

"Edelmuth eines Mohren--auf einem eroberten und nach Neapel gebrachten Algierischen Raubschiff, der einen jungen Sizilianer, mit eigener Gefahr, aus dem Wasser rettete." (360j)

Also (28), (40), (66m), (68), (84a), (118), (149),

(163).

See also <u>Pity</u>.

Duty (<u>Pflicht</u>)

Before his father permits him to play, a boy must
put his room in order. When the son refuses to do his duty, the father sends him to bed hungry (330). A ghost reminds a father of his duty to educate his son (78a). An
aunt writes her niece of her domestic, religious and social obligations and advises her always to do her duty
and not to follow her inclination (241). The adopted son
of Herr Marbel intends to go to India in order to help
his bankrupt father even though his bride is sick and the
farmers need him (389). Meister Liebreich does not par-
ticipate in a pleasure trip, because he has not yet completed his planned work (235).

> "Die Erzählung <u>Schuldigkeit</u> stellt einen jun-
> gen Officier von Adel auf, der ein frommes, wohl-
> erzogenes Kammermädchen um ihren guten Ruf und
> also ihr Glück bringt; nicht etwa durch förmli-
> che Entehrung; sondern bloß dadurch, daß ein
> nächtlicher Besuch, der ihrer Gebieterinn galt,
> auf Rechnung der Ärmsten geschoben wird. Ein
> Nothbehelf von so schrecklichen Folgen für das
> Kind, daß auch des Hauptmanns Gewissen darüber
> erwacht, und sich nicht anders will beruhigen
> lassen, als in dem er seinen Abschied nimmt,
> und dem unschuldigen Geschöpfe die Hand giebt."
> (291a)

Feeding (<u>Nahrung geben</u>)

> "Berta, ein bejährtes Weib mit halb verfaul-
> ten Zähnen, drückt den Brey aus ihrem Mund ek-
> kelhaft, wie aus dem Hintertheile des Leibes

auf den Löffel hin, und bekleckst den zarten
Mund des Kindes mit dieser verunreinigten Nahrung." (91)

Fidelity (Treue)

Young Lina lives with Gumal and the missionary who
had saved her from starvation and protected her in spite of
her father's warnings and curse (234). Elisa sells her jewels so that her husband will not go into debt, even though
he has been an adulterer (365).

> "Schön sind die Beyspiele der Dankbarkeit,
> des Edelmuths, der Treue, . . . da sie nicht
> Ideale sind, sondern aus dem Reiche der Wahrheit
> stammen." (3)

Forgivenness (Vergebung)

A tribal chief attacks another village, but is defeated. The victorious chief offers him friendship, but the
aggressor refuses. He dies of convulsions and with a curse
on his lips (234). A boy breaks another boy's hobby-horse.
They do not fight, but mend the broken toy (154k). Simon
Blaukohl forgives his slaves who had not worked because they
had been punished by the slave drivers. Now they love Simon
and work more than ever before (381).

> "In der zweyten [Geschichte] faselt die Toch-
> ter eines Landgeistlichen, die zu Hause verzogen,
> und in der Stadt verführt wird; am Ende jedoch
> einen Apotheker heyrathet, den es nicht im ge-
> ringsten kümmert, was mit seiner Braut ehedem
> vorgegangen. Eine feine Nutzanwendung." (193)

Also (220i).

Friendship (Freundschaft)

The wife of his employer attempts to seduce Gustav, the tutor; he reminds her of her duty to her husband, but forgives her. She is grateful and offers him her friendship (258). A father educates his son Ferdinand. He advises and persuades; he does not command and force his son: they become inseparable friends (261). An old man writes his son letters about the values of friends and the dangers of enemies (178b).

A student gambles--and loses. His good friend pays his debts (156a). Two friends can manage the same household without quarreling (225). Wicked people destroy their friends (245). Eduard von Waller travels and writes letters about true friendship among the people he meets (285). Adelheit von B** is such a good friend of Gustav that she finds him a woman who is closer to his age than herself (270).

> "Die [Geschichte] schwatzt vom hohen Werthe der Freundschaft, und bringt einen Orest und Pylades zum Vorscheine, die schlechterdings Niemanden den geringsten Antheil abgewinnen." (193)

> "In der Noth erkennt man den Freund." (251h)

Also (121d), (320b), (334).

Happiness and Satisfaction (Glück und Zufriedenheit)

Various stories uncover the causes of misfortune, misery and wretchedness to show people the way to happiness

(166), (375). Gustav Mehrwelt searches for satisfaction in a foolish way: in the company of scholars and courtiers, in love and honor, with the Muses and the freemasons. He ultimately finds happiness with his family (33). A discontented man leaves the false pomp of the cities and finds happiness with the good people in the village (201). Wallmont also avoids towns and lives happily in the country (204). A father writes seventeen letter to his son about true happiness (197).

One can find bliss on the farm (341), (276), (381), (388) and in the town (389). A beggar (310b), a servant (127), (368), a farmer (174), (177), (188), (370), an artisan (235), (281), (390), a ruler (308), (384), an old man (384), a father (295), a mother (95), (140), and their sons and daughters (129) are happy.

"Reichthum allein macht nicht glücklich." (154g)

"Ein, im Ganzen genommen, nicht ganz übler Roman, der unter andern die Wahrheit auf eine ziemlich anziehende Art vorträgt und einkleidet, daß wir, wenn wir wirklich glücklich seyn wollen, das Glück nicht ausser uns, sondern in uns suchen müssen." (24)

"Der Verf[asser] hat, wie er sagt, bey Herausgabe dieses Buches, die Absicht, seine Menschen durch seinen Schaden glücklich zu machen, und ihnen, durch Darstellung seiner Fehler und Verirrungen, diejenigen Klippen zu zeigen, welche sie vermeiden müssen, wenn sie glücklich werden wollen." (299)

"Warum lebe ich und so viele Menschen auf der Welt?--um glücklich zu seyn. . . . Der arme Traugott ist glückselig und der reiche Ludwig un-

glückselig. Was hat man nöthig, wenn man stets
glückselig seyn soll? Gottfried und Christian
haben nicht einerley Gesinnungen." (322)

"[Die Geschichten] haben alle den Zweck,
. . . Arbeitsamkeit, Ordnungsliebe und andere
häusliche Tugenden, als Verbesserungsmittel des
häuslichen Wohlstandes und der bürgerlichen
Glückseligkeit anschaulich zu machen." (311)

"Ein kluges Verhalten im menschlichen Leben
kann unsere Glückseligkeit befördern. Einige
Regeln dazu." (322)

"Es wird auf eine lehrreiche und zugleich unterhaltende Art gezeigt, wie die hier aufgestellten natürlich und wahr gezeichneten Personen, bey
allem Streben nach Zufriedenheit und Vollkommenheit, doch nicht einmal kluge, verständige, glückliche Menschen, sondern dieß alles erst durch immer fortgesetzte Übungen, durch heilsame Erfahrungen, durch begangene Fehler und widrige Ereig-
nisse, und nach und nach wurden." (243)

Also (198), (230), (312), (360c).

Health (Gesundheit)

A man drinks cold water after dancing. He faints and
dies. A boy drowns because he swam too far. Another one
drowns because he jumped into the water before cooling off.
A little girl has stomach pains because she swallowed a
sewing needle which she had put in her mouth (205).

Abaka learns from his father the skills of a doctor,
heals the Sultan Mahomet and becomes the chief physician
in the serail. He loves Fatme and tells her why she is so
obese, why bosoms drop, why her hips are wide, her feet are
flat and her skin is pale. He prescribes certain baths and
cures her. He also tells her how to keep good teeth. Final-

ly the two flee from the palace and marry (75)

Health and beauty can be retained by sleep, frequent washing and fresh air (186).

Malchen bears Conrad Kiefer without a midwife and nurses him herself. She does not have sore nipples, because she has raised and hardened them by gall-apples soaked in alcohol. Conrad does not wear socks nor is he ever wrapped tightly in diapers. To stop him from crying he is moved about and burped (295). A woman drinks from stagnant water and swallows nine frogs. She vomits them and five continue to live. In January 1780 someone vomited forty lizards. However, he soon swelled up again; he had new ones in his stomach. In Frankfurt a man was afflicted with a shrew-mouse (9).

> "Es fehlte uns bisher noch immer an einem Bu-
> che, das für angehende Lehrer eine kurze Anlei-
> tung enthielte, wie sie ihre Schüler, in Absicht
> der Gesundheit, unterrichten und belehren können.
> Diesem Mangel hat Hr. Klinger auf eine so gute
> Art abgeholfen, daß ihm jeder Jugendlehrer dafür
> herzlichen Dank wissen muß. . . . Iß nicht, was
> du nicht kennst." (205)

> "Das Büchelchen zerfällt in vier Abschnitte,
> in welchen über die Sorge für die Gesundheit
> . . . manches Gute und für Kinder Brauchbare
> gesagt wird." (94)

> "Das Gespräch ist durchaus den Fähigkeiten
> der Kinder angemessen, und hat ohnfehlbar beygetra-
> gen, die Kinder auf die Verwahrungsmittel gegen
> die Krankheit [die Ruhr] aufmerksam zu machen."
> (189b)

Also (273e).

Honesty (<u>Ehrlichkeit</u>)

The carpenter Meister Liebreich refuses to buy stolen
lumber even though he could thereby save much money (235).
Martens, led by the principles of honesty, never has a bad
conscience; he is always at peace, happy and sleeps well
(310a). A man tempts a poor boy to steal, but the boy refuses, tells the owner and is rewarded by him (154b),
(329f). Carl Pilger's teacher asks the boy to bring a larger
benefice from his parents if he wants to be punished less
than other pupils. The honest boy refuses (334).
A poor old couple complains about their poverty. Suddenly
they find several goldpieces and return them to the right-
ful owner who is their long lost son (336a).

> "Geradezu ist der Wahrheit Straße, und guter Weg
> um ist keine Krümme." (334)

Also (119a), (360b).

Industriousness (<u>Arbeitsamkeit</u>)

Under the guidance of a teacher the farmers of a village stop drinking and start work in order to pay off their
debts which they had accumulated by their former drunken-
ness. Through their industry and co-operation they clean
their village and it soon becomes a favorite stop for travelers (276), (308), (388).

Gumal and Lina, the two happy tribal children in Africa, till the soil, plant and raise vegetables and grain
so that they have enough to eat (234). Lorenz Stark tries

197

to instill in his son, whom he considers to be a failure, the conviction that man was made for work which alone keeps him happy (120). Children are overjoyed when their father breaks an arm. Now they can work for him and please him (45). The biography of the industrious wife of an Hungarian pastor, Theresia Theschedik, illustrates how good deeds help other people (40).

"Morgenstunde hat Gold im Munde." (251e)

"In eine angenehme Geschichte eingekleidet, werden hier . . . wichtige moralische Lehren, die auf Beförderung der Arbeitsamkeit, Genügsamkeit und ächter häuslicher Glückseligkeit abzielen, vorgetragen." (31)

Also (3), (245), (311).

Innocence (Unschuld)

Virtuous girls in all social classes can perform many noble deeds (14). Innocence is necessary for a successful marriage (157), (245). A mother sacrifices her innocent daughter to Carl Pilger. He does not accept the "gift," but supports both, mother and daughter, for a while. (334)

See also Innocent girl.

Love of the Enemy (Feindesliebe)

Father Roderich tells his grandchildren stories which illustrate the advantages of loving the enemy (294b).

Models (Beyspiele zur Nachahmung)

Biographies are good models which can be imitated:
Jesus Christ (234), banker Frege of Leipzig, merchants
Hasenclever and Wedgewood, bookdealers Lakington of Lon-
don and Bolangero, the philosophical farmer Jakob Guyer
from Switzerland, Theresia Theschedik, the industrious
wife of a Hungarian pastor (40), and burghers and farmers (25), (274c).

"Neue sittliche Erzählungen zur Nachahmung,
Lehre und Warnung des unbedachtsamen Mädchens."
(66)

"[Gustav Salden] gehört zu dem zahlreichen
Mittelgut unter den Romanen, von denen man nichts
Böses, aber auch wenig Gutes sagen kann. Einfa-
che Begebenheiten, wie sie im wirklichen Leben
sich ereignen können, werden in einem reinen,
nur mitunter etwas geschraubten Style erzählt;
und das Bestreben des Verfassers, Sittlichkeit
und Herzensreinheit zu preisen und durch Beyspiele zu empfehlen, verdient Aufmunterung und
Beyfall." (265)

"[Hier] sind . . . zwanzig Geschichten, wo-
runter auch einige Märchen sich befinden, bald
mehr, bald weniger langweilig erzählt, und mit
moralischen Reflexionen durchwebt, enthalten."
(284)

"Dieses Bändchen enthält eilf Erzählungen,
die nach der Absicht des Verf[assers] die Stelle
einer Klugheits- und Sittenlehre in Beyspielen,
zum Gebrauch junger Leute, vertreten sollen."
(63)

"Eben weil es Thatsachen sind, die hier als
Beyspiel zur Nachahmung oder zur Warnung aufgestellt werden, muß man ihre möglichsten Verbrei-
tungen wünschen." (154)

Moderation, Contentment (Mäßigung)

One should not make a habit of unnecessary things
(154p). A poor organ-grinder does not squander the few
pennies he receives on trinkets and drinking and therefore can give an orphan a small sum of money just before
he dies (161b).

Also (258), (263).

Modesty (Bescheidenheit)

Father Roderich tells his grandchildren also stories
about the benefits of modesty (294b).

Moral Conduct (Sittlichkeit, Moralität)

A girl of fourteen observes and judges the moral conduct of people (345). The goodness of a person is deter-
mined by the excellence of his education (6). Bad com-
panions ruin the morals of good people (245), (251b).

> "Das Possierlichste [dieses Buches] ist eine
> moralische Rede, die der Verf[asser] einem unge-
> borenen Kinde an seine Eltern in den Mund legt."
> (167)

> "Ein geschmeidiges, ungekünsteltes und an-
> ziehendes Büchlein; zur Weckung und Bildung des
> Tugendsinns jedem ordentlichen Hause zu empfeh-
> len, und jedes unordentliche fühlen zu machen,
> woran es ihm gebreche." (2)

> "So einfach und doch hinlänglich belehrend
> der Titel dieses kleinen Buches ist, so ein-
> fach und belehrend, dabey aber doch auch un-
> terhaltend ist die Geschichte selbst. Wer frey-
> lich auf Geister und Unholden lauert, und gern sei-
> ne Haare bergan gezogen haben will; wer gern zwi-
> schen betrunkenen Rittern, auf Turnierplätzen, in
> zerstörten Burgen, verbrannten Klöstern, zwischen

geilen Mönchen, vollen Humpen, Rüdengebell wei-
let, und Mönchs- und Knappenwitz gern hört, der
findet hier seine Rechnung nicht; wohl aber der,
welcher gern unter Menschen seiner eigenen Art
und Gattung sich aufhält, und mit seinen Glei-
chen vorlieb nimmt; er findet hier ein unterhaltendes, wahres, sprechendes Gemälde des alltäglichen Menschenlebens, voll gesunden Räsonne-
ments, und feinen geschliffenen Witzes." (56)

"[Die Erzählungen] schildern mit Wahrheit,
und haben alle irgend einen praktischen Nutzen,
begründen einen moralischen Grundsatz, und lehren Philosophie des Lebens in einem gefälligen
Tone." (62)

"Die moralischen Erzählungen enthalten drey,
in einem schleppenden Tone und einer von Sprach-
fehlern wimmelnden Schreibart vorgetragenen Er=
zählungen, die eher alles andere als moralisch
sind." (115)

"Der Verf[asser] wählt eine moralische Sen-
tenz, oder Maxime--wie er sie gewöhnlich nennt
--und giebt, zur Erläuterung derselben, eine Erzählung, ein Geschichtchen, eine Anekdote, auch
wohl einen Schwank." (175)

"Die Absicht dieser Sammlung moralischer Erzählungen und Schilderungen . . . geht nach des
Verfassers Angabe dahin, theils seine Schüler
dadurch in richtiger Deklamation zu üben, theils
die Erzählungen selbst beym moralischen Unterrich-
te zu nutzen." (313)

Also (1), (63), (94), (110), (217), (265), (277),

(282), (305), (313), (330), (333), (356).

Neatness (Sauberkeit)

Only after the farmers clean their homes and gardens,

repair and sweep the streets, and after their wives mend

their torn clothes and wash their children is their vil-

lage changed into a model community (276), (308), (388).

Herr Marbel takes care of his clothes and immediately repairs even a minor hole. Since his clothes last him a

long time, he spends little on them and becomes rich (389).

> "Wann Philippinchen ein Loch im Strumpfe oder
> in einem anderen Kleidungsstücke hatte, so lief
> sie ängstlich zur Mutter und sagte: Gucke, Mut-
> ter, das Loch da! Gieb mir eine Nähnadel, ich
> will es zustechen.
> Aber die Mutter wies sie zurück und sagte:
> Hum, ich habe jetzt keine Nadel! Ich habe keine
> Zeit dazu, daß ich dir immer aufwarten kann.
> Philippinchen ging bisweilen in Gesellschaft.
> Wann sie nun zurückkam, so bat sie die Mutter
> um den Schlüssel zur Kommode, daß sie ihre Sa-
> chen aufheben könne. Aber die Mutter sagte oft,
> dazu ist ja morgen auch noch Zeit genug. Du kannst
> ja diesen Abend deine Sachen da auch auf die Bank
> oder auf das Bett werfen.
> Und das gehorsame Philippinchen befolgte die
> Winke, die ihr die Mutter gab, auf das pünktlich-
> ste; sie kümmerte sich nicht mehr um ihren
> Schrank; die Bücher und Spielsachen warf sie
> bald auf den Herd, bald auf den Abtritt, bald
> in den Garten. Durch viele Selbstüberwindung
> brachte sie es soweit, daß sie mit durchlöcher-
> ten Strümpfen, schmutziger Wäsche und zerrissenen
> Kleidern ausgehen konnte, ohne rot zu werden. Und
> wo sie sich auszog, da ließ sie ihre Kleider lie-
> gen." (296)

> "Die Erzählungen haben alle den Zweck . . .
> Ordnungsliebe, Reinlichkeit und andere häusliche
> Tugenden . . . anschaulich zu machen." (311)

Also (182).

See also Cleanliness.

Obedience (Gehorsam)

Elisa obeys her mother to marry a man whom she does

not love. She tries to please him, and he honors her (365).

Also (296).

Obligations (Schulden)

Besides financial debts one has also obligations to
one's Stand (84b). Adolph and Sidonie von Wappenkron wrongly believe that they have a claim on position and honor because they happen to be born into nobility (361).

Patience (Geduld)

The biography of M. Mendelsohn, a skilled flute-maker
from Iburg in Osnabrück, shows that patience can lead to
wealth (40).

Patriotism (Vaterlandsliebe)

> "Die Erzählungen haben den Zweck Vaterlands-
> liebe . . . und andere häusliche Tugenden als
> Verbesserungsmittel des häuslichen Wohlstandes
> und der bürgerlichen Glückseligkeit anschau-
> lich zu machen." (311)

Also (247).

Pity (Mitleid)

Natalis is the victim of circumstances and commits
crimes against his will. When seized, the authorities pity
him and forgive him (90). Herr Marbel adopts an orphan
whom he has pitied because he had been cheated by an of-
ficer (389).

Also (294a), (296).

See also Consideration.

Promise (Versprechen)

A nun is tempted to betray her vows, but a ghost appears

and warns her. She heeds the warning and soon is selected
to the position of Mother Superior (53). A little girl
promises not to eat sweets anymore. Therefore the father
rewards her on Sunday with a walk in the country (296).

Also (326).

Punctuality (Pünktlichkeit)

Gustav Reinwald is late for supper. His father sends
him to bed hungry, but his mother secretely brings him
food and the boy never learns to be punctual (258). Teacher Richard Lorenz always starts his classes on time and the
children imitate his punctuality at home and on the play-
ground (309).

Also (182).

Racial Toleration (Rassenduldung)

The Negro children Gumal and Lina are brought up
by a white missionary (234). After many adventures Herr
Astor finally marries an American Indian girl (133).

Also (380).

Religiosity (Religiosität)

A missionary introduces Gumal and Lina, the two uneducated tribal children, to the truths of Christianity.
They call him "father." They hear that he always talks
with someone in a cave; but they do not see anyone. They
ask him, and the "father" tells them that he talks with

God, the creator of the sun, the moon and the trees. When Pedro, a servant, dies, Gumal and Lina cry, but the "father" reassures them that the loss is not forever (234).

Heinrich Gottschalk tells his children every evening about the beauty of nature and the order of the world. Without God man would decay like an old hut, but through Jesus all of us will see each other after death (379).

> "Die Erzählungen haben eine so rein sittliche Tendenz, schildern auf eine ungekünstelte Weise den Werth einer ächten Religiosität, und verbereiten sich über das Gute, welches die Tugend gewährt." (157)

> "Dabey werden überall so faßliche Lehren über . . . ein christliches Verhalten im Umgange mit dem Nebenmenschen, und in den Geschäften dieses Lebens eingestreut, daß, . . . wenn dieses Buch gelesen wird, die Absicht des Verfassers, . . . Verbreitung weiser und christlicher Grundsätze unter dem Landvolke, gewiß bey vielen erreicht werden wird." (190)

> "Die Aufsätze haben den Zweck, Religiosität . . . als Verbesserungsmittel des häuslichen Wohlstandes und der bürgerlichen Glückseligkeit anschaulich zu machen." (311)

> "Erzählungen . . . geben hier jungen Gemüthern Stimmung für mitleidiges Wohlthun und Religiosität." (38a-c)

Reverence (Ehrfurcht)

A ghost reminds sons and daughters to love and to honor their parents and other people (78a).

Self-Control (Selbstbeherrschung)

Whenever Gregorius Schlaghart is irritated by a crying

baby, his nagging wife or the cold classroom he thrashes
his pupils and his punishment becomes meaningless. Lorenz
Richard on the other hand punishes bad deeds because his
pupils deserve it, not because he is in ill humor (309).

Also (154c).

Self-Sufficiency (Selbstversorgung)

Rather than paying an incompetent man to fix the roof,
Meister Liebreich thatches his own roof (235).

Thankfulness (Dankbarkeit)

The carpenter Meister Liebreich refuses to take a
customer away from his neighbor, who is also a carpenter,
but who is careless and drinks. The drunkard is so thankful that he promises to stop his evil habit (235).

"Der Dank mit dem bloßen Munde ist noch kein
Dank." (208¢)

Also (3), (154f, m).

Thrift (Sparsamkeit)

A father gives some money to his son with which he
has to manage. Since the son must do small chores in return,
he appreciates the money more and does not spend it foolishly (235), (389). Farmers become thrifty when they discover
that the money they refuse to spend on drinking can improve
their farms (308), (388). The tinsmith Jonas Jordan receives
a contract from the court, because his bid is honest (390).

Ernst Haberfeld rather walks than takes a carriage. This
way he exercises his legs and his will to withstand the
temptations of luxuries. He also saves money (377).

Also (31), (182).

Virtue (_Tugend_)

Virtue is always rewarded (141a). It alone secures
eternal life (157). An unprotected heart can be seduced
easily. Great effort is then necessary to return from vice
to virtue (271). Louise, in contrast to her two sensuous
sisters, remains virtuous (131).

A moral soul always searches for virtue and tries to
avoid all vice (182). Virtue is achieved in deed, not only
in the mere avoidance of vice (182). Noble goals can only
be attained through noble means (182).

> "Ein Orden, wird mit vollen Backen empfoh-
> len, der nichts geringeres zur Absicht hat, als
> --die Menschen tugendhafter zu machen." (113)

> "Die Beyspiele der Weisheit und Tugend . . .
> sind der beste Theil dieser Sammlung." (4)

> "Die hier aufgestellten Beyspiele enhalten
> musterhafte Handlungen einzelner Personen. Ar-
> beitsamkeit, Menschenliebe und andere Tugenden,
> die ausgeübt sind, können zur Nachfolge reit-
> zen, und es ist besser, daß solche Lektüre all-
> gemein werde, als manche Romane und Schauspie-
> le, die den Sitten schädlich sind, die Einbil-
> dungskraft erhitzen, und gute Lehren und Grund-
> sätze aus der Seele treiben." (3)

Also (2), (81), (83a), (220a), (266a), (275), (294b),
(359).

Wisdom, Practical (<u>Lebensweisheit</u>)

Eduard von Bernau meets many people. He learns to distinguish between good and bad people (180). Ultimately the bad are punished and the good rewarded (80), (303). A father warns his children of bad people who can often be discovered from their manner (200). Three brothers visit the university. Kasimir studies all the time and avoids people, Ernst goes to many balls and studies little. Neither can find good employment when he leaves the university. Friedrich, the third brother, has studied, but also met many people. Because he is both intelligent and friendly he obtains a very good position (375).

Jonas Jordan gives his son keen advice: people can be judged by the cleanliness and the appearance of their towns, villages and houses (390). One should, however, beware of judging too quickly (186). Young people are warned of bad and foolish people (332). The farmers and burghers of Schleswig-Holstein receive special advice for the soil and climate of their region (275).

"Durch Schaden wird man klug." (64)

"In zwölf Briefen eines Greises an seinen Sohn giebt es über Freund und Feinde, Lebensweisheit . . . manches unstreitig sehr brauchbare zu lesen." (178b)

"Hier und da ein psychologischer Sprung . . . macht man gern mit; sieht man doch, wie [der Verfasser] allenthalben poetische Gerechtigkeit, und praktische Lebensregeln durch Beyspiele predigt." (303)

Also (114), (168), (251c), (345), (359), (212a).

C. Vices and other bad examples

Adultery (Ehebruch)

Students satisfy their evil desires with the prostitutes, servant girls and some of the married women in town.
The venereal disease they contract drives them to insanity
(346), (347). Her mother forces Natalie Normann to marry a
man who is twenty years older than she. Since she is very
lonely she commits adultery. Her husband throws her out of
the house. Still lonely she continues her shameful way of
life until the happiness of a virtuous couple arouses bitter remorse in her. Finally a teacher marries her and she
becomes his loyal and happy wife (52). Emilie von Wallenthal is frivolous, keeps bad company and becomes a prostitute (216). Lucien commits adultery, runs away with her
lover, but becomes sick. While she dies on the rotting
straw in a hospital she writes her confessions as a warning to other wives (245).

A husband whose wife had given her favors to a student for 100 thalers returns the money to the student and
gives his wife eight groschen "for her trouble" (383).

> "[Des Verfassers] Röschen sinkt von der ho-
> hen Stufe jungfräulicher Unschuld bis zur Ko-
> kette, und bald bis zur Ehebrecherinn herab.
> Den Gang, den der Verf[asser] sie nehmen läßt,
> wird jeder, der die Fallstricke unseres luxu-

riösen Zeitalters und die laxe Moral der höheren Stände kennt, ganz dem wirklichen Leben getreu geschildert finden." (305)

Also (320a).

See also Passion.

Boasting, Bragging (Prahlerey)

One should not brag about the knowledge and education which one has (385).

Calender, Belief in (Kalenderglaube)

The Kalendermann tells August how calendars are made and of the falseness of prognostications, astrological predictions and weather forecasts which appear in them (337).

> "Dieser Immerwährende Calender soll dem so
> lange und so allgemein durch die gewöhnlichen
> Calender verbreiteten Aberglauben und Unsinn
> in den niedern Ständen entgegen arbeiten." (176)

Carelessness, Thoughtlessness (Nachläßigkeit)

Disadvantageous results of carelessness warn those who desire to learn from the mistakes of others (64). Joseph Freeland runs away from home, because he believes that his parents mistreat him. He wants to go to America. Slave-traders sell him in Surinam where he leads a miserable life (103). A sweating boy drinks from a swampy pond and becomes sick (9). Carelessness leads Julchen Grünthal (348) and Emilie von Wallenthal (216) to immorality and an Englishman even to crime (7a). Carelessness in children's games is dangerous and leads to accidents (329a).

> "Der unvorsichtige Knabe." (66c)

> "Einige von den Gegenständen, über welche hier ein gelegentliches Wort der Ermunterung, des Unterrichts, oder der Warnung geredet wird sind . . . Unvorsichtigkeit mit dem Schießgewehr und Unvorsichtigkeit mit Baarschaften." (146)

> Also (55), (87a), (154a), (182), (220h).

Credulity (Leichtgläubigkeit)

Theodor Hardenberg believes the lies of merchants, Jews and goldmakers until he loses his inherited fortune (69). A teacher tells his students how some of his previous students were defrauded and seduced because they did not think (76a-d).

> "Nur ist der Held, Eduard Humber, zuweilen gar zu leichtgläubig und schwachköpfig um volle Theilnahme zu erregen." (142)

Cruelty to Animals (Tierquälerey)

A father laughs about a beheaded chicken which still runs about, brings his son a young bird whose legs and feathers he has cut off and twists a pigeon's wings before he kills it. When his son Kilian grows up, he lifts his dogs by their ears, digs his spurs into his horse until they draw blood, and beats the horses who are unable to pull heavy loads twice the size of those of other farmers (296).

Also (89).

Curiosity (<u>Neugierde</u>)

Curiosity leads to harm (360c). Gumal explores the dangerous surrounding woods and loses his way, for curiosity made him forget his path (234).

> "Gräfin Ulrike, schön, wohl erzogen, edel, sonst sehr verständig, geistreich, aber neugierig; nicht etwa ein Kind, sondern 16 Jahre alt, geht in die einmal nicht verschlossene Kammer des Sekretärs ihres Onkels, und durchstöbert aus Neugierde seinen Mantelsack. Wie plump! Die Rache, die Friedel, der Sekretär, dafür an ihr nimmt, ist eben so plump.--Ulrike entschnürt und durchkramt den Bündel einer Zigeunerinn, die eben zu Ulrike's Onkel gerufen war und von ihm verhört und als Gesindel über die Gränze gebracht werden soll. Die Zigeunerinn ertappt sie dabey, und mißhandelt sie mit ächt zigeunerischen Schimpfworten. . . . Horchen ist der edlen Gräfin [Ulrike] eine Kleinigkeit. Auch jetzt behorcht sie die ganze hochverehrliche Versammlung von Vater, Mutter, Onkel und quasi Bräutigam. Aber der Verf[asser] weiβ sie auch zu bestrafen. Hr. v. St. öffnet plötzlich die Thür, und die liebenswürdige Horcherinn fällt der Länge nach, ihm entgegen,ins Zimmer hinein." (182)

Cursing (<u>Fluchen</u>)

On the fifteenth of August, 1793, a farmer plowed a field of peas. He came upon a stretch of very hard soil and wished that a thunderbolt would strike him. Immediately a lightning killed not only him but also his horses (278). Parents teach their children how to curse by doing so themselves (296).

Dancing (<u>Tanzsucht</u>)

A dying woman warns young girls of excessive dancing

(98d).

    "Der Abend könnte richtiger überschrieben seyn: Folgen des übermäßigen Tanzens; doch vielleicht hat der Verfasser nicht durch allzu viel moralischen Überschriften eine gewisse Klasse von Lesern verscheuchen wollen." (141c)

    "Pastor Brand verliert auf einmal durch die physischen und moralischen Folgen des übertriebenen Tanzens, eine Tochter und zwey Schwiegertöchter. Alles, was sich nur gegen die Tanzwuth des andern Geschlechts sagen läßt, ist hier concentrirt." (245)

Deception, Fraud, Theft (Betrügerey)

The devil in disguise of a handsome page is the pleasant companion to a lady. She believes his vows of love, is deceived and seduced (301). Theodor Hardenberg becomes the prey of goldmakers, astrologers and peddlers (69).

    "[Die] Historien, die alle irgendeine Sittenlehre zu treulicher Befolgung dadurch empfehlen, daß sie dem Leser den damit verbundenen Nutzen anschaulich darstellen . . . oder einen Betrug, dem diese Claße von Lesern so oft ausgesetzt ist, enthüllen. . . " (277)

    "Dieses kleine Buch (ein Wort zur rechten Zeit!) soll in einem ganz populären Style den Bürger und Bauersmann lehren, was für Folgen aus dem unbesonnenen Empörungsgeiste und Rebellionsfieber entspringen, und dass man nicht jedem Unruhestifter und Ohrenbläser ein williges Ohr leihen dürfe." (169)

    "[Das Buch] enthält zwar keine Thatsachen, aber es ist nicht weniger nützlich, durch die muntere . . . Darstellung des Spiels und den Folgen des Betrugs und Aberglaubens." (145)

Also (146), (182), (294b).

Dirtiness (<u>Unsauberkeit</u>, <u>Unreinlichkeit</u>)

"Frau Andreas Zaunemann war eine saubere Hausfrau; wenn sie Essen auf den Tisch brachte, konnte man, ohne lange zu suchen, nach Belieben einige Raupen,auch Fliegen oder Schnecken darin finden; ehe man sichs versah, fischte man hier ein
Päckchen Haare, dort einen Waschlappen, einen
Strumpf vom Kinde, und dergleichen appetitlichen
Sachen mehr." (350)

"Bringen nur solche Weiber ihre Männer durch
Unreinlichkeit früh unter die Erde, und richten
die Haushaltung dadurch zu Grunde? die, wie Hannchen, das sonst so gute Hannchen, ihr Schlafzimmer des Jahres nur zweymal reinigen? in deren
Schlafzimmer Stroh, Kleider, schmutzige und wei-
ße Wäsche, Überreste verbrannter Unschlittlichter,
von Moder halbverzehrte Schuhe, Äpfel- und Birnen-
schalen, Pflaumenkerne und dgl. in wilder Mischung
durch einander liegen? die die Fässer und Wasser-
kannen mit einer Decke von Schmutz sich überzie-
hen lassen? deren Männer von einem Teller wohl
20 Gerichte essen müssen, ehe das Weib es einmal
für gut findet, ihn abzuwaschen, oder abwaschen
zu lassen? die ihre schmutzigen Handschuhe oder
dergleichen in der Suppe mit kochen, und in der
Terrine mit zu Tisch bringen??" (182)

Also (296).

Disgrace (<u>Schänderey</u>)

Karl Eckrodt disgraces himself because he despises

his mother (161c).

Drinking (<u>Trinken</u>, <u>Saufen</u>)

A doctor whose father drank himself to death cures

farmers who have been infected by a contagious disease:

the <u>Brannteweinpest</u>. He forms a voluntary prohibition so-

ciety which avoids the poison (387). Students in their

drinking bouts wreak havoc with a town (346), (347). Farm-

ers drink and neglect their work; their village goes down
and they fall into debt (276), (388). A drinker seduces a
girl. She becomes pregnant and both commit suicide (387).
Drinkers can be cured by a pastor (378), a teacher (388),
a doctor (387), a bailiff and a wife (276). They can also
cure themselves (85), (375), (387). Laukhard drinks, fails
as a student, as a candidate for a pastorate, as a vicar
and as a private tutor and stops his habit only when he
is a soldier (226).

> "Die Geschichte eines ungerathenen Sohnes
> der sich durch das Brannteweinsaufen ganz unglück-
> lich gemacht hat, wird erzählt, und nachher wird
> auch noch in einem langen Commentarius darüber
> ein Langes und ein Breites über die Geschichte
> geschwatzt, welches den Eindruck, den die Ge-
> schichte etwa überhaupt machen konnte, ganz wie-
> der zerstöret." (275)

Envy (Neid)

Eleonore is envious of the good fortune of other
people: they win in lotteries, they marry rich men, they
inherit much money. Her daughter becomes sick because she
also turns out like her mother and is envious of other
people (296).

Fear (Ängstlichkeit)

Fearful Tonchen, a five year old boy, runs away from
home, because he is afraid of being slapped by his aunt.
He is robbed, beaten and adopted by gypsies. He again runs
away from them, because he is afraid to go and beg for them.

Finally his father finds him and takes him home (324).

Folly (<u>Thorheit</u>)

Theodor Hardenberg, whose parents never made him perform his chores, lacks judgement, makes fast and thoughtless decisions and is frivolous and careless. After his wife, who tried to cure him, dies in childbed, prostitutes, merchants, goldmakers and visionaries cheat him until he is bankrupt (69). A man writes letters to fools in order to punish them and bring them to their senses (11).

Also (50), (322), (332).

French Governess (<u>Französische Erzieherinn</u>)

German daughters are raised by French girls who themselves have neither education nor culture (25). The innocent Julchen Grünthal is educated by a French governess in Berlin. She becomes a harlot (348).

> "Dieß Gemälde soll die nachtheiligen Folgen
> der Erziehung schildern, wie sie ehemals unsere
> Töchter von den als Erzieherinnen angenommenen
> Französinnen erhielten. Eine Erziehungsart, die
> . . . im Ganzen und dem größten Theile nach
> nichts taugte. . . . Schäferstunden heißen hier
> die glücklichen Tage, die Mariane . . . in ih-
> rer frühesten Jugend . . . durchlebt, nachdem
> sie vorher in Gefahr war, durch eine gewisse La-
> tour an Leib und Seele verkrüppelt zu werden .
> . . . Mariane fällt doch endlich als ein Opfer
> der Lüste eines Prinzen." (106)

French Democracy (<u>Französisch-demokratischer Schwindel</u>)

Ernst Haberfeld wants to travel to France, but a soldier who has just returned from that country warns him and

Ernst stays in Germany (377).

"Der französisch-demokratische Schwindel,
der, wie die neuphilosophischen Sparren, vor
einigen Jahren die Gehirne unsrer jungen und
alten Kraftgenies verwirrte, wird hier in der
Freyheitsapostelgeschichte eines Würtemberger
Magisters mit vielen treffenden Zügen, und
nicht ohne sarkastische Laune geschildert.
Höchst possierlich äußert Ulrich Höllriegel
durch Worte und Thaten seinen Freyheitswurm;
artet jedoch nie in Karrikatur aus, wird auf
mancherley Weise für sein demokratisches Apo-
stelment gestäupt und gezüchtigt, und vielfäl-
tig und schmerzlich in seinen Hoffnungen von
dem französischen Vernunftshimmelreich betro-
gen, eh' er, durch Schaden klug, zum gesunden
Menschenverstande wieder zurückkehrt." (366)

Also (121b).

French Revolution (Französische Revolution)

Pächter Martin discusses the bad effects the French
Revolution has on his neighbors Peter Rundans and Pastor
Ernst. All would have come differently had the people
kept clean homes, practiced religion, regularly gone to
church and avoided unnecessary luxuries (55). A Parisian
tailor leads the happy farmers of Heidenau into a revolution. They believe his catch-words. The army has to
bring order to the village (108). Wilhelm Friedwald tells
the farmers of Fröhlichhausen that anarchy, not democracy,
rules in France (358).

Honest Adam Gutman struggles against the evils which
penetrated Germany after the French Revolution: polygamy,
neglected children, selfishness, immorality and dishonest

servants (206). A man visits France. His hope for freedom, equality and human rights is frustrated. He finds
deception, vice, injustice, immorality and mistreatment
(67). A soldier tells a farmer about the true conditions
in France (377). A married couple in peaceful Switzerland
write to their parents in Paris about the "sins" of the
Revolution (371).

> "In diesem Buche ist Klarheit in der Zeichnung
> der mancherley Lagen, worinn ein junges durch
> Barbareyen des französischen Revolutionskrieges
> in die weite Welt gestoβenes, sich selbst über-
> laβenes Mädchen kommen konnte. . . . Röschen
> sinkt von der hohen Stufe jungfräulicher Un-
> schuld bis zur Kokette, und bald bis zur Ehe-
> brecherinn herab." (305)

> "Der Roman Henriette Duford dient die zu Lyon
> und in der Nachbarschaft vorgefallenen Revolutions-
> greuel zur Einfassung." (87b)

Gambling, Speculation (Spielsucht)

When a student loses in a game his friends pay his
debt. The thankful student promises not to play anymore
(156a). A gambler wrongly believes that he can stop this
habit any time. He finally commits suicide, while his
friend Adolph, also a habitual gambler, cures himself,
because he loves a girl (290a). Edwin gambles and loses.
His father, a rich goldsmith, pays his debts until he is
bankrupt himself. Edwin's sister marries a Polish count
in order to pay her family's obligations, but the count
deceives her. Since the family cannot find any creditors,
it finally disintegrates (brothel, suicide) (390). A ha-

bitual gambler loses and becomes a robber. He is cured

only after his father has almost killed him (25).

"Reinwald, Doktor der Rechte, ein leichtsinniger leidenschaftlicher Spieler, wird--was Spieler
zu werden pflegen--nach und nach arm, und bis zu
den empörendsten Niederträchtigkeiten Betrüger,
wozu er als Doktor der Rechte mehrere und bedeuten-
dere Veranlassungen finden konnte, als ein Anderer;
muß von Spielernoth und Spielerleidenschaft gedrun-
gen, wider Neigung und besseres Bewußtseyn ein Weib
nehmen, das mit zehn tausend Thaler Vermögen alle
widrigen Eingenschaften verbindet, welche eine
schlechte Erziehung und ungezähmte, pöbelhafte Leidenschaften zum Gefolge haben. Die Ehe ist, was
eine solche Ehe seyn kann . . . wenn der Vater
ein leichtsinniger Spieler und die Mutter eine
Buhlerinn ist. Die Mutter stirbt, und der Vater,
noch immer Spieler, endet, wie Spieler oft enden,
in verzweifelnder Armuth sein Leben als Selbstmörder." (258)

"Die erzogene [!] einzige Tochter Marie kommt
nach dem Tod ihres Vaters in das Haus ihres stren-
geren Onkels, der sie bald auf eine, für Eltern
und Erzieher nachahmungswürdige Art zur Arbeitsamkeit und Tugend zurückbringt. Er hat das Unglück,
daß sein Sohn auf Akademien ein Spieler wird, und
da Marie darüber den Kummer ihres Pflegevaters
merkt, thut sie ihm den Vorschlag, ihn nach Hause
zu nehmen, und nimmt sich vor, seine leidenschaft-
liche Spielsucht durch eine andere Leidenschaft,
Liebe zu ihrer Person, zu heilen. Die Cur gelingt
und Marie bittet sogar den Vater um seine Einwil-
ligung zur Heyrath, der sie nach vielen Warnungen
vor dem Rückfall eines Spielers ertheilt. Die ersten Jahre der Ehe entsprechen Mariens Erwartun-
gen; nachher ziehen Erbschafftsgeschäffte den Mann
in die Stadt, wo seine Spielwuth heftiger als je
wird; er verspielt seiner Frau Vermögen, und ver-
läßt sie. Eingezogen und dürftig lebt sie nun auf
dem Lande mit ihrem Pflegevater und dreyen Kindern.
Gebeugt, aber reuevoll kehrt der bekehrte Spieler,
doch mit erworbenen Vermögen, wozu Romandichter so
leicht verhelfen können, in den Schooß seiner Familie, und macht Vater, Kinder und Gattinn durch
seine Rückkehr glücklich. ... . Die Handlungsart
des Spielers ist richtig getroffen." (219d)

"Wie der junge unbefangene Mann bey den besten Vorsätzen dennoch sinkt; wie seine Phantasie, und selbst sein edles Herz den Verstand
überlistet, und lange Zeit über ihn siegt; wie
er seine Handlungen bald entschuldigt, bald ver-
dammet; wie er mit sich selbst zankt, und dennoch von dem Wirbel seines Gefühls fortgerissen
wird ... ist psychologisch richtig aufgestellt."
(290)

Also (89), (145), (161d), (245).

Gluttony (Völlerey)

A pastor and a judge decide that it is the parents'
fault if their children are gluttons (338). Heinrich's
father lets him eat whenever he is hungry. The boy becomes
a useless soldier who cares nothing for honor and father-
land (378).

> "Frau Sibylle, ein gutes, ehrliches Weib, war-
> tete den kleinen Adolf, wie wenn er ihr eigenes
> Kind wäre.
> Sie hatte von ihrer Großmutter gehört, kleine
> Kinder könnten noch nicht sagen, was ihnen fehle,
> man könnte also auch nicht wissen, wenn sie satt
> wären, und müsse ihnen deswegen so lange einstrei-
> chen, bis sie kotzeten. Deswegen fütterte Frau Si-
> bylle den kleinen Adolf allemal so lange, bis er
> kotzete, und um recht sicher zu gehen, strich sie
> ihm das Gekotzete auch wieder ein paarmal ein, bis
> sie ganz gewiß wußte, daß nichts mehr hinunter woll-
> te.
> Als er nun zu sprechen anfing, so war alle Mor-
> gen das erste Wort: Semmel! und Frau Sibylle eilte,
> sie ihm zu verschaffen. Sobald sie verzehrt war,
> ging er nach dem Zimmer des Papa, der nun seinen
> Kaffee verzehrte, gab ihm ein Mäulchen und bekam
> dafür ein--paar Tassen Kaffee und ein paar Pfenni-
> ge zu einem Weckchen. . . .
> Auf diese Art gingen die ersten Lebensjahre des
> kleinen Adolf mit Essen und Verdauen hin, wodurch
> er in diesem Geschäfte eine bewundernswürdige Fer-
> tigkeit erlangt hat." (296)

Also (329c).

Ghosts and Witches, Belief in (<u>Geister- und Hexenglaube</u>)

A young count believes in miraculous things. One day
he leaves his house to inspect an apparition in his father's
garden. Thieves attack and rob him. Not until he falls in
love is he healed from his madness (48). Meister Martin
tells his children tales of ghosts and witches. His son
Peter sees many when he grows up (296). Pastor Heilmann,
teacher Liebreich and Vogt Ehrlich chase the white "ghost"
out of the village after he had scared the farmers for many
weeks (308). Children who love their teacher believe him
that there are are neither ghosts nor witches (71).

> "Manche Thorheiten, z. E. die Furcht vor Ge-
> spenstern sind gerügt und die Nichtigkeit der-
> selben gut aus einandergesetzt." (287b)

> "Einige von den Gegenständen, über welche
> hier ein gelegentliches Wort der Ermunterung,
> des Unterrichts, oder der Warnung geredet wird,
> sind . . . Gespensterfurcht und Goldmacherey."
> (146)

> "In [einigen Nummern] werden die Verirrungen
> der Gespensterfurcht entwickelt." (147b)

Also (145), (154a), (357).

Gossip (<u>Geschwätz</u>)

A mother complains about her neighbors while her children listen. They spread the gossip and the neighbors do
not talk to her anymore (296).

Also (171a).

Greed (<u>Habsucht</u>, <u>Geiz</u>)

Euphrosine never shared her presents with her sisters.
Once she received a basket of fruit. She hid it in her clos-
et and forgot it. It rotted and spoiled her clothes. For two
winters she had to spin her own yarn and sew to replace her
ruined wardrobe (375). Herr Harpax praises his son Gottfried whenever the boy saves money. Gottfried does not buy
new clothes, does not attend church, eats poorly and finally
dies without having tasted the pleasures of life: good food,
the joys of nature and religion. But he saved 7000 thalers
(296).

> "Georg Carleton, Jussuff, Albert Angely sind
> wahre Heroen ihrer Art, als Geizige, als Hab-
> süchtige. Man kann ein braver Nichtswürdiger
> seyn, und gegen diese gehalten, sich beynahe
> tugendhaft finden." (182)

> "Züge eines unerhörten Geizes."(279a)

Idealism, Philosophic (<u>Idealismus</u>)

Buttervogel, a Kantian, and Ostwind, a Fichtean, de-
bate the philosophical systems of Kant, Fichte, Schelling
and Schlegel: "Die Inconsequenzen ihres verba magistri be-
schworenen philosophischen Systems; tolle Tendenzen des
a-priori Schwindels werden ans Licht gestellt." The "Ber-
liner Kriegsrath," representing common sense, decides the
argument and triumphs over such philosophical nonsense (58).
Adelheit B** heals Gustav, her beloved who is ten years
younger than she, of the disease of idealism, poesy, abso-

lutism and freedom, in short, the products of the new philosophy and leads him to a woman who is of his own age
(270).

Indignation (Empörung)

Students rebel against the authorities, are caught
and jailed (346), (347). Farmers revolt after a rabble-
rouser has stirred them up. Several are beaten and hurt
(169).

Inconstancy (Unbeständigkeit)

> "Die Geschichte eines jungen Unbesonnenen,
> der von seinem Vater seiner eigenen Wahl über-
> lassen, einen Stand nach dem andern wählte,
> und immer mit Reue wieder verließ, und darüber
> an den Bettelstab gerieht." (360d)

Injustice (Ungerechtigkeit)

Pupils who bring large fees are not punished and receive good marks while good pupils whose parents are poor
are always punished and get bad grades (309). A landlord
cannot relieve an old and poor woman suffering from gout
from paying her rent, because it would be "unjust" to the
other tenants (235).

> "So gern der Recensent der guten Absicht der
> Verfasserinn bey Abfassung dieses . . . Werk-
> chens, Gerechtigkeit wiederfahren läßt: so kann
> er sich doch nicht überzeugen, daß ein langwei-
> liger Predigerton, der durchgängig in demselben
> herrscht, bey der erwachsenen Jugend Glück ma-
> chen werde." (151)

Jealousy (Eifersucht)

Seltener and Korde control and defeat jealousy:

"In Seltener ist der Eifersüchtige wohl mit zu starken Zügen geschildert. Korde ist die Kopie eines ehrlichen weiblichen Charakters." (227)

Laziness, Idleness (Faulheit)

The traveler Eduard von Waller also writes to his friend Carl about idle persons (285). A lazy housewife neglects her home and her children (146). Farmers are idle and go into debt (276). Meister Piger talks about his hard life, rests every fifteen minutes and does not work on holidays. His son remains a student for thirty-eight years and waits for the death of his rich brother (296).

"Müßigkeit lehret Böses." (245)

Also (121a).

Litigeousness (Prozessucht)

Jacob, a mean landowner who punishes his farmers frequently, tries to discourage Hallo from treating his farmers with love and seeks to bring legal action against him. He dies before a warrant can be delivered to Hallo (384).

Also (146).

Lying (Lügen)

Lying is the worst vice; others may be excused (335). A father tells his wife that he merely went for a walk while he had actually been drinking and was accompanied by his six year old son (297). At dinner Lottchen asks for wine, but she is too young. She complains about a stomach ache. The entire company laughs about the cunning girl and her mother gives her wine. From then on Lottchen often received praises and rewards for lying (296).

> "Die Geschichte will . . . den sehr richtigen Satz lehren, das man Kinder zur strengsten Aufrichtigkeit und Wahrheitsliebe gewöhnen müsse, weil laut der erzählten Geschichte eines Unglücklichen, aus der Verletzung derselben die schlimmsten Folgen und Gewohnheiten entspringen können." (335)

Also (66o).

Murder (Mord)

A soldier cannot die peacefully (he awakens twice after an apparent death) before confessing the three murders he has committed (330). A murderer punishes himself (329d). Students murder. They are dismissed from the university (346), (347). A man kills another in a duel. He feels so guilty that he goes insane (375).

Negative Examples (Warnende Beyspiele)

> "Die mannichfaltigen Fehler und Verdorbenheiten der menschlichen Natur werden von ihrem Entstehen an entwickelt, gründlich und größtentheils richtig bestimmt, ihre Äusserungen, dem Wesen derselben gemäß theils allgemein, theils in Beyspielen anschaulich gemacht und ihre traurigen Folgen zur Warnung vor denselben dargestellt." (152).

Also (28), (110), (139), (256), (266), (267a-f), (334).

Novels, Reading of (<u>Romanleserey</u>)

Biographies should be read, not novels; these destroy the morals (5). Eduard von Waller comments on the harmful effects of reading popular novels (285). Rath Dose gives Cecilie Wieland's <u>Oberon</u>, Wetzel's <u>Herrmann und Ulrike</u>, Langbein's <u>Schwänke</u>, Cramer's <u>Wacker</u>, Schilling's <u>Guido von Sohnsdom</u> and finally Lafontaine's and J. G. Müller's novels so that the young girl loses the habit of reading "schlüpfrige und sittenverderbende Bücher." (100)

> "Die traurigen Folgen des frühen Romanlesen
> . . . werden geschildtert." (294a)

Also (170), (214), (295).

Onanism (<u>Selbstbefleckung</u>)

To aid boys in practicing the "secret sin," their parents permit them to stay in bed in the morning and see to it that two sleep together (296). A teacher tells his students that they should use the "Dessauische Handschuh" to stop the habit and prevent harmful effects (334). A young man who practiced onanism cures himself and tells others of his success (99). Poor parents care more for the language abilities of their children's tutor than his virtue (296).

> "Der Hauptinhalt beschäftigt sich mit den geheimen Sünden der Jugend. . . . Der wahrhaft ehrwürdige Pfarrer zu Eggstädt nimmt Gelegenheit mit den Landburschen über das Laster der Onanie zu sprechen, sie zu warnen und zu heilen. 'Onanie auf dem Lande?' Nicht anders; 'denn sogar unter den Bauersleuten ist dieß Laster in einem sehr hohen Grade eingerissen.'" (83)

"'Bekannt mit der Verführung der Jugend, und
durch ein Buch auf eine gewisse, von derselben
öfters begangene Sünde aufmerksam gemacht, welche die Selbstbefleckung genannt wird, und welche
in ihren Folgen um so schädlicher ist, weil sie
oft lange unentdeckt und ungewarnt getrieben wird,
suchte Christine ihre Kinder vor derselben, so
viel wie möglich, zu verwahren. Es waren aber
nur Winke, die sie ihnen, in Ansehung dieses Lasters,
bey dieser oder jener Gelegenheit geben zu müssen
glaubte; ausführlich hierüber zu reden, hielt sie
nicht für gut!' Nun werden diese Winke beschrieben,
nebst den Veranlaßungen dazu." (128)

"Wenn es gerathen wäre, jungen Leuten, um sie
vor zu frühem und unregelmäßigen Gebrauch der Ge-
schlechtstheile zu warnen, hiernächst sie gegen
Selbstbefleckung mit Abscheu zu erfüllen, den
ganzen modus procendi bey der Begattung darzulegen:
so würde Rec[ensent] diese ärmliche Compilation
dazu am wenigsten wählen." (65)

Also (214).

Pampering (Verzärteln).

Karl Eckrodt's mother coddled her son so much that as

an adult he despises and scorns her (161c).

"Die Waldorfsche Familie, oder die Folgen der
Verzärtelung [ist] eine gut durchgeführte Erzählung, die eben so gut unterhalten, als heilsam
belehren kann." (227d)

Passion, Lust, Prostitution (Hurerey)

A teacher goes with his students to a hospital in or-

der to show them the sad results of prostitution: women and

men crippled by venereal disease (334). Franz Weichenberg,

a student, goes to many prostitutes and contracts venereal

disease (26). A Catholic girl is offended. Because her se-

ducer bribes her she accuses a priest. Driven by lust

and encouraged by the profitable outcome of her first immoral act she becomes a prostitute and steals from churches.
She is caught and convicted to death. Only on the scaffold
she tells of the priest's innocence and reveals her first
seducer. Neither can benefit from her confession; both
have already died (267e). The traveling philosopher Eduard
von Waller naturally writes to his friend Carl also of his
observations on passionate and immoral women (285). An amo-
rous country girl tries to seduce Carl Pilger. She does not
succeed because he loves another girl (334).

> "Es ist die Geschichte eines guten Menschen
> von gutem Herzen und glücklichen Anlagen; der
> aber gewohnt ist, bloß nach Instinct und erregter
> Leidenschaft, oder nach seinem Gefühl fürs Gute
> und Schöne zu handeln, ohne seine Tugend auf be-
> währte Grundsätze zu stützen. Bey dieser Hand-
> lungsweise geräth er dann auf Schulen und Uni-
> versitäten durch übel angebrachten Großmuth
> und Freygebigkeit, Nachgiebigkeit gegen Lockun-
> gen seiner Freunde zu Spiel und Theater und an-
> deren Vergnügungen, in Schulden und Unordnung;
> wird ein Betrüger an seinem rechtschaffenden Va-
> ter, wird flüchtig, tritt in eine Schauspieler-
> gesellschaft, muß auch die Schulden wegen ver-
> lassen, geräth endlich . . . unter eine Räuber-
> und Bettlerbande, und dann ins Zuchthaus." (160a)

Also (245), (275).

See also Adultery.

Predictions (Prophezeihungen)

Dreams do not predict the future (357). One can, however, "predict" a person's fate from his earlier behavior
and must warn him (143).

"Ein harter Winter ist zu erwarten, wenn um
Martini herum die Brüste der gebratenen Gänse
braun aussehen." (337)

Also (210).

Prejudice (<u>Vorurtheil</u>)

Georg Reinhard (174) and Georg Treumann (144) plant

when the weather is good and not on the date which the cal-

endar advises. They are not afraid of thunder, but build

lightning rods. The Jew Schmuel and Doctor Ehrenmann dis-

cuss their means and methods of earning money. Soon it be-

comes evident that the Jew is honest and that the doctor

charges exorbitant fees (269a).

> "Wärend [Küster Ehrentrauts, der den Stand ei-
> nes Dorf-Schulmeisters erwählt hatte] Amtsführung
> hat er indessen oft mit den Honoratioren des Ortes,
> z.B. dem Gutsherrn, Gerichtshalter, Förster, und
> deren Frauen, Gespräche über religiöse, moralische,
> pädagogische und andere Gegenstände geführt, um
> manche Vorurtheile in ihnen zu bekämpfen." (325)

> "<u>Hannchen, oder die verkannte Unschuld</u>, worin
> die Lehre, daß Niemand nach dem Schein beurthei-
> len müsse, gut dargestellt ist . . . " (161a)

> "[Die Erzählungen] sind alle in der nützlichen
> Absicht gewählt um Unarten und Vorurtheile, wie
> sie unter den ganz gemeinen Ständen leider noch
> herrschen, zu widerrathen und zu widerlegen." (17)

> "[Der Verfasser] will . . . den Bürgers- und
> Bauersleuten auf eine unterhaltende Art nützliche
> Lehren und gute Gesinnungen beybringen, und durch
> eben dieses Mittel Vorurtheile und Irrthümer zer-
> streuen." (277)

Also (7a), (50), (182), (220g), (293), (330).

Pride (<u>Stolz</u>, <u>Hochmuth</u>)

A little girl loses all her friends because she is too proud (66f). Droste asks Evchen to be his wife, but her father gives her to another man. The proud Droste does not complain (2201). A soapboiler wins in a lottery. He becomes very proud, commits a crime and is imprisoned (147a). A ghost warns a proud daughter not to hire servants to perform her duties, the housework (78a). A rich old woman asks a poor but honest man to bury her jewels and to tell her daughter when she is old enough. The mother dies, the poor man suddenly becomes sick and asks the daughter to visit him. But she is too proud to step into the hut of the poor man. He dies without telling her about the buried treasure (336c).

Also (66i).

Principles, Lack of (<u>Prinziplosigkeit</u>)

Eduard Wallstedt is a passionate and unprincipled young man. He squanders his money, follows his passions, goes into debt, joins a theatrical troupe, becomes a robber and forms a band of thieves. Finally he is caught and jailed (160a).

Punishment (<u>Züchtigung</u>)

Conrad Kiefer's father (295) and the teacher Lorenz Richard (309) punish very seldom. When they do, it is effective. The teacher Gregorius Schlaghart punishes fre-

quently and the children merely laugh at him (309). A
dissolute person who has nevertheless a good heart is
punished often and severely until he commits suicide
(253a).

> "Am Ende des zweyten Theils hat [der Verfas-
> ser] alle im Buche vorkommende schlechte Menschen
> gehörig bestraft, und die goldene Wahrheit auf
> eine sehr einleuchtende und doch unterhaltende
> Art gelehrt, daß das Laster nie glücklich seyn
> könne." (303)

Quackery (Quacksalberey)

A good doctor from Würzburg cures the farmers of
Traubenheim. They had always consulted imposters who did
not help, but harm them (308). Jakob Ehrenmann discusses
with the farmers of Wiesenthal the harm done by quackery
(210). Doctor Ehrenmann, a quacksalver, treats the coun-
selor of commerce Beil with smoke, poisons and incanta-
tions (269b). Farmers who consult a quack become deformed
(16). A pregnant woman does not consult a quack, but a
good mid-wife. She bears a healthy son (295).

> "16 Beyspiele erweisen den unersetzlichen,
> oft erschrecklichen Schaden, welchen die Quack-
> salberey, im ganzen Umfange des Wortes, anrich-
> tet; schildert die Ursache der Anhänglichkeit,
> besonders des Landmanns and diese mörderische
> Kurart, und thut einen gut gemeinten Vorschlag,
> wie diesem Unwesen zu steuern wäre."(274a)

> "Des Verfassers Räsonnements über . . .
> Quacksalberey ist gewiß sehr wahr und richtig."
> (321)

> "Jakob Ehrenmann kämpft gegen die Vorurtheile
> der Quacksalberei und des Wahrsagens." (210)

Also (107).

Seduction (Verführung)

A nobleman seduces the daughter of a hunter. He promises to marry her, but she dies of grief. The nobleman has
no regrets until she returns as a ghost to tell him that
he has made two families very unhappy (220h). A girl should
always be on guard when she is with men (245), for a man
can be the devil in disguise and seduce her (301). Meister
Liebethat practices intercourse with his wife while their
son Heinrich watches. They believe that he is asleep. Since
Heinrich takes his father as an example, he becomes a man
at thirteen, father at eighteen, an old man at twenty-four
and dies at thirty (296).

Fikchen must marry the rich Heckert although she
loves the teacher Knauf. Knauf tells her that in a certain
village future husbands bring their brides like wine-barrels
to the teacher to have them opened and tested. He seduces
Fikchen. The bride confides in Heckert. On the wedding
day Knauf finds a foul liquid in his glass--part of the wine
from the keg he has opened (375).

"Ein schönes unschuldiges Bauernmädchen, wird
von einem adeligen Wohllüstling verführt in seinem Hause die Stelle eines Kammermädchens anzu-
nehmen, und kurz darauf von ihm entehrt. Nach
allmählich überwundener Gewissenhaftigkeit nimmt
sie von ihm Geld, um einen Pater, an dem sich
der Edelmann seiner Strafpredigten wegen rächen
wollte, als Urheber ihrer Schande anzugeben.
Dieser wird sofort eingesperrt, und erliegt in
einem fünfjährigen Gefängnis. Röschen geht in-

dessen von einer Schande zur andern fort, wird
verstoßen, und endlich aus Mangel eine Diebin
und Kirchenräuberin, und bekennt noch auf dem
Blutgerüste die Unschuld des Paters, der aber
bereits im Kerker verschieden, und der Edelmann
gleichfalls durch den Tod seiner Strafe entgan-
gen ist." (267f)

Also (219e), (245).

Self-deception (Selbsttäuschung)

An old man warns his son of the dangers of self-de-
ception (178b).

Selfishness (Selbstsucht)

Rouelle, a French nobleman, leaves his wife and takes
their younger son with him to Paris so that he may be educated. The most important principle in the son's education
becomes selfishness. The boy seduces a young painter's
wife and murders her. She was his brother's wife (220o).
Old man Saalfeld writes letters to Claudine Lahn. He seeks
to be praised for his wit and his intelligence, but gets
no satisfaction from his egotism (232).

Also (283f).

Sentimentalism (Schwärmerey)

Sentiment is listed as a vice that ought to be
avoided (182), (286b).

"Speeding" (Zu schnelles Fahren)

A drunken coachman drives so fast that the carriage

turns over and he breaks his arm (387).

> "Welcher Bewohner großer Städte und Reisende
> kennt und bewundert nicht die Gewandtheit der Kut-
> scher und ihrer Kutscherrollen spielenden Herren
> unter unsern vornehm tuenden Equipagenklassen von
> Einwohnern, mit welcher sie, ohne daß es sonder-
> lich viel Rippen-, Arm- und Beinknochen kostet,
> durch die engen mit Menschen vollgepfropften Gas-
> sen, in ihren Kutschen, Cabrioletten u. dgl. hin-
> stürmen, und den emsigen, arbeitsfleißigen Fußgän-
> ger, den Hunden gleich achten, die sich instinkt-
> artig bey einem nahenden Wagengerassel zu wahren
> und durch einen Sprung hinter die Straßenabweiser
> zu retten wissen? . . . Mit noch ganz glimpflich
> angelegter Geissel der Satyre, wird die schnell-
> fahrende und reitende Race in volkreichen Städten
> in diesen Bogen gezüchtigt."(41)

Squandering (Verschwendung)

Augustine, the only daughter of a rich father, buys
expensive clothes, gives parties and attends many balls.
When she marries she continues to lead her life of luxury
and hires many servants to take care of her children and
her house. Finally her husband goes bankrupt and dies because he lost his honor. Augustine becomes insane; the
children are raised in a poorhouse (375). A Parisian
couple uses paper money for a spill and bathes in Rhine
wine to outdo their neighbors who bath only in milk (371).
The traveler Eduard von Waller finally writes his friend
Carl about the evil effects of luxury (285).

> "[Es ist] die Geschichte eines jungen Hambur-
> gers, der nach Paris geht, anfags ein ungeheurer
> Verschwender ist, aber am Ende gebessert wird."
> (137)

Also (38a), (55), (119), (245).

Superstition (<u>Aberglaube</u>)

A woman in childbed believes that she is bewitched.
She asks a shepherd to free her of the spell. He fills the
room with smoke; the sick woman chokes and dies (107). The
traveler Eduard von Waller finally also writes his observations about the poor people who are guided by supersti-
tions (285).

> "Aberglaube und Unglaube, zu denen schon in der
> Kindheit und bey der Erziehung der Grund gelegt
> wird, sind die ersten Ursachen, warum man die Hül-
> fe des Arztes verachtet, und an Beschreyen, Anthun,
> u.s.w. glaubt." (107).

> "An diesem Noth- und Hülfsbüchlein ist nun be-
> sonders zu loben, daß es dem Aberglauben kräftig
> und doch auf eine behutsame, den katholischen
> Glauben nicht antastende Art entgegen arbeitet."
> (85)

> "Die Gegenstände der Beleuchtungen mit eingemisch-
> ten Beyspielen sind: Die Täuschungen der Einbildungs-
> kraft--das Doppelterscheinen--das Alpdrücken--das
> Traumdeuten--Geistercitiren--Bannen--Schatzgraben--
> Feuerbesprechen, u.s.w."(135)

> "Der Abergläubische leitet die Erscheinungen
> in der sichtbaren Welt nur von den Wirkungen in
> der unsichtbaren her, und will allem Übel nur durch
> geheime Künste entgegenarbeiten und abhelfen." (152)

Also (86), (145), (182), (219g), (210), (341).

Thoughtlessness (<u>Leichtsinn</u>)

> "Ein Knabe setzt zwey Reihen Lichter auf den
> Tisch . . . brennt erst die Hand seiner Gespie-
> len damit, fährt hernach mit seinem schönfrisir-
> ten Kopfe durch die Reihen, um seinen Muth zu zei-
> gen, und hat das Unglück, seine Haare anzuzünden.

235

In der Zeit aber, daβ er in der Stube herumlief,
--den Kopf ins Bett steckte,--eine Bouteille Li-
queur sich auf den Kopf gieβt,--daβ der Vater
Wasser holt, muβten die Haare längst verbrannt
seyn." (156a)

Vanity (Eitelkeit)

A vain bachelor marries a girl from the Nobility, but
since his wife does not come up to his expectations he is
not happy (283f). Friends laugh at a vain little girl, because she dresses like a young lady (21a). Justitiarus Edel-
wald marries a virtuous girl from the country. In the town
she becomes vain, adulterous and squanders his money. He
throws himself from a bridge and shoots himself (259a).

> "Benjamine . . . stellt die Nachtheile der
> Eitelkeit, vorzüglich in Absicht der (weiblichen)
> Sucht glänzende Stände zu ersteigen, dar." (315a)

Also (21a), (66f), (121d), (186), (314), (316), (341).

Vice (Laster)

Farmers and burghers hear stories of various vices
and their bad consequences (274a), (277). Ludwig Waghals
has some vices and consorts with other people of bad habits.
The downfall of these friends concerns him greatly, he seeks
to mend his ways (50). All people who have bad habits are
unhappy and receive their punishment (303). Vice never
leads to happiness (303). An old man becomes insane because his sons have destroyed themselves through their
passions. A youth who sees and pities the old and innocent

man recalls the horrible sight whenever he is tempted. He will never send his father to an asylum (121g).

> "Heinrich von Wild ist die Geschichte eines gebesserten Lasterhaften." (254)

Wrath, Ill Temper (Zorn)

Gregorius Schlaghart beats his students from sheer bad temper (309). Lina's mean father is so enraged when his daughter refuses to go with him, that he must pay for his ill temper with his life: he dies of convulsions (234). Braus is insulted by his friend and kills him in a duel (377).

Also (89), (162a).

Writing (Schriftstellerey)

Early authorship leads to bad health; the author writes too much, sleeps too little, becomes a hypochondriac, yet is paid poorly (355). Gustav fails as a tutor, a doctor, journalist and advocate, because he offends people with his writing (167).

CHAPTER III

FORMAL CHARACTERISTICS

This final chapter contains a list of recurring formal characteristics of the novels of education and the introductions by their authors. It is again based on the Neue Allgemeine Deutsche Bibliothek as well as our own reading. Although some of the characteristics are also common to other novels of the eighteenth century, notably the epistolary novel, satire and dramatic novel, there remain some which recur so frequently that they may almost be said to define the Novel of Education. Only a wider comparative study would, however, allow definite conclusions.

The parenthesized numbers refer again to the bibliography and the quotations are taken either from the books themselves ot their reviews in the Neue Allgemeine Deutsche Bibliothek.

<u>List of Formal Characteristics</u>

A. Titles

1. Titles indicate the person for whom the book is
   written:

   für Kinder (1), (17), (81), (102), (118), (134),
       (154), (159), (164), (181), (191), (233), (234),
       (236), (272), (278), (294), (322), (329), (331),
       (341), (379);

   für gute und fleißige Kinder (29);

   für gute Kinder (38), (60);

   für fleißige Kinder (117);

   für Kinder und Kinderfreunde (71);

   für junge Kinder (207);

   für reifere Knaben (170);

   für die Jugend (9), (152), (155), (160), (161), (165),
       (175), (282), (343), (356), (359), (378)

   für die zartere Jugend (162);

   für die unerfahrene Jugend (328), (332);

   für die erwachsene Jugend (151), (182);

   für die gebildete Jugend (156);

   für die chursächsische Jugend (89);

   für junge Leute (23), (93), (118);

   für Jünglinge (5), (66), (79), (83), (211), (228),
       (245), (259), (289);

   für die Jünglingswelt (101);

   für gute Söhne (197);

   für Deutschlands Söhne und Töchter (133);

für Jünglinge und Jungfrauen (217);

für Knaben und Mädchen (4), (94);

für Leute beyderley Geschlechts (93), (118);

für studierende Jünglinge (57), (226);

für Universitätsjünglinge (82);

für die nachdenkende Jugend (256);

für die weibliche Jugend (2), (157);

für gute Töchter (273), (315);

für erwachsene Töchter (186);

für junge Frauenzimmer (98), (224);

für Frauenzimmer edler Erziehung (227);

für bürgerliche Mädchen (128);

für Töchter aus höhern Ständen (132);

für Mädchen (54a), (66), (83), (153), (168), (211), (228), (245), (259), (289);

für die Mädchenwelt (100);

für Damen (36), (75);

für das schöne Geschlecht (273);

für den gemeinen Mann (339);

für Erwachsene (17);

für junge Ehemänner (370);

für Ehegatten (148);

für Bräute (13);

für Gattinnen (13), (168);

für Mütter (13), (128);

für Bauersweiber und Töchter (15);

für Familien (129), (235);

für Eltern (5), (83), (99), (226), (259), (341);

für Eltern und Erzieher (202);

für Eltern und Herrschaften (127);

für Erzieher (5), (83), (99);

für Schullehrer (189);

für Lehrer (83), (189), (278), (309), (343);

für Landschullehrer (309);

für unstudirte Leute (284);

für Wißbegierige (208), (360);

für Schulen (8), (311);

für Volksschulen (235);

für Bürgerschulen (163);

für Bürger- und Landschulen (333), (350);

für Bürger und Landleute (8), (16), (20), (85), (169),
    (252), (274), (275), (277), (298), (317), (330),
    (338);

für Herrschaften (127);

für Bürger (8), (67), (190), (337);

für das Landvolk (190), (210);

für den Bauersmann (169), (337);

für Bauersleute (85), (227);

für den Landmann (68);

für das Volk (146), (149), (295), (308);

für Meister, Gesellen und Lehrjungen (364), (390)

<u>für Gelehrte und Ungelehrte</u> (279);

<u>für junge Kaufleute</u> (194), (250);

<u>für Handwerker</u> (74);

<u>für Herrendiener und Dienerinn</u> (314);

<u>für Dienstbothen</u> (127);

<u>für dienende Mädchen</u> (47);

<u>für alle Stände</u> (18), (147), (175), (340);

<u>für gute Leute</u> (340);

<u>für Leidende</u> (45);

<u>für leidende Mitbrüder</u> (99);

<u>für Alt und Jung</u> (10), (293), (387);

<u>für Reich und Arm</u> (387);

<u>für Denker und Edle</u> (362);

<u>für Leser feinern Gefühls</u> (28);

<u>für Wohllüstlinge</u> (26);

<u>für lüsterne Leser</u> (11).

2. Many names appearing in titles have an allegorical
   meaning:

   A benevolent farmer: Erdmann Hülfreich (15);

   an honest boy: Ehrenfels (22);

   a poor teacher: Caseus (lat. <u>n</u>. "cheese") (43);

   a daring young man: Waghals (50);

   a good man: Lebrecht (56);

   a quarreling wife: Xanthippe (92);

   a good family: Gutmann (111)

a headstrong father: Stark (120);

a farmer: Erdmann (125);

a loyal husband and father: Treumann (144);

a benevolent father: Vater Traumann (163);

an honest farmer: Ehrmann (177);

a pastor who does not have any time for the farmers:
   Eil (179);

a drinker: Barthel Most (185);

a brave German: Gutmann [1] (206);

an honest and good teacher: Ehrenmann (210);

a benevolent carpenter: Meister Liebreich (235);

a wise and homely father: Klugmann (243);

a happy farmer: Frölich (243);

a benevolent man: Gutmann (252);

an irate teacher: Schlaghart (309);

a traveler: Pilger (334);

a happy farmer: Frohmann (341);

a peaceloving son of a judge: Friedwald (358);

a man who does not think: Glaskopf (328);

a wise farmer: Landmann Kluge (380).

3. Titles and subtitles contain proverbs:
   Lügen haben kurze Beine (207);
   Handwerk hat goldenen Boden (208e), (390);

---

[1]The reviewer of this book suggests that the hero should
be called "Starkmann" or "Fest."

Durch Schaden wird man klug (64), (74b);

Schuster, bleib bei deinem Leisten (201f);

Der Schein betrügt; Morgenstunde hat Gold im Munde;

Alte Liebe rostet nicht; Wohl aus den Augen, wohl aus

dem Sinn; Wer bald giebt, giebt doppelt; Ausgeschoben

ist nicht aufgehoben, Tugend und Handwerk sind der Kin-

der bestes Erbteil (280);

Der schändet sich selbst, der seine Mutter verachtet

(161b);

Der Krug geht so lange zu Wasser, bis er zerbricht

(378);

Es ist nicht alles Gold, was glänzt (192);

Hochmuth kommt vor dem Fall; In der Noth erkennt man

den Freund (251h);

Ein X für ein U machen (36), (370).

Also (200), (236), (274a).

4. Successful earlier titles slightly varied helped
authors attract readers for their new books:
Der aufrichtige Volksarzt (107), Der aufrichtige Kalendermann (337);
Noth- und Hülfsbüchlein (84), (85), Karl C. Nencke,
Noth- und Hülfsbüchlein in politischen Rechtsangele-
genheiten fürs deutsche Volk und seine Freunde (Leipzig, 1802); Noth- und Hilfsbüchlein für alle, welche
durch Liebe oder durch Selbstbefleckung ausgeschweift

haben (Leipzig, 1795);[2] Karl Friedrich Ebers, Noth-
und Hilfsbüchlein bei Feuersbrünsten, oder bewährte
Anleitung dieselben zu dämpfen und zu löschen (Karls-
ruhe: Braun, (1818);[3] Deutschmanns Noth- und Hilfsle-
sebuch für die lieben Landleute, mit Regeln der Vorsicht geziert (Leipzig, 1804);[4] Vater Graumann, Amor.
Ein Noth- und Hülfsbüchlein für Liebende und Eheleu-
te (Cölln: Hammer, 1797);[5] Neues Noth- und Hilfsbüchlein für den Bauersmann (Klagenfurt: Walliser, 1792).[6]

Elisa, oder das Weib, wie es seyn sollte (365);
Stephan, oder der Handwerker, wie er seyn sollte
(281); Elisa's, des Weibes, wie es seyn sollte, Vermächtnis für ihre Tochter Henriette (Leipzig: Comp-
toir für Litteratur, 1801);[7] Johann Karl Gottlob
Schindler, Roberts Vermächtnis an seinen Sohn; Seitenstück zu Elisa's Vermächtnis an ihre Tochter (Cam-
burg [!]: Peterson, 1803);[8] Elisa, kein Weib, wie es

---

[2]Christian Gottlob Kayser, Vollständiges Bücher-Lexicon enthaltend alle von 1750 bis zum Ende des Jahres 1832
in Deutschland gedruckte Bücher (Leipzig: Ludwig Schumann,
1834-1836), Vol. II, pt. 4, p. 250 a.

[3]Ibid.   [4]Ibid.

[5]Neue Allgemeine Deutsche Bibliothek, Vol. XVI, p. 62.

[6]Ibid., IV, 158. Many other similar titles are listed
in Kayser's Bücher-Lexicon.

[7]Ibid. LXIII, 297.

[8]Kayser, op. cit., III, 5, 85 a.

seyn sollte. Ein höchst nöthiges Wort zur richtigen Schätzung der Schrift: Elisa, oder das Weib, wie es seyn sollte (95); Louise, ein Weib, wie ich es wünsche (49); Robert, oder der Mann, wie er nicht seyn sollte (382); Robert, oder der Mann, wie er seyn sollte (352); Fritz, der Mann, wie er nicht seyn sollte (386); Der Mann, wie er ist (304); Das Weib, wie es ist (306); Die gute Frau (302); Anonymous, Mann und Weib in ehelichen Verhältnissen. Oder wie sie seyn sollten (Leipzig: Lauffer, 1801);[9] Die ganze Familie, wie sie seyn sollte; ein Roman wie er seyn kann (318); Moritz und Auguste, oder die Kleinen, wie sie seyn sollten (351); Erwin Müller, Das Unterröckchen, wie es seyn sollte (Leipzig, 1803).[10]

Christoph Martin Wieland, Der goldene Spiegel, oder die Könige von Scheschian, eine wahre Geschichte (Leipzig: Weidmann, 1772);[11] Angenehmer goldener Spiegel (66), Fürstenspiegel (119); Spiegel menschlicher Leidenschaften (87); Spiegel für die Bildung junger Herzen (79); Spiegel für Ehegatten (148); Sittenspiegel für die Jugend (152); Sittenspiegel für Kinder (272); Spiegel menschlicher Leidenschaften (347).

---

[9] Neue Allgemeine Deutsche Bibliothek, LXXVII, 539.

[10] Kayser, op. cit. III, Romane, 142 a.

[11] Ibid., 133 a.

<u>Die gute Christine</u> (127); <u>Die gute Christine die</u>
<u>Zweyte</u> (128).

B. Introductions

Many reviews indicate that a work has an introduction.
Of the books I have myself read these have introductions:[12]
(76), (85), (86), (119), (211), (212), (224), (234),
(235), (276), (295), (296), (370), (371), (375), (376),
(377), (383), (385), (386).

1. Some introductions give the technique and the plan of
the book:

"[Ich wollte] die Grundwahrheiten der Religion,
insbesondere der christlichen, auf eine den Kindern
faßliche und zugleich angenehme Art vortragen. . . .
Ich bediente mich der sokratischen Methode . . . und
um diesen Unterricht anziehend und angenehm zu machen,
kleidete ich ihn in das Gewand der Geschichte, dachte
mich an die Stelle eines christlichen Greises, der .
. . Kindern, die noch nicht die richtige und gegrün-
dete Erkenntniß von Gott und den Wahrheiten der Religion hatten, diese so nach und nach beizubringen
und eine Gesellschaft von Verehrern Gottes nach
christlichen Grundsätzen um sich zu versammeln." (234)

"So, wie besondere Sittenlehren, so giebt es auch
besondere Erfahrungen von Menschen, besonders praktische Kenntnisse, die für gewisse Stände, ganz un-
entbehrlich, für andere desto brauchbarer sind. Wer
das Scepter und wer den Pflug, wer den Degen und wer
den Richterstab führt, hat jeder seine Beobachtungen,
Grundsätze, Warnungsregeln nöthig.--
Die Absicht bei nachstehenden Aufsätzen ist: jungen Prinzen, und besonders solchen, die zum Regieren
bestimmt sind, manche eben ihnen nützliche Wahrheit
zu sagen; nicht wie gewöhnlich, in Bildern, als wodurch der Vortrag zwar feiner, aber zugleich auch un-
kräftiger wird, sondern mit aller Offenheit, die sich

---

[12]For a good study of introductions of novels see
Hans Ehrenzeller, <u>Studien zur Romanvorrede von Grimmelshau-</u>
<u>sen bis Jean Paul</u> (Bern und München: A Francke, 1955).

ein Erzieher zur Pflicht machen würde, wenn nicht diesen die Furcht vor Anwendungen bände.

Ist der Ton in manchen dieser Aufsätze spottend, oder selbst bitter, so hat ihn wahrscheinlich weder Muthwillen, noch Galle dazu gemacht; bloß die Wirkung, die der Aufsatz bezielte, hat ihn so vorgeschrieben. Durch zu bescheidene Verschleierung wird keine Scham, und durch zu furchtsame Schonung wird keine Abscheu erregt.

Die einzige pflichtmäßige Schonung war die: Beispiele von Fehlern und Lastern nicht aus der Mitwelt, sondern aus einer schon entfernten Vorwelt zu nehmen." (119)

"Ich stelle dieses System in eine Reihe von Handlungen auf, und concentrirte sie auf eine Person, weil ich gewiß glaube, daß Mann oder Weib, wer dieses System befolgt, glücklich ist." (365)

"Ein Menge von geringen, unschicklichen, unartigen und meistentheils zweckwidrigen Handlungen würde ich erzählen müssen [um die Kindheit zu schildern], und dadurch den unangenehmen, verhaßten Gedanken an unsere kindische Schwachheit rege machen, keineswegs aber belehrend und unterhaltend seyn." (369)

"Selbst die denkende Klasse der Menschen nimmt in gewissen Beziehungen, wo Lieblingsneigungen gern die Moral willkürlich zu formen suchen--die durch sinnliche Darstellungen mitgetheilte Belehrung williger an, als den Unterricht, welchen sie in gerader Beziehung auf sich erhält. Aber noch ungleich mehr bedarf die nicht denkende Klasse auf welche die kalte Moral weit seltener vortheilhaft würkt, einer sinnlich anschaulichen Belehrung."(314)[13]

"[Meine Absicht ist] durch die hier aufgestellten Beyspiele zu zeigen, wie unverkennbar die Richtung sey, welche unser Charakter durch die Erziehung bekommt; wie diese Richtung sich in unsern Handlungen zeigt; und wie die Erziehung überhaupt oft das glückliche oder unglückliche Schicksal einzelner Menschen, vieler Menschen oder ganzer Nationen bestimmt." (6)[14]

"Fiction [ist] die beste Lehrerinn für die lebhafte jugendliche Phantasie." (217)[15]

---

[13]Neue Allgemeine Deutsche Bibliothek,XXIX, 484-5.

[14]Ibid., XXXV, 98.   [15]Ibid., XL, 188.

"[Meine Absicht ist] die Welt zu überzeugen, daß
mehr Gutes als Böses, und in dem Leben des Menschen
mehr Glück als Unglück herrsche, daß es noch viele
glückliche Menschen gebe, und noch mehr geben könnte und unter gewissen Voraussetzungen geben würde."
(266)[16]

"[Die Absicht ist] das Gebäude des Wahnglauben
in Beziehung auf das Reich der Geister zu untergra-
ben, und insbesondere jene unwillkürlich schauder-
haften Eindrücke zu mindern, welche diejenigen Wahr-
nehmungen auf uns zu machen pflegen, die nicht auf
der Stelle, als natürliche Folgen einer in den or-
dentlichen Naturkräften gegründeten Ursache deutlich einleuchten." (357)[17]

"Ich übergebe ihnen hier ein Werkchen, das Biographien von Jünglingen und Mädchen enhält, die
theils durch Vorurtheile, theils durch eigene Übereilung und Schwärmerey unglücklich wurden. Was sie
hier lesen werden, ist nicht Erdichtung--ist Wahrheit.--Ich könnte Zeit, Ort und Personen nennen, die
ich aber aus Schonung weglasse. . . . Meine redliche
Absicht war, Ihnen, verehrungswürdige Freunde und
Freundinnen, und zugleichallen Eltern und Vormün-
dern in Beyspielen zu zeigen, wie unglücklich oft
Schwärmerey, Übereilung, rasche Jugendhitze, Eigen-
sinn und Geitz machen.--
Wer Sie also immer sind, die Sie zum Kloster eine
Neigung hegen,--ich bitte Sie, um Ihrer Glückseligkeit willen,--nehmen Sie dieß Buch, die theuern Erfahrungen eines redlichen Mannes, in die Hand, und
prüfen Sie Sich wohl, ob Sie alles darin vom Kloster-
leben Geschilderte zu ertragen im Stande sind, damit
Sie nicht einst gleiches Schicksal treffe!--
Und ihr, Eltern und Vormünder! opfert doch die
Ganze Glückseligkeit eurer Kinder oder Pflegekinder
nicht euren Vorurtheilen, eurem Eigensinne, eurem
Geitze, oder anderen unedlen Absichten auf!
Wie glücklich wäre ich, wenn ich durch meine Be-
mühung nur einen einzigen Jüngling,--nur ein einzi-
ges Mädchen vom Untergange zurückhielte!--" (211)

2. One introduction gives the history of the work (211),

(212) and the biography of its author:

---

[16]Ibid., XXII, 544.   [17]Ibid., XXXIV, 120.

"... Ein junger Mensch von ein und zwanzig Jahren, verstoßen von Eltern und Anverwandten, die sonst
mein Schicksal mit mir hätten theilen müssen, verlassen von meinen Freunden und Bekannten, wurde ich ohne
Unterstützung, ohne Aussicht in die weite große Got-
teswelt hinausgeworfen. Ohne einen Groschen Geld
machte ich zu Fuße, bey der strengsten Jahreszeit,
im Februar, den ungeheuern Weg von München bis Berlin. Wenn ich da vor Kälte steif und starr war, wenn
Schnee und Regen meinen ärmlichen Anzug ganz und gar
durchnäßt hatten, wenn mir der heulende Nordwind den
Schnee um die Ohren stöberte, wenn mein müder Fuß in
den Sandwüsten von Barnth und Mittenwalda seine Last
nicht mehr vorwärts schleppen wollte, dann sagte ich
zu mir selbst:,Du duldest für die Wahrheit!'--und dieser Gedanke goß neue Stärke in meine Glieder, und
brachte mich mit frohem Muthe an das Ziel meiner Emi-
gration.--
    Alle diese Verfolgungen, und weit mehr, die ich
hier nicht nennen kann, mußte ich meiner Klostergeschichten [(211)] wegen erdulden, die ich 1796 her-
ausgab, um die schwärmerische Jugend vor dem Abgrunde
zurückzuhalten, in dem ich selbst schmachtete, und
meinem verblendeten Vaterlande doch einmal die Augen
zu öffnen.
    Und ihr, Jünglinge und Mädchen! denen entweder Na-
tur oder Erziehung den Saamen der Schwärmerei ins
Herz gestreuet hat,--ich bitte euch bei eurer irrdi-
schen und überirrdischen Glückseligkeit, höret mich,
höret meine Warnungen und Bitten,--was ich hier nie-
derschreibe, schreibe ich nicht aus Haß, oder aus Langeweile,--nein!--die Thränen rollen mir über die Wan-
gen herunter, in dem ich dieß schreibe--mein Schicksal steht mir lebhaft vor Augen,--und ihr sollet nicht
so unglücklich werden, als ich es war, und es noch
viele andere sind!--" (212)

3. Other introductions list the themes of the book:

    "Dankbarkeit gegen Ältern, Geschwisterliebe, Men-
schenfreundlichkeit, Wohlthätigkeit, Freundschaft,
Bescheidenheit, Sinn für häusliche Freuden, sind die
Gefühle, welche ich in ihren [der Kindern] Herzen zu
erwecken strebe. Ich suche sie empfänglich zu machen
für alles, was bald das Glück ihres künftigen Lebens
abhängen wird:weise Sparsamkeit, Genügsamkeit, Häuslichkeit, Liebe zu den Wissenschaften, Verlangen ihren Geist würdig auszubilden.--Auf einer anderen Sei-
te bemühte ich mich, ihnen Abneigung gegen böse Ge-
sellschaften, Habsucht, Verschwendung, Eitelkeit, Ro-

mansucht und andere Untugenden beyzubringen.--Allenthalben wird man das Bestreben gewahr werden, meine jungen Leser nicht nur zu unterhalten, sondern sie immer besser, glücklicher und liebenswürdiger zu machen." (375)

"Dieses Büchlein hat drey Theile. Der erste lehret: wie die Bauersleute vergnügt leben können: 1) Gesundheit . . . , 2) glückliche Ehe . . . , 3) Ehre und Liebe bey den Mitmenschen . . . 4) Ein gutes Gewissen vor Gott und Menschen.
Der zweite Theil des Büchleins zeigt: wie Bauersleute welche nach Vorschriften desselben thun, reicher werden können, als sie zuvor waren. 1) Die Kunst etwas zu erwerben. 2) Das Erworbene zu erhalten.
Der dritte Theil enthält Hausmittel wider die meisten Nothfälle des Lebens, wo sich nämlich die Menschen unter Gottes Beystand selbst helfen können. 1) Solche, die das Leben, oder die Gesundheit der Menschen und des Viehes in Gefahr bringen; 2) Solche, die den Häusern und andern Gebäuden schaden; 3) Solche, die das Getreide und andere Früchte verderben.
Verstehn und Reden ist wohl gut:
Doch besser--wer auch danach thut!" (85)

Also (371).

4. Introductions are written for the parents or teachers

of young readers:

"[Dieses Buch] ist vorzüglich in Hinsicht der sittlichen Bedürfnisse für Bürgerskinder bearbeitet worden, um als ein Lehr- und Lesebuch sowohl in Bürgerschulen als Bürgerfamilien benutzt zu werden." (235)

"[Das Buch] soll eine Schutz= und Bittschrift für die armen wehrlosen Kinder seyn, deren viele durch die Unwissenheit und Unvorsichtigkeit der Eltern um ihre vergnügten Stunden, um Tugend, Gesundheit und Leben gebracht werden. Ich habe dies mit Exempeln bewiesen, von denen schwerlich jemand eines lesen wird, ohne sich an ein Haus zu erinnern, wo es ebenso zugehe, wie es in dem Exempel beschrieben wird.
Ältern, die ganz roh sind, werden nun freylich dadurch nicht gebessert werden, sie werden das Buch voll Unwillen weglegen, schimpfen, und in der verkehrten Art, die Kinder zu behandeln, fortfahren. Für

diese habe ich aber auch nicht geschrieben. Das gan-
zu Buch ist in einem scherzhaften Tone abgefaßt;
nicht deswegen, als wenn ich glaubte, daß die Thorheiten, von denen ich rede, unbedeutende, belachens-
würdige Kleinigkeiten wären . . . deswegen schrieb
ich vielmehr scherzhaft, damit ich desto mehr Leser
herbeylocken und ihnen im Scherz Wahrheiten sagen
könnte, die den mehrsten so nützlich , so unentbehr-
lich sind, damit auch diese das Büchelchen lesen
möchten, die nicht genug Geduld haben, einen ernst-
haften Vortrag auszuhalten." (296)

   "[Ich habe] nicht für den unreifen, sondern für
den gebildeten, auf die Verirrungen des menschlichen Herzens schon aufmerksam gemachten Jüngling geschrieben." (347)[18]

Also (234), (375).

5. Other introductions are addressed to the reader:

   "Mich däucht, die Warnungen, die Sie, meine jungen
Freundinnen, hier lesen, sind Warnungen, die in unser
Zeitalter gehören. Schon viele beweinten ein durch
Leichtsinn oder Schwärmerey verscherztes und zernich-
tetes Glück.--Aber wie? werden Sie, meine Lieben, die-
se Matronen-Moral auch nicht ungern von einem jungen
Mädchen hören?--Doch warum sollten Sie das? . . ."
(385)

   "Werdet wohl sehen, daß es in diesem noch mehr als
im ersten [Bande] mein Bestreben ist, nicht bloß zu
unterhalten, sondern auch zu nüzzen, und müßt's mir
eben nicht übel nehmen, wenn ich manchmal etwas frey
von der Leber spreche." (383)

   "Liebe Freunde, nicht wahr, ihr wollet durch dieses Buch verständiger werden? Ja, und besser soll
euch dieses Buch auch machen. Dazu ist es geschrieben, und gedruckt worden. Es kömmt vieles darin vor,
was eine Kenntnis berichtigen kann." (210)[19]

Also (76), (119), (211), (212), (224), (276), (296),

(370), (371), (383), (386).

---

[18]Ibid., LIV, 43-44.   [19]Ibid., LXXVII, 234.

6. An occasional introduction tries to provoke the

reader:

> "So viel ist ein Kopf werth, wenn man auch nichts
> weiter damit anzufangen weiß, als man den Hut darauf
> setzt. Weiß man aber das, was im Kopfe steckt, recht
> zu gebrauchen, so ist er noch weit mehr werth. Dann
> kann man sich alles verschaffen, was man bedarf,
> kann die ganze Welt als sein Eigenthum ansehen, und
> lächeln über alle, die reich und mächtig sind, und
> das, was im Kopfe steckt, nicht zu gebrauchen wis-
> sen.--
> Um nun zu zeigen, wie man seinen Kopf gebrauchen
> kann, und wieviel man auszurichten vermag, wenn man
> ihn recht zu gebrauchen weiß, gebrauchte ich meinen
> eigenen Kopf, setzte mich hin, und schrieb die Ge-
> schichte E. Haberfelds, der, durch den guten Gebrauch,
> den er von seinem Kopf machte, aus einem Bauer ein
> Freyherr wurde. Wer einen Kopf hat, der lese sie."
> (377)

> "Reich an unerwarteten Begebenheiten und romanhaf-
> ten Überraschungen ist dieses Buch nicht; ich gestehe
> aber, daß es weniger meine Absicht gewesen, durch
> kleine Autor-Künste die Aufmerksamkeit solcher Men-
> schen zu fesseln, die nur amüsiert seyn wollen, als
> vielmehr . . . ernsthafte, oft nicht ganz beherzig-
> te Wahrheiten in ein ganz gefälliges Gewand zu hül-
> len; nützlichen Grundsätzen auf diese Weise allgemei-
> nern Cours zu verschaffen; mein Schärflein zum fei-
> nern Studium practischer Weltklugheit beyzutragen,
> und meine Mitbrüder aufmerksam auf manche, zuweilen
> flüchtig übersehene Seiten ihres Herzens zu machen."
> (372)

7. One introduction is a dedication:

> "Die Briefe an Lina, welche ich zu den Füßen Ih-
> res [Eurer Kaiserlichen Maiestät] geheiligten Throns
> niederlege, haben durch den Beyfall der Kenner das
> Gepräge des Werths der Nützlichkeit erhalten." (224)

8. This introduction explains the genre Moralische Er-

zählung:

> "Von der poetischen Erzählung unterscheidet sich

254

die moralische, seinen [des Verfassers] Grundsätzen
nach, durch den bestimmten Zweck, ein Interesse zu
erwecken, das mehr in Aufklärung des Verstandes, in
Bildung der Vernunft, als in Spannung des Herzens
und der Imagination seinen Grund hat. Mit der unterhaltenden Erzählung in Prosa, dem kleinen Roman,
hat sie zwar manches gemein, zum Beyspiel die Sittengemälde, den historischen Styl, selbst die Absicht der Belehrung; dabey aber doch auch das Eig-
ne, daß sie ganz ausdrücklich darauf ausgeht, eine
für die Sitten wichtige Wahrheit, einen Lehrsatz
aus der Philosophie für die Welt durch die erdichtete Begebenheit zu versinnlichen. Hierdurch nähert
sie sich zwar der Fabel, dem Apolog, und der Allego-
rie; diese scheinen aber, ihrer größern Einfachheit
wegen, mehr zu Anfängern in der Lebensweisheit zu reden; hingegen die moralische Erzählung ist besonders
bequem, gebildeten Menschen in verwickelten und sel-
tenen Lagen anschaulichen eindringlichen Rath zu er-
teilen, und solche Charaktere zu entwickeln, die nicht
durch allgemein bekannte Gründe ihre, Jedem auffallen-
de, Bestimmung erhalten haben. Unter den Erfordernis-
sen dieser Gattung ist das erste Wahrheit und Über-
einstimmung in den Charakteren und Sitten. In Rücksicht der Begebenheiten vertritt Wahrscheinlichkeit
die Stelle der Wahrheit. Der Verfasser hatte übrigens durchaus nicht die Absicht, in seinen Erzählungen individuelle Personen und Lagen zu schildern;
auch erklärt er sich für einen Feind aller schwärme-
rischen Empfindsamkeit. Er arbeitet mehr für den Verstand und für die Vernuft, als für die Phantasie und
das Herz.--'Der Künstler muß bey mir dem Geschäffts-
mann, und dem Forscher durchaus untergeordnet blei-
ben; und ich lese weit mehr Akten und Lehrbücher, als
schön geschriebene Werke.'" (283)[20]

9. One introduction gives simple rules for reading:

"So oft man dieses Buch wieder von der Hand legt,
muß man die Stelle, bei welcher man aufhörte, wohl
anmerken. Man legt nämlich ein Papierlein, oder ein
vom Buchhändler angeheftetes Bändlein entzwischen,
damit man das nächste Mal gleich weiß, wo man fort-
zufahren hat." (210)[21]

---

[20]Ibid., LXIV, 364-365.   [21]Ibid., LXXVII, 234.

10. One introduction is a poem:

"Dies Buch ist mit Bedacht
Für Jung und Alte so gemacht,
Daß, wer es liest und darnach thut,
Verstand, Gesundheit, guten Muth
Erhält und wohl ein reicher Mann
Nach dessen Vorschrift werden kann.
Zur Lust für Kind und Kindeskind
Viel schöne Bilder drinnen sind,
Wohlfeilen Preises ist es auch[22]
Deshalben kauf es und gebrauch
Es fleißiglich in Fried und Ruh;
Gott gebe das Gedeihn dazu." (86)

11. One book, not included in the bibliography, does not

have an introduction:

"Da keine Vor- oder Nachrede von dem Plane und der
eigentlichen Bestimmung dieses Büchleins Nachricht
giebt, so läßt sich darüber nichts bestimmtes urthei-
len."[23]

C. The book itself

1. Allegorical names appear not only in the titles, but

also in the stories:

Herr von Mildenheim (85); Wilhelm Denker (86); teacher

Trauter (235); coachman Braus, Frau Friedliebin, inn-

keeper Wüterich, hypochondriac Heilberg, Frau Huld-

richin (376); Herr Harpax [lat. n. harpargo: "extor-

tionist"; lat. vb. "to rob," "to plunder"] (296),

(376); Herr Piger [lat. adj. "lazy"] (296); Meister

---

[22]"Sechs gute Groschen oder 27 Kreutzer rheinisch."

[23]Review of Gallerie der vorzüglichsten Künste und
Handwerker. Ein lehrreiches und unterhaltendes Bilderbuch
für die Jugend (Zürich: Trachsler, 1804) in Neue Allgemeine Deutsche Bibliothek, Vol. XCVI, p. 173.

Derb (378); drillsergeant Sackermenter, Junker Blut-
fink (377); hypochondriac Weichlich (296); Vogt Ehrlich, Vogt Schlacker (289); Pastors Wohlgemuth (86),
Friedlieb, Gutmann (376), Ehrmann (372), Fröhlich (71),
Nimmsweg (179), Frommfried (164) and Gutheim (280);
Doctors Ehrenmann (210), Süß, Mark and Sinn (121c);
Dümmler, Drangsturm (121c); farmer Fröhlich (243);
traveler Freeland (103), father Liebethat (296),
teacher Güte (71); Lottchen Früh, "ein zwölfjähriges
Mädchen mit allen den Vorzügen des Leibes und der Seele begabt." (179)

2. The setting of some educational novels is a real
town:
Berlin (348), (387), (100); Paris (137), (371); Ried
(190);
or a country:
Holland (378); Africa (234); America (133), (103);
Surinam (381); Turkey (75); France (67); Switzerland
(2), (15), (188), (263), (276), (371), (387).
Others take pleace in a fictional village:
Altenheim (390); Alteck (389); Fröhlichhausen (350);
Goldenthal (388); Langenhausen (308), (309); Mildheim
(85), (86); Traubenheim (308), (309).

3. The form
a) Some novels of education contain chiefly dialogue

between the teacher and the taught, father and son, mother and daughter, aunt and niece, pastor and farmer:[24]

"In einer ungekünstelten Sprache geben hier Erzählungen, Gespräche und kleine Schauspiele jungen Gemüthern Stimmung für Gutmüthigkeit, mitleidiges Wohlthun und Religiosität." (38)[25]

"[Das Buch] liefert Unterredungen eines Vaters mit seinen Kindern über die feine Lebensart." (200)[26]

"[Der Verfasser] hat durch den Erzählungston, durch Unterredungen, in welchen Fragen mit Beyspielen und Geschichten wechseln, seinen Zweck, verständlich zu werden, und der Wahrheit Eingang zu verschaffen, vollkommen erreicht." (205)[27]

"Kleine belehrende Vorfälle und Gespräche." (207)[28]

" . . . darüber giebt es denn . . . ein Gespräch." (208)[29]

"Der Verfasser hat seinen Unterricht in Dialoge eingekleidet . . . .: 'Lehrer: Wenn Kinder ihren Altern bey ihren Geschäfften gern helfen und dienen wollen, mit welchen Dingen werden sie wohl anfangen müssen? Schüler: Mit solchen, die nicht zu schwer für sie sind, und zu denen sie eben Kräfte genug haben. Lehrer: Wenn z.B. ein Knabe von zehn Jahren schon den Pflug am Acker regieren wollte, um dadurch seinem Vater einen Dienst zu erweisen?

---

[24] Such dialogues "locken dem anderen sie wahre Meinung ab," because "der Lehrer fängt bei gleichgültigen Sachen an und führt durch Urtheile des Kindes zum Keim." (Christian Gotthilf Salzmann, Über die wirksamsten Mittel Kindern Religion beyzubringen [Leipzig, 1787], p. 145).

[25] Neue Allgemeine Deutsche Bibliothek, Vol. VII, p. 291.

[26] Ibid., LIX, 224.   [27] Ibid., XXXVI, 62.

[28] Ibid., XCI, 443.   [29] Ibid., LXXXII, 256.

<u>Schüler</u>: So würde er seine Absicht nicht erreichen: denn er würde doch keine ordentliche Furche zu wege bringen.'" (343)[30]

"Der Schauspiele oder dramatischen Erzählungen sind zwey: Der zerbrochene Wasserkrug, und der Waise." (360f/g)[31]

". . . eine dramatisierte Scene . . ."(360h)[32]

" . . . worin passende Gesänge, Unterredungen und Anreden des Lehrers abwechseln." (189a)[33]

"Man unterhalte sich mit Kindern über sinnliche Gegenstände, die in ihrem Gesichtskreise liegen und ihre Verstandeskräfte nicht übersteigen. Die Abhandlungen sind durchaus praktisch und enthalten solche Gespräche, als Muster [(189a)]. Das Gespräch ist durchaus den Fähigkeiten der Kinder angemessen, und hat ohnfehlbar beygetragen, die Kinder auf die Verwahrungsmittel gegen die Krankheit [die Ruhr] aufmerksam zu machen." (189b)[34]

"Es sind Erzählungen und Gespräche 50." (17)[35]

"Worin besteht nun diese Form [des Buches]? Es ist die Gesprächsform. Dieß erste Bändchen enthält 16 Gespräche. . . . Diese Gespräche . . . laufen immer zwischen einem Pfarrer und einem Richter, der vermuthlich ein bloßer Bauer seyn soll, weil der Prediger ihn immer nur mit Er nennt." (338)[36]

"nur die ewige Einkleidung in Gespräche zwischen Vater und Lehrer und Kindern, die zu manchem müßigen Wortwechsel Anlaß giebt, nutzt sich, wie mich dünkt, nachgeradezu sehr ab." (282)[37]

---

[30]<u>Ibid</u>., LXVIII, II, 642.   [31]<u>Ibid</u>., XIII, 449.

[32]<u>Ibid</u>., XV, 179   [33]<u>Ibid</u>., LXII, 467.

[34]<u>Ibid</u>., LXXV, 547.   [35]<u>Ibid</u>., XXIX, 50.

[36]<u>Ibid</u>., XXXIII, 331.   [37]<u>Ibid</u>., XVIII, 107.

"Das Buch würde sich angenehmer lesen lassen,
wenn der Verfasser den geschmacklosen Gespräch-
ton und das Er, womit der Kalendermann seinen
August unterrichtet, abgeschafft hätte." (337)[38]

Also (17), (76), (89), (94),(102), (181), (234),

(235), (276), (294b), (308), (327), (375), (379).

b) A few educational books, readers, almanachs and

yearbooks contain fables with animal protagonists:

"Die Beyspiele der Weisheit und Tugend, und die
morgenländischen Fabeln, sind der beste Theil dieser Sammlung." (4)[39]

"Darauf folgen: moralische Dichtungen und Fabeln; ohnstreitig der schätzbarste Theil des
Buchs. Die Fabeln selbst werden gewiß den Kindern
viel Vergnügen machen, und die darin liegende Moral ist entweder kurz angegeben, oder läßet sich
leicht finden." (117)[40]

"Alle Erzählungen und Fabeln, welche in diesem
Buche enthalten sind, zielen auf Verbesserung
des Herzens, auf würkliche Belehrung ab . . . Das
Ganze ist in zwey Abtheilungen getheilt; in der
ersten sind die Fabeln und Erzählungen enthalten,
deren Sittenlehre hauptsächlich für das jugendliche Alter paßt; in der zweyten aber diejenigen,
aus welchen auch Erwachsene eine gute Lehre schöp-
fen können." (118)[41]

"Auch hier wechseln moralische Erzählungen, Fabeln, Feenmärchen, Träume mit allerley Anweisungen,
Lebensmaximen, und Recepte für Küche und Haushalt
ab, und gewöhnen eine hierher gehörige, zwar sehr
bunte, bisweilen tändelnde; aber doch größtentheils gemeinnützige Lektüre." (186)[42]

---

[38]Ibid., XCVI, 490.   [39]Ibid., CI, 392.

[40]Ibid., LXIX, 247.   [41]Ibid., LXII, 470.

[42]Ibid., LIV, 190.

"Zehn Fabeln in Prosa und Versen." (207)[43]

"Den Beschluß machen acht lehrreiche Fabeln."
(248)[44]

"[Daphne und Phöbus ist] eine sehr glückliche
Umarbeitung dieser bekannten Fabel, die dadurch
am Lehrreichen und Interessanten nicht wenig gewonnen hat." (283c)[45]

"Die Compilation enthält 175 ganz gut gewähl-
te Fabeln in Prosa und Versen." (367)[46]

One might also include the Krebsbüchlein (296)

though its main characteristic is satire like

Swift's Gulliver's Travels.

Also (38), (110), (359).

c) Although most novels of education contain an oc-

casional letter, some of them are actually epis-

tolary novels:

"Nach dem Titel erwartete Recensent in diesem
Buche Briefe pädagogischen oder moralischen In-
halts, die etwa zwischen Auguste und Hieronimus
gewechselt worden wären. Allein er fand bey nähe-
rer Untersuchung nichts mehr und nichts weniger
als einen Roman, in die jetzt beliebte Briefform
gefaßt." (6)[47]

"Der gesunden Vernunft wird an dem Briefwechsel
mit einem, ihr, wie es scheint, sehr fremden Menschen wenig gelegen seyn. Indessen ahnet der Herr
Briefschreiber nicht; vielmehr erklärt er mit
großer Selbstzufriedenheit, er habe die Absicht,
durch diese Briefe die Thoren zu züchtigen und
zur Vernunft zu führen." (11)[48]

---

[43]Ibid., XCI, 444. [44]Ibid., XXXI, 188.

[45]Ibid., LXIV, 364. [46]Ibid., XLIX, 264.

[47]Ibid., XXXV, 98. [48]Ibid., XII, 485-6.

"Ein Theil der nachstehenden Briefe war bereits
schon in der Monatsschrift Flora genannt, abge-
druckt, und hier finden nun die Leser die ganze
abgeschlossene Fortsetzung derselben, und werden
die auf ihre Durchlesung verwandte Zeit wohl nicht
zu bereuen Ursache haben. Obgleich der Ton dieser
herzlichen und lehrreichen Episteln nicht überall
anziehend und ästhetisch schön geformt ist, auch
hier und da durch Wiederholungen etwas eintönig
wird: so herrscht doch durchs Ganze ein lichtvol-
ler, überzeugender Vortrag, und ein Reichthum
von Menschenkenntniß, den man ja in unsern frosti-
gen und gespannten--leider! nur so genannten Er-
ziehungsromanen unserer wortreichen Literatur so
selten antrifft." (13)[49]

"Das Ganze ist, wahrscheinlich aus Bequemlich-
keit für den Autor, in Briefe abgetheilt, und diese sind an ein Frauenzimmer, Henriette, gerichtet,
die unter diesem Namen eine Vertheidigung der Leipziger Damen geschrieben hat." (35)[50]

"Diese Briefe verrathen eine sichere, und geüb-
te Hand, Bekanntschaft mit dem menschlichen Herzen und der Welt, und das edelste Gefühl für Liebe und Freundschaft." (70)[51]

"Herr F[röbing] . . . hat bey diesen Briefen,
deren einige bereits in seinem Volkslehrer mit
Vergnügen gelesen worden sind, die Absicht, leere
Stunden nützlich auszufüllen, und unvermerkt gute
Entschließungen zu erwecken." (146)[52]

"Herr C[laudius] hat seine Nachlese in 25 Send-
schreiben zertheilt, und solche einem Vater an
den Sohn in die Feder dictiert. Was die Briefform
betrifft, muß man ja nicht glauben, daß die 25
Stücke eben so viele verschiedene Gesichtspunkte
oder Absonderungen enthalten. Die meisten sind
nichts als Fortsetzung über einzelne Fälle; und
nicht selten kommt im 20ten der Verf[asser] auf
eben den Punkt zurück, der schon im 10ten hinrei-
chend von ihm war erörtert worden." (105)[53]

---

[49] Ibid., LXXXIX, 498.

[50] Ibid., LXXVII, 270.

[51] Ibid., XXVIII, 308.

[52] Ibid., XXXIX, 275.

[53] Ibid., XXXV, 276.

"[Einige brave **Schulmänner**] hätten sich ein
Buch gewünscht, das hauptsächlich zur Besserung
und Bildung des Herzens abzwecke, ohne durch
trockene moralische Aufsätze den jungen Leser
von der Lectüre derselben abzuschrecken; deswegen müße es zuvörderst erdichtete moralische
Dichtungen enthalten, weil die Fiction die beste Lehrerin für die lebhafte jugendliche Fan-
tasie sei." (217)[54]

"[Die Schrift] enthält 17 Briefe eines Vaters
an seinen Sohn, der schon über die Kinder- und
Knabenjahre hinweg ist, und jetzt im Begriff
steht, das väterliche Haus zu verlassen, um sich
einem Geschäffte zu widmen." (197)[55]

"Ein junger Graf beschreibt in einer Reihe von
Briefen die Geschichte seiner Liebe gegen die
Tochter seines Verwalters." (219a)[56]

"Der Verfasser hat diesmal zu beyden die Briefform gewählt, wodurch, bey der ersten wenigstens,
nicht die Geschichte selbst, sondern die Bogen-
zahl des Buches gewonnen hat." (219e/f)[57]

"Die Briefform trägt hier etwas bey, die ver-
schiedenen Charaktere abstechender zu zeichnen;
zerreißt aber doch den Faden der Geschichte, den
der erzählende Ton in lichterm Zusammenhange würde haben forlaufen lassen." (219f)[58]

"Diese Briefe . . . liefern, von eben so fester
als feiner Hand gezeichnet das äußerst interessante Bild einer geistreichen und edeln Frau, die
früh schon das Opfer ihrer Pflicht ward . . . und
als ein solches stirbt, wie sich es am Schlusse
dieser Briefe ergiebt." (270)[59]

"Dieß erzählt er seinem lieben Carl . . . und
theilt . . . ihm seine Gedanken in einer solchen
soliden Form mit, daß, wenn man die Apostrophe,
lieber Carl! in eine andere, andächtiger Zuhörer!
verwandelt, einige Briefe sogleich für Predigten
gelten können; die meisten aber das vollkommene
Ansehen der Aufsätze in den ehemaligen beliebten

---

[54]_Ibid._, XL, 188. [55]_Ibid._, XXIV, 103.
[56]_Ibid._, XIV, 501. [57]_Ibid._, XLII, 357.
[58]_Ibid._, XLII, 359. [59]_Ibid._, LV, 143-4.

Wochenschriften haben." (285)[60]

"Wer die Liebe in ihren natürlichen Wirkungen, nicht aber in Thorheit und Wahnsinn ausgeartet zu sehen wünscht, der wird gewiß diesen in Briefen und Dialogen eingekleideten Roman nicht ohne Unterhaltung durchblättern." (345)[61]

"Um die Geschichte des armen Herrn von Mildenburg die Trockenheit zu benehmen, und die Leser gegen die Langeweile zu waffnen, welche nothwendig durch das Winseln und Klagen meines Helden, bey allen seinen selbst geschaffenen Leiden, hätte entstehen müssen, wählte ich die Form, diesen Roman in Briefe abzufassen, in der Hoffnung, daß die Abwechselung des Styles einen Theil jener Unvollkommenheiten heben sollte." (372)

Also (37), (219k), (220a), (224), (279b), (290b), (371).

d) Although the dramatic form of presenting characters is not uncommon in the seventeenth century Gesprächsspiele and review journals (Thomasius, Freimüthige, lustige und ernsthaffte, jedoch vernunfft- und gesetzmäßige Gedanken oder Monats-Gespräche über allerhand, fürnehmlich aber neue Bücher [Halle, 1690ff];[62] and Gundling, Neue Bibliothek [1709-1721][63]), the first German "dramatic novel" is said to have been Hase's Gustav Aldermann (1780).

---

[60]Ibid., XXVIII, 60.   [61]Ibid., XIV, 483.

[62]Joachim Kirchner, Das Deutsche Zeitschriftenwesen, seine Geschichte und seine Probleme (Wiesbaden, Otto Harrassowitz, 1958), Vol. I, p. 40.

[63]Ibid., 41.

Many novels of education occasionally proceed by
dialogue, but a few educational novelists also
use the dramatic form throughout the book:

"Hipparinius, Sohn des Dion stellt die Wirkungen übertriebener Strenge gegen einen jungen Wüstling, der jedoch noch nicht alles Gefühl für das Gute ertödtet hat, in dramatischer
Form dar." (253a)[64]

". . . aber es ist nicht weniger nützlich,
durch die muntere dramatisirte Darstellung des
Spiels und der Folgen des Betrugs und Aberglau-
bens." (145)[65]

"[Die Verfasserin] thut dieses durch dialogi-
sirte Sprüchwörter, die in einem gewissen Zusammenhange stehen." (251a-h)[66]

"Die letzte seiner [des Verfassers] Erzählungen
ist von ihm dialogisirt worden, und ein kleines
Drama daraus entstanden." (88)[67]

"Worinn besteht diese Form? Es ist die Gesprächsform." (338)[68]

"Selten ist ein Gerichte für alle Gaumen, und
ein Buch für alle Stände. Es ist hier Hausmanns-
kost, von lauter unschädlichen, mitunter auch
nahrhaften Ingredienzen; nur mit einer langen
Brühe, die auch wohl ihre Liebhaber findet, aber
doch nicht nach jedermanns Geschmack ist. Der
Stoff ist theils aus erdichteten Situationen,
theils aus wahren und entlehnten Geschichten her-
beygeschafft. Das alles ist dialogisiert und dra-
matisiert." (147)[69]

---

[64]Neue Allgemeine Deutsche Bibliothek, Vol. LXII,
p. 552.

[65]Ibid., XL, 275.   [66]Ibid., LXXIX, 223.

[67]Ibid., XLIX, 116.   [68]Ibid., XXXIII, 330.

[69]Ibid., XXXIII, 406.

"Gleich die erste mitunter dramatisirte Erzählung stellt die Geschichte einer Ehe dar."
(291)[70]

ē) Many educational fictions are biographies:

"In der Vorrede eifert [der Verfasser] gewaltig
gegen die übermäßige Romanlectüre unsrer Zeitge-
nossen, und fordert deutsche Gelehrte auf, statt
der Romane Biographien großer Männer zu schreiben,
und daher will er selbst einen Versuch mit der
biographischen Geschichte seines Armins machen,
aber der Versuch ist mißlungen."(5)[71]

"In frühester Jugend schon lernet der Held dieser Geschichte Branntwein saufen, und treibt es
so unbestraft fort, daß nach mehr als 50 Jahren
erst,--einen solchen Zeitraum wenigstens brauchen
seine Abentheuer--der Tod ihn dafür bestraft."
(185)[72]

"Für [Hülfsmittel zur Betriebsamkeit] hält der
ungenannte Verfasser nicht mit Unrecht die so bekannte Brevius per exempla, und will durch Le-
bensbeschreibungen solcher Individuen, die durch
anhaltende Thätigkeit aus dem Mangel sich zum
Überfluß haben Nacheiferungen zu erwecken suchen."
(40)[73]

"Diese kleine Schrift enthält die Biographien
von zehn Kaufleuten." (249)[74]

"In einer launigen Unterredung, welche der Verfasser mit seinen zwey Onkeln, dem Pfarrer und
Apotheker, hält, zeigt er den rechten Gesichts-
punkt, woraus er diesen Roman angesehen wissen
will, nämlich als eine Biographie, oder eine Darstellung der Charaktere, wie sie wirklich sind."
(288d)[75]

---

[70]Ibid., LXXIII, 67   [71]Ibid., IV, 512.

[72]Ibid., XXIX, 234.   [73]Ibid., LXXIV, 183.

[74]Ibid., CIII, 167.   [75]Ibid., LXXXVII, 54.

266

"'Zweifelt niemand, daß das Leben gut geschriebe-
ner Biographien gelehrter Männer und merkwürdiger
Beförderer der Wissenschaften studirender Jünglinge in mehr als einer Rücksicht großen Nutzen gewäh-
re: so giebt auch gewiß jeder gerne zu, daß nicht
alles, was selbst in den besten Lebensbeschreibun-
gen vorkommt, für alle gleich interessant ist und
daß es Jünglingen, so lange sie auf Schulen und
Universitäten den Wissenschaften obliegen, oder
als Kandidaten mehr für andere, als für sich und
ihre Studien leben, bald an Zeit und Gelegenheit,
bald an Gelde, bald an Einsicht fehlt, sich einen
wohlgewählten Apparat guter Biographien ausgezeich-
neter Menschen anzuschaffen, ihn zu lesen, und das
Wissenswürdigste daraus zu Bildung ihres Verstandes und Herzens, und zu glücklicher Betreibung der
Wissenschaften, welchen sie sich gewidmet haben,
zu verwenden.'" (57, Vorrede)[76]

"Dieser schwülstige Anfang einer wirklichen Lebensgeschichte schien dem Rec[ensent] nichts weniger als eine gute Vorbedeutung von der Schreibart des Verf[assers] zu seyn." (334)[77]

"Der Herausgeber dieser Sammlung hat, . . . so
mühsam es in der That ist, von einem Kaufmanne eine nützliche und interessante Biographie zu liefern, so gut hat er doch diese Schwierigkeit zu
bekämpfen gesucht." (349)[78]

Also (34), (43), (46), (89), (96), (109), (174),

(193), (216), (226), (263), (309), (340), (364).

f) One novelist introduces dialect:

"'Nehme he't mie nich öbbel, gnädiger Herre, det
sin luter Nierungen. Un kurt und gut, wat soll det?
Late he's bin Ollen!'" (384, pt. I, p. 167)

g) Others use slang and colloquial **language:**

"'Infamer Rakker, ochsendummer, du verfluchtes
Pack, ihr tausendsapperment'sches Zeug.' . . .

---

[76]Ibid., LXXIII, 461-2.   [77]Ibid., I, 271.

[78]Ibid., XXIX, 51-52.

Plitz, Platz, hast du nicht gesehen--karbatschen,
daß sie Baumöl geben mögen--nach Nothen durch-
hauen--Hiebe aus dem Salz bekommen, usw." (338)[79]

"Nippernäpperey; zusammenhabern; Kömmst endlich
Parischen; du Fillig; daß dich alle Kobolde."
(261)[80]

"Glimmernde Laffen, junge Lecker." (36a)[81]

"Unedle Ausdrücke wie schnacken, gnötteln, er-
kuppeln sollten billig in einer für die Jugend bestimmten Schrift mit vorzüglicher Sorgfalt vermie-
den werden." (151)[82]

"Er schimpfte wie ein Rohrsperling, er schalt
den Bedienten einen Eselskopf, das Kammermädchen
eine verdammte Tschruphel." (156)[83]

h) Some novels of education are satires:

"Die Satyre ist treffend, ohne Personalität,
und die kleinen Streifereyen inns Gebiet der Moral fallen nirgends in einen ermüdenden Prediger-
ton." (10)[84]

"Dieses Buch wimmelt gleichsam von kleinen abge-
rissenen Zeichnungen großer und kleiner Narren un-
term Monde; aber der ächte Geist der Satyre wohnt
nicht in ihm. . . . Unser Verf[asser] zählt fast
auf jedem Blatte seines sogenannten satyrischen
Romanes die Fehler und Schwächen der Menschen mit
ernster bisweilen zu ernster Stimme auf; aber das
Lächerliche mit der subtilen Geißel der Satyre
hervorzuheben, und den weisen Lacher zu unterhalten, versteht er wenig." (33)[85]

"Wie der Titel des Buches, so auch sein Inhalt,
derbe, handfeste Satyre, in Form und Ton. [Der
Verfasser] verschmäht auch das Gemeinste nicht,
sobald es auch nur seinem Spotte dient, und dieser Spott ist größtentheils plump und unmanier-
lich."(269)[86]

---

[79]Ibid., XXXIII, 333.

[80]Ibid., CII, 360.

[81]Ibid., LXXIII, 548.

[82]Ibid., LXVII, 258.

[83]Ibid., XCVIII, 86.

[84]Ibid., XCII, 91.

[85]Ibid., XLVII, 328.

[86]Ibid., CIII, 224-5.

"Daß der Verf[asser] es durchweg auf Ironie an-
legte, sieht man freylich, und schon auf dem Ti-
telblatte; nicht jeder Gegenstand aber ist deren
empfänglich, und eine mehr als alphabetlange Ironie gehört unter die langweiligsten Dinge, die
sich denken lassen. Nicht ironisch, sondern plump
benimmt sich Wenzel bey Auswiegelung der Bauern,
in seiner Antwort an den würdigen Geistlichen, in
der Bittschrift an den desto unwürdigern Kirchen-
patron." (43)[87]

"Mit noch ganz glimpflich angelegter Geissel
der Satyre, wird die schnellfahrende und reitende
Race in volkreichen Städten in diesen Bogen ge-
züchtiget." (41)[88]

"Was die darin vorkommenden persönlichen Saty-
ren und die Anspielungen auf einige neuere Welt-
begebenheiten betrifft: so gehört die Beurtheilung
lung derselben nicht vor unser Forum." (50)[89]

"[Die Abentheuer und Liebesgeschichten] ereignen sich viel zu natürlich, und sind überhaupt dem
(wenn der Rec[ensent] so sagen darf,) satyrisch-
didaktischem Zwecke des Verf[assers] nur untergeordnet." (58)[90]

"[Der Verfasser] parodiert und persifliert nämlich darinn die gewöhnlichen Horoscope und Pro-
gnostica der Calender. . . . Dergleichen Ironie
und seynsollenden Witz, wäre er auch etwas weniger schaal als er hier ist, verfehlt ganz seinem
Zwecke." (176)[91]

"Menschenkenntniß, richtiger Blick ins weibliche Herz, Laune, Witz und glückliches Talent zur
Satyre zeichnen den Verf[asser] vortheilhaft aus."
(92)[92]

Also (42), (167), (296), (309).

---

[87]Ibid., LXVII, 329.

[88]Ibid., XLIX, 406.

[89]Ibid., XXIV, 93.

[90]Ibid., LXXXII, 395-60.

[91]Ibid., XX, 276-7.

[92]Ibid., CI, 169.

i) Good and bad models in the same story emphasize

   the right and the wrong paths by contrast:

   "Den Pfarrer Cornelius gewinnt man lieb. . . .
Er gewinnt viel, da er in Contrast mit einem ge-
wissen Ehren Beyerus gesetzt ist, der als ein
Schriftgelehrter von gewöhnlichem Schrot und
Korn auftritt." (262)[93]

   "Daß [der Freund des kurierten Spielers], durch
eine ähnliche Leidenschaft hingerissen, zu einem
niedrigen Diebstahle, und endlich zum Selbstmorde
verleitet wird, scheint als ein Theaterkunstgriff
benutzt zu seyn, um dem Schlusse der Erzählung
mehr Eindruck und Anziehung zu verschaffen."
(290a)[94]

   "[Herr Pfarrer Schlez] schildert uns hier in
Schlaghart und Richard zwey Dorfschullehrer von
entgegengesetzten Charakter und Werth. Dieser ist
ein würdiger, schätzbarer Mann; jener ein Tölpel
in aller Absicht. Beyder Lebensgeschichte, Charakter, Lebensart, Amtsführung, Betragen in verschie-
denen Verhältnissen werden . . . auf das lehr-
reichste verwebt und dargestellt." (309)[95]

   "Alle diese Charaktere sind so vortheilhaft gezeichnet, daß man an ihrem Gemälde beinahe keinen
Flecken gewahr wird. . . . Dagegen sind nun die
entgegen stehenden Charaktere eines jungen Grafen
von Lenz . . . u.s.f. so äußerst schlecht, daß
sie eher eingefleischten Teufeln als Menschen ähn-
lich sahen." (6)[96]

Also (98a), (131), (139), (181), (294a), (308),

(310d), (369), (388).

j) Some educational novels use the first person nar-

   ration:

   "'Das Dutzen ist in der Welt stark Mode, etc.

---

[93] Ibid., IX, 26.

[94] Ibid., LXIII, 302.

[95] Ibid., XXIII, 55.

[96] Ibid., XXXV, 99.

Nur Geduld! die erste Nacht; ja ja die Braut-
nacht, ich weiß es noch von Alters her, bringt
gemeiniglich das liebe Du zuwege (S. 30). Hatte
ich für keine Reparatur zu sorgen, und es war
Sommer, so strickte ich, was das Zeug halten
wollte.'(S. 42)" (326)[97]

Also (43), (137), (287), (295), (358), (377),

(380), (387).

k) Few authors appear as authors amidst their char-

acters:

" . . . Man verzeihe mir hin und wieder eine kleine Anmerkung; ich möchte nicht, daß dies Buch bloß
unterhalten, sondern es auch nutzen und dem Men-
schenkenner manchen Wink geben möge." (383, p. 38-9)

" . . . Es gefällt mir doch nicht so ganz vom
Herrn Burck, daß er schon als Student so trefflich
für die Zukunft sorgte. Es wäre dann, wenn er ein
Ämtchen gehabt hätte, auch noch Zeit gewesen, sich
eine Geliebte zu wählen. Merkt euch das, ihr Herren
Studenten und Kandidaten, ihr seid in dem Falle
manchmal sehr übereilt und voreilig.--Es ist mein
völliger Ernst, ich bin sehr unzufrieden damit,
und will mir's von meinen hochgeehrten Herren Söh-
nen stark ausbitten, sich nicht eher nach den hüb-
schen Mädchen umzusehen, bis sie im Stande sind,
eine zu wählen, und auch hübsch zu ernähren."
(369, p. 26-7)

Also (96), (275), (284), (344), (379).

D. Plagiarisms

"Der Unfug, den man seit einiger Zeit mit Büchertiteln
treibt, wird in Wahrheit doch gar zu arg! Womit meint der
Leser wohl, dass er obrigen Küchenzettel zu Folge, hier
bewirtet werde?--Mit nichts anderm als der bekannten Leo-
poldine des Herrn Schulz, der ein geschmackloser Sudel-
koch das Blut abzapft, und ihr Mark ausgesaugt hat, Haut
und Knochen aber, als eine für Kinder überaus gesunde
Nahrung, dem heranwachsenden Publiko aufdringen will." (1)[98]

---

[97]Ibid., IX, 117.   [98]Ibid., VI, 508.

"Dieses Buch ist blos ein Nachdruck von des Herrn geheimen Kirchenraths Seiler Lesebuch für den Bürger und Landmann, den der famose Nachdrucker Strobel in München besorgt hat." (8)[99]

"Nur der erste Abschnitt . . . gehört der Verfasserinn eigenthümlich. Alles übrige ist aus Rousseau's neuer Heloise entlehnt. . . . Wer also Rousseau's neue Heloise, allenthalben auch nur in der Cramer'schen Übersetzung besitzt, und daraus die Briefe (namentlich den 20ten des 3ten Theils, den 10. und 11ten des 4ten, den 2. und 3ten des 5ten Theils) nachlesen will, dem wird die Julie Wolmar unsers Verfassers, bis auf Nr. 1, sehr entbehrlich seyn. Billig hätte diese Entlehnung aus R. auf dem Titel deutlich angezeigt werden sollen." (37)[100]

"Diese Anzeige war schon niedergeschrieben, als wir entdeckten, daß die Menschheit in besonderen Zügen bloß ein neuer Umschlag für ein Buch ist, das den Titel hat Eduard von Wallers Briefe an seinen Freund, oder der reisende Philosoph (Augsburg: akademische Handlung, 1791). So etwas sollte doch wohl jedesmal, um die Käufer vor Schaden zu hüten, auf dem Tittelblatt oder dessen Rückseite bemerkt werden, und der Freyherr von Reichlin . . . hätte recht gethan, sogleich gegen eine so unredliche Handlung des Verlegers zu protestieren." (285)[101]

"Eine Leihbibliothek des Ortes, wo der Rec[ensent] sich aufhält, setzte auch seine Vermuthung außer allen Zeifel. Das Buch fand sich, es heißt Julius, ein Seitenstück zu Guido von Sohnsdom, und erschien im Jahre 1798 zu Freyberg in der Crazischen Buchhandlung. Es hatte in dieser Gestalt zwey Theile, und die Haupthelldinn dieses Buches , die hier, statt Lottchen, Cordchen heißt, spielt eine weit schlüpfrige Rolle, und nimmt ein weit tragischeres Ende. Und unter gegenwärtiger Firma bekehrt sich Cordchen, und wird, nach ihren Verirrungen eine gute brave Hausfrau.
Wie soll Rec[ensent] sich nun dieses Erscheinen erklären? Vom Verf[asser] selbst kann sie kaum herrühren. Warum hätt' er uns wohl ein altes, bloß verändertes, bloß zusammengezogenes Buch für ein neues verkaufen, warum dem Helden desselben, ohne Zweck und Ziel, einen andern Namen geben, und das Alles verschweigen sollen?

---

[99] Ibid., XXII, 406. [100] Ibid., XCIV, 130.

[101] Ibid., XXVIII, 61.

Hat aber ein fremder Verf[asser] sich diese berufene
Freyheit genommen, so ist diese Unverschämtheit ohne
dergleichen, und der verkappte Schleichhändler verdient nicht nur des geplünderten Autors schärfste Ahn-
dung; auch Rec[ensent] muß erklären, daß dieser dop-
pelte Betrug, ein altes Buch, ohne alle Notiz, für ein
neues zu geben, und mit fremden Eigenthume so eigen-
mächtig zuverfahren, zu den schaamlosesten Taschenspie-
lerstreichen des Autorenhandwerks gehört." (303)[102]

Also (30), (79), (281), (348).

---

[102]Ibid., LXX, 355-6.

BIBLIOGRAPHY OF THE DISSERTATION

Novels

Anonymous. Launthal und Burks Jugendgeschichte. Augsburg:
       C. F. Bürgien [Bürglen?], 1795.

Adlerjung, Johann Ludwig. Unterhaltungen eines Lehrers mit
       seinen Schülern, in belehrenden und warnenden Er-
       zählungen, zum Unterrichte der erwachsenen Jugend
       beyderley Geschlechts. Prag und Leipzig: Widtmann,
       1792.

B., Ernst. Der Wechsel. Eine Morgenlectüre für geplagte
       Männer, deren Weiber gern ein X für ein U machen.
       Leipzig: Joachim, 1800.

Becker, Rudolph Zacharias. Noth- und Hülfsbüchlein für
       Bürger und Bauersleute, darin für den Bürger- und
       Bauernstand viel Nützliches, Angenehmes und Beleh-
       rendes verzeichnet steht. Grätz: Zaunrith, 1793.

_____. Noth- und Hülfsbüchlein. Oder lehrreiche Freuden-
       und Trauergeschichte der Einwohner zu Mildheim.
       Gotha: Becker, 1798.

Engel, Johann Jakob. Der Fürstenspiegel. Vol. III of J.J.
       Engels Schriften, Classiker-Ausgabe. Frankfurt:
       M.L.St.Goar, 1857.

_____. Herr Lorenz Stark. Ein Charaktergemälde. Vol. XII
       of J.J. Engels Schriften, Classiker-Ausgabe. Frank-
       furt: M.L.St. Goar, 1857.

_____. Der Philosoph für die Welt. Vols. I-II of J.J.
       Engels Schriften, Classiker-Ausgabe. Frankfurt:
       M.L. St. Goar, 1857.

Herrmann, Friedrich. Die Familie Angely. Eine Geschichte
       aus den Zeiten des französischen Revolutionskrie-
       ges. Lübben: Christian Traugott Gotsch, 1804.

Knigge, Adolf Freyherr von. Geschichte des armen Herrn
       von Mildenburg. 3 Theile. Hannover: Hahn, 1789-
       1797.

_____. Die Reise auf die Universität. Ein Seitenstück zu der Reise nach Braunschweig. Neuburg: Joachim, 1805.

Kraus, Ulrich. Klostergeschichten für Jünglinge und Mädchen. Freyburg, 1796.

_____. Neue Klostergeschichten. Frankfurt: Diez, 1799.

LaRoche, Sophie von. Briefe an Lina als Mutter. Ein Buch für junge Frauenzimmer, die ihr Herz und ihren Verstand bilden wollen. Leipzig: Gräff, 1795.

Lossius, Kaspar Friedrich. Gumal und Lina. Eine Geschichte für Kinder, zum Unterricht und Vergnügen, besonders um ihnen die ersten Religionsbegriffe beyzubringen. Erster bis dritter Theil. Neue Auflage. Gotha: Justus Perthes, 1809.

Lossius, Rudolph Christoph. Meister Liebreich. Ein nützliches Lesebuch für Volksschulen und bürgerliche Familien. 3 Theile. Gotha: Justus Perthes, 1800.

Meißner, August Gottlieb. Skizzen. 11. und 12. Sammlung. Leipzig: Dyk, 1796.

Meynier, Johann Heinrich. Kleine Geschichten zur Besserung und Veredlung jugendlicher Herzen. Neue Auflage. Nürnberg: Friedrich Campe, 1820.

Nicolai, Friedrich. Vertraute Briefe von Adelheit B** an ihre Freundinn Julie S**. Berlin und Stettin: Friedrich Nicolai, 1799.

Pestalozzi, Heinrich. Lienhard und Gertrud; ein Versuch die Grundsätze der Volksbildung zu vereinfachen. Ganz umgearbeitet. Zürich und Leipzig, 1790-1792.

Salzmann, Christian Gotthilf. Conrad Kiefer, oder Anweisung zu einer vernünftigen Erziehung der Kinder. Vol. IV of Salzmanns Werke. Stuttgart: Hoffmann'sche Verlagsbuchhandlung, 1845.

_____. Ausführliche Erzählung wie Ernst Haberfeld aus einem Bauer ein Freiherr geworden ist. Vol. VII of Salzmanns Werke. Stuttgart: Hoffmann'sche Verlagsbuchhandlung, 1845.

_____. Heinrich Glaskopf. Ein Unterhaltungsbuch für die Jugend. Vol. V of Salzmanns Werke. Stuttgart: Hoffmann'sche Verlagsbuchhandlung, 1845.

_____ .Heinrich Gottschalk in seiner Familie, oder erster Religionsunterricht für Kinder von 10 bis 12 Jahren. Vol. VI of Salzmanns Werke. Stuttgart: Hoffmann'sche Verlagsbuchhandlung, 1845.

_____ . Geschichte Simon Blaukohls. Vol. XI of Salzmanns Werke. Stuttgart: Hoffmann'sche Verlagsbuchhandlung, 1846.

_____ . Krebsbüchlein oder Anweisung zu einer unvernünftigen Erziehung der Kinder. Leipzig: Philipp Reclam jun., 1894.

_____ . Moralisches Elementarbuch nebst einer Anleitung zum nützlichen Gebrauch desselben. Erster Theil. Neue verbesserte Auflage. Leipzig: Siegfried Lebrecht Crusius, 1785.

_____ . Sebastian Kluge's Lebensgeschichte. Vol. XII of Salzmanns Werke. Stuttgart: Hoffmann'sche Verlagsbuchhandlung, 1846.

Schindler, Johann Carl Gottlob. Robert oder der Mann, wie er nicht seyn sollte. Ein Gegenstück zu Robert, der Mann, wie er seyn sollte. 3 Bände. Leipzig: Schladebach, 1800-1802.

Siede, Christian Friedrich. Raritäten von Berlin und merkwürdige Geschichten einiger Berlinischen Freudenmädchen auch dem unschuldigsten Mädchen lesbar. Zweyter Theil. Berlin: Christian Gottfried Schöne, 1794.

Schlez, Johann Ferdinand. Geschichte des Dörfleins Traubenheim. Für's Volk und für Volksfreunde. 2 vols. Nürnberg: Grattenauer, 1791-1792.

_____ . Geschichte des Dörfleins Traubenheim. Für's Volk und für Volksfreunde. Zum Gebrauche für Katholiken bearbeitet von einem Pfarrer in dem Herzogthum Neuburg. 2 vols. München: Deutscher Schulfonds-Bücherverlag am Rindermarkte, 1801.

_____ . Gregorius Schlaghart oder die Dorfschule zu Langenhausen. Nürnberg: Felseckersche Buchhandlung (Neudrucke Pädagogischer Schriften, Vol. II. Ed. Albert Richter. Leipzig: Richard Richter, 1890).

Sintenis, Johann Christian S. Hallo's glücklicher Abend.
     Zwey Theile. Frankfurt und Leipzig: Erich Flei-
     scher, 1786.

Spieβ, Christian Heinrich. Meine Reisen durch die Höhlen
     des Unglücks und die Gemächer des Jammers. 4 vols.
     Leipzig: Leo, 1796-1799.

Steinbeck, Christoph Gottlieb. Der aufrichtige Kalender-
     mann. Ein gar kurioses und nützliches Buch. Für
     die Jugend und den gemeinen Bürger und Bauers-
     mann. Gera: Rothe, 1792.

_____. Der hundertjährige Kalender oder Schnurpfeife-
     reien. Ein Volksbuch. Gera: Deutsche Volkszeitung
     und Wilhelm Heinsius, 1795.

Timme, Christian Friedrich. Faramonds Familiengeschichte
     in Briefen. 4 vols. 2d. ed. Erfurt: Keyser, 1782.

Unger, Friederike Helene. Julchen Grünthal. 3d. ed. Berlin:
     Unger, 1798.

Wahl, S. W. Adolphine. Leipzig: Gräff, 1794.

Wallenrodt, Johanna Isabella Eleonore. Fritz der Mann wie
     er nicht seyn sollte; die Folgen einer üblen Er-
     ziehung. 2 vols. Gera: Haller, 1800.

Wobeser, Wilhelmine Karoline von. Elisa oder das Weib wie
     es seyn sollte. Allen deutschen Mädchen und Weibern
     gewidmet. 3d. ed. Leipzig: Gräff, 1798.

Zschokke, Heinrich. Die Brannteweinpest. Eine Trauerge-
     schichte zur Warnung und Lehre für Reich und Arm,
     alt und jung. Vol. XV of H. Z.'s Novellen und Dich-
     tungen. 11th. ed. Aarau: Sauerländer, 1874.

_____ Das Goldmacherdorf. Eine anmuthige und wahrhafte Ge-
     schichte.Vol. XVI of H.Z.'s Novellen und Dichtungen.
     11th. ed. Aarau: Sauerländer, 1874.

_____. Das Loch im Ärmel. Vol. III of H.Z.'s Novellen
     und Dichtungen. 11th. ed. Aarau: Sauerländer, 1874.

_____. Meister Jordan, oder Handwerk hat goldenen Bo-
     den. Ein Feyerabend-Büchlein für Lehrlinge, ver-
     ständige Gesellen und Meister. Vol XIII of H.Z.'s
     Novellen und Dichtungen. 11th. ed. Aarau: Sauer-
     länder, 1874.

Other primary sources and reference books

Allgemeine Deutsche Bibliothek. Edited by Friedrich Nicolai.
    Vols. I, IV, VIII, LII and "Anhänge" to vols. XII,
    XXXVI and LXXXVI. Berlin: Friedrich Nicolai, 1765-
    1791.
    Edited by Carl Ernst Bohn. Vols. CVI and CVII.
    Kiel: Carl Ernst Bohn, 1792.

Germer, Helmut. "The German Novel of Education from 1792 to
    1805: A Bibliography." Unpublished Master's thesis,
    The Graduate School, Vanderbilt University, Nash-
    ville, Tennessee, 1965.

Holzmann, Michael, and Bohatta, Hanns. Deutsches Anonymen-
    Lexikon 1501-1850. 7 vols. Hildesheim: Georg Olms
    Verlagsbuchhandlung, 1961. Reprographic reprint of
    the Weimar edition 1902-1911.

Journal der Romane. Vol. I, Berlin: Johann Friedrich Unger,
    1800.

Kayser, Christian Gottlob. Index Locuplentissimus Librorum
    . . . Vollständiges Bücher-Lexicon enthaltend alle
    von 1750 bis zum Ende des Jahres 1832 in Deutsch-
    land gedruckte Bücher. Vols. I-III. Leipzig: Ludwig
    Schumann, 1834-1836.

Kosch, Wilhelm. Deutsches Literatur-Lexikon. Biographisches
    und Bibliographisches Handbuch. 2d ed. 4 vols. Bern:
    A. G. Francke Verlag, 1949-1958.

Neue Allgemeine Deutsche Bibliothek. Edited by Carl Ernst
    Bohn. Vols. I-LV. Kiel: Carl Ernst Bohn, 1793-1800.
    Edited by Friedrich Nicolai. Vols. LVI-CVII. Berlin
    und Stettin: Friedrich Nicolai, 1801-1806.

Salzmann, Christian Gotthilf. Über die wirksamsten Mittel
    Kindern Religion beyzubringen. Leipzig, 1787.

Secondary Sources

Beaujean, Marion. Der Trivialroman in der Zweiten Hälfte
des 18. Jahrhunderts. Die Ursprünge des modernen
Unterhaltungsromans. Bonn: H. Bouvier u. Co., 1964.

Becker, Eva. Der Deutsche Roman um 1780. Stuttgart: J. B.
Metzlersche Verlagsbuchhandlung, 1964 = Germanisti-
sche Abhandlungen 5.

Borcherdt, Hans Heinrich. Geschichte des Romans und der No-
velle in Deutschland. 2 vols. Leipzig: J. J. Weber,
1926.

Dibelius, Wilhelm. Englische Romankunst: Die Technik des
Englischen Romans im 18. und zu Anfang des 19. Jahrhunderts. Berlin und Leipzig: Mayer und Müller,
1922 = Palaestra XCII / XCVIII.

Ebeling, Friedrich W. Geschichte der komischen Literatur
in Deutschland seit der Mitte des 18. Jahrhunderts.
Vol. III. Leipzig: Eduard Haynel, 1869.

Ehrenzeller, Hans. Studien zur Romanvorrede von Grimmels-
hausen bis Jean Paul. Bern und München: A Francke,
1955.

Frambach, Oskar. "Zur Jenaer Allgemeinen Literatur-Zeitung
(JALZ)" in DVLG, XXXVIII (1964), pp. 576ff.

Halperin, Nathalie. Die deutschen Schriftstellerinnen in
der zweiten Hälfte des 18. Jahrhunderts. Frank-
furt/Main, 1935.

Jahresberichte über die Erscheinungen auf dem Gebiete der
germanischen Philologie. Edited by Gesellschaft
für deutsche Philologie. Neue Folge. Vols. XVI-
XIX.

Jenisch, Erich. "Vom Abentheuerroman bis zum Bildungsroman"
in GRM, XIV (1926), pp. 339-351.

Kirchner, Joachim. Das Deutsche Zeitschriftenwesen, seine
Geschichte und seine Probleme. 2 vols. Wiesbaden:
Otto Harrassowitz, 1958.

Kunze, Horst. Gelesen und geliebt. Aus erfolgreichen Büchern
1750-1850. Berlin: Rütten & Loening, 1959.

Nutz, Walter. Der Trivialroman, seine Formen und seine Hersteller. Ein Beitrag zur Literatursoziologie = Kunst und Kommunikation, Nr. 4. Köln: Opladen, 1962.

Parthey, Gustav. Die Mitarbeiter an Friedrich Nicolais Allgemeinen Deutschen Bibliothek nach ihren Namen und Zeichen in zwei Registern geordnet. Ein Beitrag zur deutschen Literaturgeschichte. Berlin: Nicolai, 1842.

Raumer, Karl von. Geschichte der Pädagogik vom Wiederaufblühen klassischer Studien bis auf unsere Zeit. Vol. III. Stuttgart: Sam. Gottl. Liesching, 1849.

Schneider, Ferdinand Josepf. Die Freimaurerei und ihr Einfluß auf die geistige Kultur in Deutschland am Ende des 18. Jahrhunderts. Prag, 1909.

Sommerfeld, Martin. Friedrich Nicolai und der Sturm und Drang. Ein Beitrag zur Geschichte der deutschen Aufklärung. Halle/Saale: Verlag von Max Niemeyer, 1921.

Stadelmann, Rudolf und Fischer, Wolfram. Die Bildungswelt des deutschen Handwerkers um 1800. Berlin: Schokken Verlag, 1955.

Thalmann, Marianne. Der Trivialroman des 18. Jahrhunderts und der romantische Roman. Ein Beitrag zur Entwicklungsgeschichte der Geheimbundmystik. Berlin: Ebering, 1925

Touaillon, Christine. Der Deutsche Frauenroman des 18. Jahrhunderts. Wien: Braunmüller, 1919.

Wessenberg, J. H. von. Über den sittlichen Einfluß der Romane. Ein Versuch. Constanz: Wallis, 1826.